D0090578

THE REAL PETER PAN

Also by Piers Dudgeon

Maeve Binchy

THE REAL PETER PAN

J. M. BARRIE AND THE BOY WHO INSPIRED HIM

PIERS DUDGEON

THOMAS DUNNE BOOKS

St. Martin's Press ✺ New York

THOMAS DUNNE BOOKS.
An imprint of St. Martin's Press.

THE REAL PETER PAN. Copyright © 2015 by Piers Dudgeon. All rights reserved.
Printed in the United States of America. For information, address St. Martin's Press,
175 Fifth Avenue, New York, N.Y. 10010.

www.thomasdunnebooks.com
www.stmartins.com

Library of Congress Cataloging-in-Publication Data

Names: Dudgeon, Piers, author.
Title: The real Peter Pan : J. M. Barrie and the boy who inspired him / Piers Dudgeon.
Other titles: J. M. Barrie and the boy who inspired him
Description: First U.S. edition. | New York : Thomas Dunne Books, 2016. | British edition
    has subtitle: the tragic life of Michael Llewelyn Davies. | "First published in Great Britain
    by The Robson Press, an imprint of Biteback Publishing" [London, 2015] — Verso title
    page.
Identifiers: LCCN 2016001233| ISBN 9781250087799 (hardcover) | ISBN 9781250087805
    (e-book)
Subjects: LCSH: Davies, Michael Llewelyn. | Barrie, J. M. (James Matthew), 1860–1937—
    Friends and associates. | Barrie, J. M. (James Matthew), 1860–1937—Family. | Upper
    class—Great Britain—Biography. | BISAC: BIOGRAPHY & AUTOBIOGRAPHY /
    Literary.
Classification: LCC DA574.D38 D83 2016 | DDC 942.083092—dc23
LC record available at http://lccn.loc.gov/2016001233

Our books may be purchased in bulk for promotional, educational, or business use.
Please contact your local bookseller or the Macmillan Corporate and Premium
Sales Department at 1-800-221-7945, extension 5442, or by e-mail at
MacmillanSpecialMarkets@macmillan.com.

First published in Great Britain by The Robson Press, an imprint of Biteback Publishing

First U.S. Edition: July 2016

10 9 8 7 6 5 4 3 2 1

Contents

Foreword   ix

Chapter One   1905: An Awfully Big Adventure   1

Chapter Two   1860–1900: A Rich Harvest of Possibility   11

Chapter Three   1895: A Key to Kensington Gardens   17

Chapter Four   1897: Spellbound   25

Chapter Five   1897: Barrie Comes Out   31

Chapter Six   1897–99: Lost Boy   41

Chapter Seven   1900: Peter and Michael Break Through   47

Chapter Eight   1901–03: Island Games   57

Chapter Nine   1901–03: Unrest Within the Family   69

Chapter Ten   1903–04: The Real Play   81

Chapter Eleven   1904–05: Arthur's Retreat   87

Chapter Twelve   1905–07: Death Takes a Hand   97

Chapter Thirteen   1906: Barrie's Scotland   109

Chapter Fourteen   1907: The Widow Sylvia   123

Chapter Fifteen   1908: Dependence and Uncertainty   137

Chapter Sixteen   1909: Mind Games and Manoeuvres   153

Chapter Seventeen   1910: No Idle Steer   167

Chapter Eighteen   1910–11: Scourie: Learning to Fly   181

Chapter Nineteen   1912: The Outer Hebrides: Catching Mary Rose   195

Chapter Twenty   1913–14: Broken to Eton   207

Chapter Twenty-One   1914–15: Loving, J. M. B.   225

Chapter Twenty-Two   1915: The Blue Bird of Happiness   235

Chapter Twenty-Three   1916–17: Home Fires Burning   257

Chapter Twenty-Four   1917–18: Michael Turns Away   267

Chapter Twenty-Five   1918: The Real Peter Pan   281

Chapter Twenty-Six   1918: Within the Gothic Chamber   297

Chapter Twenty-Seven   1919: Oxford   307

Chapter Twenty-Eight   1919: Garsington   315

Chapter Twenty-Nine   1920: Romance   323

Chapter Thirty   1920: Michael Breaks Out   333

Chapter Thirty-One   1920: Between Earth and Paradise   345

Chapter Thirty-Two   1920–21: Barrie Gets His Way   355

Chapter Thirty-Three   1921: Disposal   363

Afterword   375
Acknowledgements   385
Sources   389
Index   391

A lovely youth, – no mourning maiden decked,
With weeping flowers, or votive cypress wreath,
The lone couch of his everlasting sleep:
Gentle, and brave, and generous, – no lorn bard
Breathed o'er his dark fate one melodious sigh:
He lived, he died, he sung in solitude.

'Alastor' by P. B. Shelley (1816)

Foreword

O F THE LLEWELYN Davies boys who were the inspiration for *Peter Pan*, Michael was J. M. Barrie's favourite. 'We all knew Michael was The One,' wrote his younger brother Nico. Barrie loved him with 'a great love', as Michael's friend at Eton and Oxford, Robert Boothby, recalled.[1]

The Real Peter Pan is the story, both joyous and tragic, of a beautiful boy who was chosen by Barrie to be his gateway to the magical world of childhood, which he longed to recapture, and to the strange spiritual world of his later work.

Unlike Alice Liddell and Lewis Carroll (in the context of *Alice in Wonderland*), and Alastair Grahame and Kenneth Grahame (*The Wind in the Willows*), Michael was not simply the audience of stories

---

1   Interviews with the film-maker Andrew Birkin in the 1970s.

related by Barrie. He was a participant in a creative improvisation that produced *Peter Pan*, a collaboration that continued into Michael's teenage years and the writing of the later plays.

There have been films, novels, biographies and plays aplenty since Peter first made an appearance in Barrie's 1902 novel, *The Little White Bird*, but no perfect accord as to what 'the poor little half-and-half' – this half human, half supernatural boy – means.

Barrie's play opened in London in 1904, and played annually to huge audiences for many decades into the future. In America it opened the following year and was just as popular nationwide. In 1911 came Barrie's *Peter and Wendy*, the equally famous novel, and in 1924 the first film, a silent movie faithful to the original.

Barrie was surprised by what audiences and critics in America read into the play, particularly about their own history and culture, in which of course Tiger Lily and the American Indians feature more meaningfully than elsewhere. But he could not have wished for more *gravitas* than he got from Mark Twain's note to *Peter Pan*'s American star, Maude Adams, that the play was 'a great and refining and uplifting benefaction to this sordid and money-mad age'.

The feeling in America in 1905 was that Peter Pan was a significant symbol of something that society was in danger of losing, even that already we in the West had lost.

But then Walt Disney seized upon the more saccharine elements of the story and produced an animated film which far from censuring our money-mad age turned them to huge commercial advantage.

So pervasive did the Disney interpretation of Peter Pan become in the national consciousness that even today there is for many no incongruity in the eternal boy, the child in all of us, being associated with a pleasure park designed by the singer Michael Jackson, a

bus company in Springfield, Massachusetts, a make of peanut butter, and Hummingbird egg candy.

Other animated films followed – one from Australia in 1988, and
Disney's sequel *Return to Neverland* in 2002.

There was however also a different movement, an increasing interest in the life of Peter's creator, J. M. Barrie, and of the Llewelyn Davies
boys with whose lives Barrie made the play 'streaky', as he put it.

Andrew Birkin's brilliant docudrama mini-series, starring Ian
Holm as Barrie, led the way in 1978. And Marc Foster's fictional
Finding Neverland again featured Barrie in 2004, this time played
by Johnny Depp.

But *Finding Neverland* was not as true to life as it made out. The
biographical aspect had been sanitised so that Barrie came upon
the Llewelyn Davies family *after* the boys' father had died; thereby
removing any possible suggestion that he might have come between
Sylvia and her husband.

This phenomenon of writers and makers deftly dampening down
or altering facts to idealise Barrie is another pervasive element. Possibly lurking behind it is the fear of the curse levelled at all who
would write about him. Even Andrew Birkin admitted to this: 'I feel
somewhat felled by Barrie's curse – "May God blast any one who
writes a biography of me."'

But the curse was not going to stop it happening because there
were now two theatres of interest – the fantasy story of Peter and
the reality of the Davies boys' lives. It was only a matter of time
before someone noticed that the creative improvisation that led to
Peter Pan had not only effected the fiction it had affected the boys
who were part of it, deeply.

The first germ of the idea of Peter, long before the original play
was written, was a vision of a boy lost in a wood, singing for joy

because he knew now that he could be a boy forever and not be compelled to grow into a man.

In the world of film this seemed like the perfect theme for a musical. Dwight Hemion's 1976 adaptation of *Peter Pan* starred Mia Farrow and Danny Kaye. Joseph Weinberger's version appeared in 2001, and in 2014 Phil Willmott's *Lost Boy*.

Willmott's *Lost Boy* was interesting not only because it was a musical, but because it reunited some of the characters of the original play as young adults on the eve of the First World War, that great watershed which separated the old world from the new. There is something about Peter Pan that makes him eternally part of the new, with potential for growth and hope for the future.

Meanwhile, the analytical psychology movement had got hold of him and declared Peter a *puer aeternus*, one of the archetypal ideas that define the 'primordial, structural elements of the human psyche'.

Inevitably there followed attempts to show him at work in the modern world. Damion Dietz's 2003, award-winning *Neverland: Never Grow Up, Never Grow Old*, was set in an amusement park, with Peter an older, androgynous teenager, and Steven Spielberg's *Hook*, 1991, presented Robin Williams as a corporate lawyer who discovered the Peter Pan in himself.

Many a production started out with high hopes and ground to a halt before being revived with heavily revised scripts, as if there remained in the minds of their ageing creators an uncertainty of who or what Peter Pan is.

Barrie knew this would be a problem. When it was all over with the boys, he wrote that the 'tree of knowledge in the wood of make-believe vanishes if you need to look for it'. This, of course, is why he had needed Michael.

In search of an anchor in authenticity, every so often a production returns to the Barrie prototype. P. J. Hogan's 2003 *Peter Pan* was faithful to it, but the audience had been led astray so often now that it failed to break even at the box office.

Ten years later Ella Hickson for the Royal Shakespeare Company produced *Wendy and Peter Pan*. Hickson admitted how difficult it was to convince people that the sentimental, heroic, Disney adventure was not the whole story. She looked hard at the scripts and the book of *Peter Pan* and noticed how much the theme of death features. With Peter it began with his speculation at the mermaid's lagoon, faced with the possibility of drowning, that death would be 'an awfully big adventure'.

In his life with Michael and in two of his later plays – *A Well-Remembered Voice* and the ghostly *Mary Rose* – Barrie became ever more concerned with the question, and the feeling we get is that childhood and death, like two ends of a circle, meet somewhere, and that it is here in this misty arena that the deeply meaningful half of Peter – the supernatural half – really lies.

It was in this arena that with joy in his heart Michael alone was able to explore the real Peter Pan, and it was here that he met his destiny.

Meanwhile, in 2015, well over 100 years after Peter first appeared, the cinematic and theatrical bandwagon rolls on. Ella Hickson's *Wendy and Peter Pan* returns as this book is published. Piers Chater Robinson's musical *Peter Pan* has a USA Arena Tour. Harvey Weinstein's theatrical musical production of the Johnny Depp film *Finding Neverland* has its premiere in America. And Joe Wright's *Pan*, a film starring Hugh Jackman, Amanda Seyfried, Rooney Mara, Garrett Hedlund and Levi Miller, is scheduled to open across the world.

Piers Dudgeon, February 2015

The Highlands and Islands of Scotland
Michael's Arcadia

Chapter One

1905: An Awfully Big Adventure

LOOKING AT THE photographs taken in the summer of 1905 of James M. Barrie and Michael Llewelyn Davies in the garden of his country retreat, Black Lake Cottage in Surrey, one cannot help but be reminded that Edwardian England (1901–10) was an era distinct in time for reasons other than that it spanned the reign of Edward VII.

It isn't only the straw hats of the men and the long, waisted skirts and floppy hats of the women that speak so eloquently of our graceful, peaceful past, nor the boyish, snake-linked belt holding up Barrie's cricketing whites. It is something to do with the laziness of the scene, which echoes in our minds with the sound of leather against willow and the hum of bees, that tells us that this was an age unperturbed by time – held in stasis like the clock that stands at ten to three in Rupert Brooke's nostalgic evocation of it in 'The Old Vicarage, Grantchester'.

The era portrayed itself as one of innocence, in contrast to the worldliness of the Victorians and before the carnage of the First World War. The Edwardian age was the last gasp of old rural England. After 1918, nothing here would be quite the same again. Small wonder, then, that it took the eternal image of Peter Pan, the archetypal innocent who would never grow up, to its heart.

The play, written on the back of Barrie's games with four of the five sons of Arthur and Sylvia Llewelyn Davies, met in London's Kensington Gardens, was always a work of improvisation and underwent constant revision from the moment of its first rehearsal, so that it was not published between book covers for twenty-four years.

In the summer of 1905 Barrie was still reeling from the success of its first London showing. It had premiered at the Duke of York's Theatre on 27 December 1904, run for 145 performances, and would return annually to similar success for decades afterwards.

But already he had it in mind to write a whole new act, making more of 'the Neverland'. It was with this in mind that, in July 1905, he sent for Michael Llewelyn Davies.

He wanted the boy to revisit the scenes in Black Lake forest from which 'the chief forces' of the play – the lost boys, Captain Hook, the crocodile and so on – had emerged. He wanted to remind Michael of the real haunts that inspired the play, to return him to the roots of the Neverland, and use him once more as the creative catalyst for a new Act III.

Michael had taken to Barrie's world of make-believe and imagination into which he, alone of his brothers, was actually born, as if it were second nature. It was no coincidence that Michael is the first to 'let go' in the play, when Peter Pan teaches the children to fly.

And now that his elder brother George, at age twelve, no longer believed in fairies, Michael, at five, was coming into his own. Of course, Michael knew the play intimately. It had been re-enacted time and again in the boys' nursery at home. He had visited the theatre back-stage, been introduced to the cast as one of the creators of it. He had even flown in the harnesses that transported Peter, Wendy, John and Michael to the Neverland and, like the other Llewelyn Davies boys, he knew the difference between Tinkerbell, the fairy, and Tinkerbell the light that danced on stage, which was really shone by one of the stage staff. But he didn't yet consciously question the difference, and that was why Uncle Jim, as Barrie was known within the family, needed him.

Barrie needed to become a boy again, to re-enter that unconscious, unreflective, mysteriously self-contained mind-set of boyhood, insulated against the real world and so soon mislaid, but from which the naturally curious, inquisitive, imaginative and in every sense beautiful Michael never strayed.

The playwright had decided that the Neverland, which had only twice been mentioned in the original script, was to be made more the focus of the play as a magical environment of heavenly moments and with a very special element of danger.

Michael was to be 'the golden ladder into the dream', as Barrie had long ago imagined introducing his own son to 'the old lair' of his boyhood exploits. In Michael's company, the Black Lake would be more than 'this tiny hollow where muddy water gathered'. The pine forest environs of Barrie's cottage would become once again 'an impregnable fortress full of pirates and redskins, their war-like voices breaking the air as they came and went'.

Many a time in the two years that had passed since the last Black Lake holiday, Barrie himself had lost his way to the golden ladder, 'though all the time he knew that the spot lay somewhere over there. When he stood still and listened he could hear the boys at play, and they seemed to be calling: "Are you coming, Captain?" … but he never could see them, and when he pressed forward their voices died away.'

When Michael arrived, Barrie wanted him to say: 'Take my hand, father, and I will lead you there; I found the way long ago for myself.'[2]

Even at five years of age, Michael had something unique. His older brother Peter, who became a fine scholar and publisher, remembered his having 'the true stuff of the poet in him from birth'.[3] Michael's famous cousin, Daphne du Maurier, at fourteen wrote of him in her first story as 'a boy who is searching for happiness, at least not exactly happiness, but that something that is somewhere, you know. You feel it and you miss it and it beckons and you can't reach it … I don't think anyone can find it on this earth.'[4]

In a few years, people would be talking of Michael as gifted, sensitive, charming, impressionable and with an aura around him not of this world. Barrie realised that he was a chip off the du Maurier block more than any of the other boys. It was this 'something' in Michael that he was after, whether less for his own salvation than for his work we will never know.

But there was a price to pay. While a new Act III of *Peter Pan* did come out of their liaison at Black Lake Cottage in July 1905,

---

2   Barrie in *Tommy and Grizel* (1900).

3   Peter Llewelyn Davies in the unpublished family history, which became known as *The Morgue*.

4   *The Seekers* by Daphne du Maurier, unfinished and unpublished, was written in 1921 after Michael's death.

embedded in it was something disastrously formative for Michael personally. It was, as we shall see, from this time that the boy's nightmares began.

Flying was of course a metaphor for finding your way into the Neverland. In a letter to a friend, Michael's cousin Daphne described how, when she was brought low during the Second War, she lay in bed, 'looking at the world through the wrong end of a telescope, the world itself and the people on it being very small and ant-like, and all their activities a little futile' and then 'centred her mind on an island, the island of her dreams ... an island just surfacing from the sea'.[5] And it was this same technique that Barrie played with the Davies boys, whom he dubbed 'the boy castaways of Black Lake Island'. Never mind that there was no island in the Black Lake in fact: there was in their mind's eye. Bit by bit, as the island emerged from the water, their focus on it increased, and eventually 'the little people' of the island also emerged and soon you had the rudiments of a story.

'They do seem to be emerging out of our island, don't they, the little people of the play,' wrote Barrie, 'all except that sly one [referring to himself, the model for the pirate captain, Hook], the chief figure, who draws farther and farther into the wood as we advance upon him? He so dislikes being tracked, as if there were something odd about him, that when he dies he means to get up and blow away the particle that will be his ashes.'

The island game was the perfect, light-hypnotic environment for the creative process. But this time, after Michael and Barrie were left to themselves, the focus was switched from islands to the Black Lake itself:

---

5   Margaret Forster, *Daphne du Maurier* (1993).

If you shut your eyes and are a lucky one, you may see at times a shape-less pool of lovely pale colours suspended in the darkness; then if you squeeze your eyes tighter, the pool begins to take shape, and the col-ours become so vivid that with another squeeze they must go on fire. But just before they go on fire you see the lagoon. This is the near-est you ever get to it on the mainland, just one heavenly moment; if there could be two moments you might see the surf and hear the mermaids singing.

With the Black Lake a mermaids' lagoon and the surrounding fir trees a tropical forest, together Uncle Jim and the boy began tell-ing a story. This was his way, always had been since he was a child, when one of his friends would tell half of a story he had read, and someone else had to work out the end.

'First I tell it to him,' said Barrie, 'then he tells it to me, the under-standing being that it is quite a different story; and then I retell it with his additions, and so we go on until no one could say whether it is more his story or mine. A story had to be told together.'

It is intriguing to read the story of what became the new Act III of *Peter Pan* and wonder who contributed which parts. Peter and Wendy are marooned on a rock in the mermaid's lagoon and must surely drown. We may see Michael's contributions among the pret-tier parts, including Wendy's rescue by means of a kite, which he had made only a few days before. Barrie, on the other hand, was always the provocateur in the games with the boys, responsible for the story's more menacing aspects, and plainly there is his trade-mark, mock-heroic whimsy here too.

As for the very last line of the story about death being an adven-ture, which in an extraordinary way predicts Michael's own last act on this earth fifteen years later, it is anybody's guess who put the idea in Peter's mind. It had been tossed to and fro since its first utterance. While walking one day in Kensington Gardens one of Michael's brothers had pointed to two headstones with 'W St M' and '13a PP 1841' inscribed on them – they can still be seen on the west side of the Broad Walk in the Gardens today. Uncle Jim said they were gravestones for two children (Walter Stephen Matthews and Phoebe Phelps) who had fallen out of their prams and died. Peter Pan had his work cut out burying dead children, apparently, after 6 p.m. lockout in the Gardens, and would dance on their graves, playing on his pipes to make them laugh as they began their journey in the afterlife.[6]

Barrie had a fascination with the afterlife, and where better to explore it than in the company of the beautiful mermaids of the Black Lake lagoon in such an innocent spirit of adventure as this?

It is the end of a long playful day on the mermaids' lagoon. The sun's rays have persuaded him to give them another five minutes, for one more race over the waters before he gathers them up and lets in the moon. There are many mermaids here ... and one might attempt to count the tails did they not flash and disappear so quickly. At times a lovely girl leaps in the air seeking to get rid of her excess of scales, which fall in a silver shower as she shakes them off. From the coral grottoes beneath the lagoon, where are the mermaids' bed-chambers, comes fitful music. One of the most bewitching of these blue-eyed creatures is lying lazily on Marooners' Rock...

Here the mermaids love to bask, combing out their hair in a lazy way. Peter often chats with them and sits on their tails when they

---

6   The official line is that the stones indicate the old boundary line for the parish of Westmin-ster St Mary's and the parish of Paddington.

get cheeky. He has already given Wendy one of their combs. The most haunting time at which to see them is at the turn of the moon, when they utter strange wailing cries; but the lagoon is dangerous for mortals then.

'Mermaids are such cruel creatures, Wendy, that they try to pull boys and girls like you into the water and drown them.'

Wendy is uneasy as she surveys the rock, which is the only one in the lagoon and no larger than a table. Since she last looked around a threatening change has come over the scene. The sun has gone, but the moon has not come. What has come is a cold shiver across the waters which has sent all the wiser mermaids to their coral recesses. They know that evil is creeping over the lagoon.

Peter of course is the first to scent it … The pirates are coming. (This is the moment for Hook and Peter.)

HOOK 'Pan! Into the water, Smee. Starkey, mind the boat. Take him dead or alive!'

The fight is short and sharp … Hook's iron claw makes a circle of black water round him from which opponents flee like fishes. There is only one prepared to enter that dreadful circle. His name is Pan. Strangely, it is not in the water that they meet. Hook has risen to the rock to breathe, and at the same moment Peter scales it on the opposite side. The rock is now wet and as slippery as a ball, and they have to crawl rather than climb. Suddenly they are face to face. Peter gnashes his pretty teeth with joy, and is gathering himself for the spring when he sees he is higher up the rock than his foe. Courteously he waits; Hook sees his intention, and taking advantage of it claws twice. Peter is untouched, but unfairness is what he never can get used to, and in his bewilderment he rolls off the rock. The crocodile, whose tick has been drowned in the strife, rears its jaws, and Hook, who has almost stepped into them, is pursued by it to land. All is quiet on the lagoon now, not a sound save little waves nibbling at the rock, which is smaller than when we last looked at it. Two boys appear with the dinghy, and the others despite their wounds climb into it. They send the cry 'Peter – Wendy'.

When their voices die away there comes cold silence over the lagoon, and then a feeble cry.

'Help, help!'

Two small figures are beating against the rock; the girl has fainted and lies on the boy's arm. With a last effort Peter pulls her up the rock and then lies down beside her. Even as he also faints he sees that the water is rising. He knows that they will soon be drowned, but he can do no more.

As they lay side by side a mermaid who had dared to come back in the stillness stretches up her arms and begins slowly pulling Wendy into the water to drown her. Peter, feeling her slip from him, wakes with a start, and is just in time to draw her back.

Wendy rouses herself and looks around her. 'Peter! Where are we, Peter?

'We are on the rock, Wendy, but it is growing smaller. Soon the water will be over it. Listen!' They can hear the wash of the relentless little waves.

'I can't help you, Wendy. Hook wounded me. I can neither fly nor swim.'

'Do you mean we shall both be drowned?'

'Look how the water is rising.'

They put their hands over their eyes to shut out the sight. They think they will soon be no more. As they sit there something brushes against Peter as light as a kiss, and stays there, as if saying timidly, 'Can I be of any use?' It is the tail of a kite, which Michael had made some days before. It had torn itself out of his hand and floated away.

'Michael's kite,' Peter says without interest, but next moment he has seized the tail, and is pulling the kite toward him.

'It lifted Michael off the ground,' he cries. 'Why should it not carry you?'

'Both of us!'

'It can't lift two; Michael and Curly tried.'

Wendy knows that if it can lift her it can also lift Peter too, for she has the secret from the boys – Peter is no weight at all. But it is a deadly secret…

'Let us draw lots,' Wendy says bravely.

'And you a lady; never.'

Already he had tied the tail round her. She clings to him; she refuses to go without him; but with a 'Good-bye, Wendy,' he pushes her from the rock; and in a few minutes she is borne out of sight.

Peter is alone on the lagoon, but with something much more exciting in mind than flying to safety on a kite string.

The waters are lapping over the rock now, and Peter is aware that it will soon be submerged. Pale rays of light mingle with the moving clouds, and from the coral grottoes is to be heard a sound, at once the most musical and the most melancholy in the Neverland, the mermaids calling to the moon to rise.

Peter is afraid at last, and a tremor runs through him, like a shudder passing over the lagoon; but on the lagoon one shudder follows another till there are hundreds of them, and he feels just the one.

Next moment, with the lagoon suffused with moonlight and that smile on his face and a drum beating in his breast as if he were a real boy at last, Peter stands erect on the rock again and calls:

'To die will be an awfully big adventure.'

Chapter Two

1860–1900: A Rich Harvest of Possibility

MICHAEL, THE FOURTH of five sons of Arthur and Sylvia Llewelyn Davies, was born on 16 June 1900, at 31 Kensington Park Gardens, on the north side of what were once the private gardens of Kensington Palace.

Sylvia was a du Maurier, the third of five children born to Emma and George du Maurier. Her father had risen from a penurious and rootless childhood to become a famous cartoonist, notably for the society pages of *Punch* magazine, and the author of three bestselling novels: *Peter Ibbetson* (1891), *Trilby* (1894) and *The Martian* (1896).

Before he had found fame on *Punch*, he had trained as an artist in Paris, smoked opium, exercised his beautiful tenor voice and engaged in séances and experiments in hypnotism. Arriving in London in 1860, he shared an apartment with James McNeill Whistler, mixed with Pre-Raphaelite artists such as Rossetti, Millais and Edward Burne-Jones and became something of a touchstone in London's literary and artistic community, with Henry James his closest friend.

Sylvia was her father's favourite child. Brought up in an enlightened, bohemian atmosphere at New Grove House on the edge of sprawling Hampstead Heath, high above the city, she was 'a graceful beauty, her charm enhanced by the endearing crookedness of her mouth and a tip-tilted nose', according to the biographer Diana Farr.[7]

> Her skin was white, her shoulders wide and splendid; her hair very dark, a fine frame for that pale face which in repose had a noble almost Grecian quality. But perhaps her most remarkable feature was her eyes, set wide apart with a serenity which attracted the young, the shy and the hesitant.

Sylvia's unusual beauty, charm and grace, matched by a mocking wit and sense of fun, were already welcomed in London society when, at twenty-three, she first met Arthur, her future husband. They were the perfect foil to Arthur's dark good looks and more serious demeanour: 'We used to think he was a young warrior in an Italian picture,' the composer Sir Hubert Parry, a family friend, once said of him.

Three years older than Sylvia and a rising barrister, Arthur was the second of seven children of the Reverend John Llewelyn Davies and his wife, Mary. The family home was miles to the north in Kirkby Lonsdale, a village between the Lake District and the Yorkshire Dales.

---

7   Diana Farr, *Gilbert Cannan: A Georgian Prodigy* (1978).

The Llewelyn Davieses were Christian, highbrow, but politically progressive. Arthur's father had been President of the Cambridge Union and more recently Chaplain to Queen Victoria. Ottoline Morrell, one of the original Bloomsbury set, wrote of him:

> He had been a friend of F. D. Maurice and Robert Browning and even Thomas Carlyle. He was a shy, sensitive reserved man, and had rather a stiff, dry, unsympathetic manner, but after a time I had broken the ice. I found this old man, sitting in his little study, a great solace and very interesting…

Besides the intellectual prowess and unsympathetic manner, the Reverend John Llewelyn Davies was an original member of the famous Alpine Club, and was the first to climb the highest peak within the Swiss frontier (the Dom, 14,911 feet). He was also a supporter of women's rights and workers' rights, a champion of trade unionism and had nerve enough to lambast imperialism from the pulpit while the Queen herself was in the congregation – the reason he found himself living hundreds of miles to the north in 1889 as Rector of Kirkby Lonsdale.

Dolly Parry, one of Sir Hubert's daughters, wrote of the appointment:

> It was regarded as a sort of banishment. He was a Broad Churchman, and on a very high moral and intellectual plane. Mr Gladstone [who was on his fourth stint as Prime Minister] was criticised for this appointment. I heard so much of it from my father and mother, though only thirteen – that I had my own reasons for disliking Mr Gladstone in my youth. He didn't approve of Mr Llewelyn Davies and he cut down trees.

For his part, John Llewelyn Davies was never in the least bitter and grew to love Kirkby and his walks over the Fells, where he turned the vicarage into a hive of reformatory endeavour.

Dolly's close association with the family had begun with her mother's great liking and admiration for Arthur's sister, Margaret, who was General Secretary of the Women's Co-operative Guild from 1889 to 1922. The intellectual and social achievements of the Llewelyn Davieses knew no bounds. Arthur's Aunt Emily founded Girton College, Cambridge, and his own list of accomplishments, before being called to the Bar, included Junior and Senior Scholarships at Marlborough School (a major English public school), Minor and Foundation Trinity Scholarships at Cambridge University, where he took a First Class Degree in the Classical Tripos and won the Lebas Essay Prize in 1884, the First Whewell International Law Scholarship in 1887 Law, and the Inner Temple Pupil Scholarship in Common Law in 1889.

His brothers Crompton and Theodore had both been Apostles at Cambridge – members of a secret society to which only select undergraduates were elected and which would shortly include the philosopher G. E. Moore (*Principia Ethica*), the poet Rupert Brooke, and many members of the Bloomsbury set, such as John Maynard Keynes, Leonard Woolf, Lytton Strachey and his brother James.

Crompton's story is an especially adventurous one. He became a successful lawyer, friend of Lloyd George and supporter of Sinn Féin and married Moya O'Connor, an attractive, dynamic woman who smuggled guns during the War of Independence and was reputed to have been one of Irish revolutionary leader Michael Collins' many lovers. Crompton actually helped Collins draft the Free State constitution and knew him well. After he was ambushed and shot through the head in August 1922, Crompton was appointed Arbitrator and Inspector General in Land Matters for the Free State.

Arthur and Sylvia were a handsome couple with diverse and attractive strains in their character and background, which seemed to predict a lasting, dovetail attraction between them, rather than any serious kind of conflict, and a rich harvest of possibility for the generations to follow.

Fate, in the shape of Mr Barrie, was to determine otherwise.

Chapter Three

1895: A Key to Kensington Gardens

MOST AFTERNOONS FROM his house at 133 Gloucester Road, James Matthew Barrie, a boyish figure with a
round, full, sensitive-looking head and a faraway look in
his eyes, would make his way by means of Palace Gate on the south
side of the Kensington Gardens on to the Broad Walk, dressed in
overcoat and scarf to protect his chest. His constant pipe-smoking
had produced a ticklish cough, which friends associated with him
as surely as his thick, high-pitched Scottish accent.

At this stage a bowler hat and a stick completed the ensemble,
creating an image strangely like that of Charlie Chaplin, the south
London export to Hollywood whom Barrie would later entertain at

home and invite to play Peter Pan on film (which, alas, never happened). Like Barrie, Chaplin was short, although at five feet five he had one and a half inches on the little writer.

In those days, the Kensington Gardens were wild, the paths rougher than they are today; and it was quieter: no bandstand even played. It was 'a tremendous big place, with millions and hundreds of trees', as one regular user described it, and although in the distance one could just hear the rumble of horse-drawn vehicles along the Bayswater Road, on the northern border, it was a peaceful, rural retreat, remote from metropolitan London, which swept past it. There were even sheep grazing there.

Entering the gardens from the south with his pretty young actress wife, Mary Ansell, and huge St Bernard dog, Barrie came at once upon the main north–south axis of the gardens. The Broad Walk was nanny-central between two and four in the afternoon, when Kensington Gardens was commandeered by a number of young, middle- and upper-class children, many of the latter gathering in the more select area at the top of the Walk, called The Figs.

All perambulators seemed Gardens-bound then, although there were fewer people than you would see there today, and at first the Barries would walk in some solitude with their gigantic companion and, as they liked to do, play hide-and-seek and countless other games for a St Bernard's delight.

Porthos, for that was his name – vast, gentle and apparently melancholy, but not really – was more or less the child that they never had.

After their marriage in 1894, which followed three nervous breakdowns and an emergency dash by Mary Ansell to Barrie's bedside in the family home at Kirriemuir, ostensibly for a last goodbye, Barrie made a lightning recovery and a marriage ceremony was undertaken at the house (as was allowed under Scottish law). Afterwards, a much-recovered Mr Barrie and his new wife had honeymooned in Switzerland and bought the St Bernard there, and their London house the following year.

The Barries' home at No. 133 was a well-appointed, three-storey town house, the first outward sign of his success since buying a one-way ticket to London almost ten years earlier, clutching an article for the *St James's Gazette* entitled 'The Rooks begin to Build'.

When he and Mary first lived there they wouldn't see many people in the evenings, so the games with Porthos would continue, running breakneck races up and down the stairs, or playing 'finding his favourite author'. Or Porthos might do the tricks his master had taught him, like drinking milk out of a tumbler, or shaking hands, or removing a glove from a pocket and bringing it back to him. And Mary would come alive and dance for Porthos, who would watch her every movement with solemn, worshipping eyes.

Porthos was the child in their house, but he wasn't the only one. It was, in the opinion of a few observers, all a bit 'unnatural'. But it was perfectly natural for them.

A toyshop en route to the gardens was a regular stall. Porthos would come to a halt there and wave his tail, so that one or other of them would buy him a toy. He liked dolls mostly, not balls. It all began after Barrie bought himself a toy for his own amusement.

It represented a woman, a young mother, flinging her little son over her head with one hand and catching him in the other, and I was entertaining myself on the hearthrug with this pretty domestic scene when I heard an unwonted sound from Porthos, and looking up, I saw this noble and melancholic countenance on the broad grin. I shuddered and was putting the toy away at once, but he sternly struck down my arm with his, and signed that I was to continue. The unmanly chuckle always came, I found, when the poor lady dropped her babe, but the whole thing entranced him; he tried to keep his excitement down by taking huge draughts of water; he forgot all his niceties of conduct; he sat in holy rapture with the toy between his paws, took it to bed with him, ate it in the night, and searched for it so longingly next day that I had to go out and buy him the man with the scythe…

The dame in the temple of toys which we frequent thinks I want them for a little boy and calls him 'the precious' and 'the lamb', the while Porthos is standing gravely by my side. She is a motherly soul, but over-talkative.

'And how is the dear lamb today?' she begins, beaming.

'Well, ma'am, well,' I say, keeping tight grip on his collar.

'This blighty weather is not affecting his darling appetite?'

'No, ma'am, not at all.' (She would be considerably surprised if informed that he dined today on a sheepshead, a loaf, and three cabbages, and is suspected of a leg of mutton.)

'I hope he loves his toys.'

'He carries them about with him everywhere, ma'am.' (Has the one we bought yesterday with him now, though you might not think it to look at him.)

'What do you say to a box of tools this time?'

'I think not, ma'am.'

'Is the deary fond of digging?'

'Very partial to digging.' (We shall find the leg of mutton some day.)

'Then perhaps a weeny spade and pail?'

Once Porthos was let off his leash in the gardens, his master would play with him, and soon children would gather round to watch. The huge dog, up on his hind legs, was as tall as the little man in the bowler hat. Man and dog boxed, circled, and stopped to go off running, then walked on again to play hide-and-seek among the trees.

Pamela Maude, daughter of West End actors Cyril Maude and Winifred Emery, who were starring at the time in Barrie's hit play *The Little Minister* remembered: 'Mr Barrie had a pale face and large eyes and shadows round them; he looked fragile. But he was strong when he wrestled with Porthos.'

But then all of a sudden he'd stop and become like ordinary people again and make jerky jokes or do tricks with match-boxes or talk about cricket. He tried to show Pamela's sister Margery how to bowl and to bat, but she always refused to learn; she stood with a stubborn look on her face and her hands on her hips. 'I am a girl,' she said, 'and girls don't play crickets.'

Mr Barrie's face showed he thought girls were stupid.

Pamela remembered that his wife Mary 'was lovely'.

> Her cheeks were the colour of a wild rose and we liked to stare at her. She wore pretty clothes that seemed different to those worn by other people, dresses in brown and green that some woodland fairy-lady could have worn. She made us think of the Flower Ladies in our books, which were illustrated by Walter Crane – she was 'Queen Summer'. But we could not feel at ease with her. She did not talk to us and she never smiled when we were with her.

Mary, the daughter of a licensed victualler and a woman who kept a boarding house on the south coast, had given up a promising career in the theatre to become Barrie's wife. She had even had her own company at one time. The sight of children about her husband soon began to arouse mixed feelings. 'I am not quite happy with them,' she wrote with honesty.

Something about them puts me off, their humanness to tell the truth.
They are little people. I have never been really happy with people.
Some constraint tightens me up when I am with them. They seem so
inside themselves, so unwilling to reveal their real selves. I am always
asking for something they won't give me; I try to pierce into their
reserves; sometimes I feel I am succeeding, but they close in again,
and I am left outside.

Truth was that Mary far preferred dogs to children. 'An animal is so
helplessly itself … perhaps my love for the dogs, in the beginning,
was a sort of mother-love…'

Few had much either good or bad to say about Mary Ansell. Dolly
described her as 'commonplace, 2nd rate & admirable'.

Besides having an interest in cricket and playing with toys, Barrie confessed to having taken a few simple lessons in conjuring in a
dimly lit chamber beneath a shop from 'a gifted young man with a
long neck and a pimply face, who as I entered took a barber's pole
from my pocket, saying at the same time, "Come, come, sir, this
will never do."'

Whether because he knew too much, or because he wore a trick shirt,
he was the most depressing person I ever encountered; he felt none
of the artist's joy, and it was sad to see one so well calculated to give
pleasure to thousands not caring a dump about it.

The barber's pole was successfully extracted from many a child's
mouth in the Kensington Gardens, even though the difficulty of
disposing of it Barrie found considerable.

Then there was the magic egg-cup. 'I usually carried it about with
me, and with its connivance I did some astonishing things with

pennies; but even the penny that costs sixpence is uncertain, and just when you are saying triumphantly that it will be found in the eggcup, it may clatter to the ground...'

The next moment he was pretending to hypnotise a child with his eyebrows. He had an unusual ability to elevate and lower his eyebrows separately, like two buckets in a well, while gazing into the face of a child intently with his large, morose, staring eyes, not unlike those of Porthos. It was a trick that almost never failed to give him a chance to check a screaming boy's tears.

The boy would stop mid-scream and consider the unexpected movement without prejudice, his face remaining as it was, his mouth open to emit the frozen howl if the trick did not surpass expectation. The fair-minded boy was giving the odd little man a chance. It was all Barrie needed. Next minute he was telling him about fairies as though he knew all about them.

He had a favourite haunt called the Story Seat and told a new fairy tale there every afternoon for years. Asked when was the first fairy, he would say: 'When the first baby laughed for the first time, his laugh broke into a million pieces, and they all went skipping about. That was the beginning of fairies.'

Nannies would press their charges upon him, making no connection at all with the stories coming out of the Old Bailey about Oscar Wilde and his young friends.

Indeed, so innocently was he regarded that, in 1902, Lord Esher, Secretary to His Majesty's Office of Works, who was responsible for the gardens and who for reasons perhaps best kept to himself took to calling Mr Barrie 'the furry beast', presented him with his own key so that he could go there whenever he liked, even unattended after lock-out time.

'Lock-out time is fairy time in the gardens,' Barrie would tell his young charges.

You can be looking at fairies during the day without knowing. I have heard of children who declared that they had never once seen a fairy. Very likely if they said this in the Kensington Gardens, they were standing looking at a fairy all the time. The reason they were cheated was that she pretended to be something else. This is one of their best tricks. They usually pretend to be flowers, because the court sits in the Fairies' Basin, and the Fairy Basin, you remember, is all covered with ground-ivy (from which they make their castor-oil), with flowers growing in it here and there. Most of them really are flowers, but some of them are fairies. You never can be sure of them, but a good plan is to walk by looking the other way, and then turn round sharply. Another good plan, which I sometimes follow, is to stare them down. After a long time they can't help winking, and then you know for certain that they are fairies. There are also numbers of them along the Baby's Walk (which as you know runs off the bottom of the Broad Walk towards the Serpentine Lake). There are so many flowers there, and all along the Baby's Walk, that a flower is the thing least likely to attract attention. They dress exactly like flowers. The beginning of the tulip weeks is almost the best time to catch them.[8]

---

8   J. M. Barrie in *The Little White Bird* (1902).

Chapter Four

1897: Spellbound

I T WAS NOT until 1897 that the Llewelyn Davies family arrived at 31 Kensington Park Gardens, on the north side of the gardens. After their wedding in 1892 and a honeymoon at Porthgwarra in deepest Cornwall, Sylvia and Arthur had set up home at 18 Craven Terrace in Paddington, close to where Arthur had been renting lodgings.

Craven Terrace was 'a dear little house (or Sylvia made it so), a sort of maisonette', as Dolly Parry described it. Sylvia had a flair for design and created soft furnishings for their home as well as lovely clothes for herself and her sons, often evolved from whatever lay to hand. 'I remember Arthur telling me that Sylvia gave away his trousers for plants which a man brought round on a barrow,' wrote Dolly years later. In fact, money had been so short at this time, so early in Arthur's career, that Sylvia had been working for a well-known theatrical costumier, Ada Nettleship, who made clothes for the famous actress Ellen Terry (a great friend of du Maurier) in a dressmaking business set up by her father.

Then, in October 1896, du Maurier had died and the family benefited from legacies, mainly derived from the huge sales of du Maurier's second novel, *Trilby*, which tells of the fate of a young, bohemian artist's model in Paris when a man by the name of Svengali inveigles his way into her life and exercises his hypnotic power over her. With more than a touch of irony, the royalties from *Trilby* brought Sylvia and her sons within Barrie's orbit for the first time.

The extra money also brought Nanny Hodgson on to the scene. At Craven Terrace, two children had been born to Sylvia in successive years – George on 20 July 1893, Jack on 11 September 1894. Her third son, Peter, was born on 25 February 1897, and as Sylvia now had three boys claiming her full-time attention, the decision was taken to employ a nanny.

Mary Hodgson (Dadge to her family) was the eighth of ten children born to Thomas, a stonemason, and his wife Mary, at Kirkby Lonsdale. Nanny was twenty-one going on twenty-two when she arrived. Inevitably, being so close to the Kensington Gardens, she joined the throng between two and four each afternoon, with George and Jack conspicuous in bright red tam-o'-shanters, blouses and breeches, made by Sylvia, and little Peter in his perambulator pushed by Nanny. It was only a matter of time before Barrie caught George's eye.

He claimed first to have seen the four-year-old on the sward behind the Baby's Walk. Originally George was, he said, 'a missel thrush, attracted there that hot day by a hose that lay on the ground sending forth a gay trickle of water'. George was lying 'on his back in the water, kicking up his legs'.[9]

The boy never tired of this story, and soon it was he who told it to Barrie rather than Barrie to him. All children were birds once apparently, and all children in this part of London were originally birds in Kensington Gardens:

> Solomon Caw, the wise old crow on Bird Island in the Serpentine, was responsible for choosing a bird for each new mother and sending it to her. And the reason there are bars on nursery windows and a tall fender by the fire is because very little people sometimes forget that they no longer have wings, and try to fly away through the window or up the chimney.

Young George's delight on a summer afternoon was to go with him to some spot in the gardens where the unfortunate mothers who have no children may be seen trying to catch one with small pieces of cake.

> That the birds know what would happen if they were caught, and are even a little undecided about which is the better life, is obvious to every student of them. Thus, if you leave your empty perambulator under the trees and watch from a distance, you will see the birds boarding it and hopping about from pillow to blanket in a twitter of excitement; they are trying to find out how babyhood would suit them.[10]

The saddest sight is the birds who never find a mother. He chose

---

9   J. M. Barrie, *The Little White Bird* (1902).

10   Ibid.

the original title of a book he published in 1902 called *The Little White Bird*, because 'the little white birds are the birds that never find a mother'. Sad because Barrie never would have a child of his own flesh, though he had the fantasy of a boy called Timothy and wrote about him, wishing that he could have played just once in the Kensington Gardens, 'and have ridden on the fallen trees, calling gloriously to me to look; that he could have sailed one paper galleon on the Round Pond, [or] chase one hoop down the laughing avenues of childhood, where memory tells us we run but once…'

Barrie claimed that he had the fairy language from George after thinking back hard and pressing his hands to his temples.

'"Fairy me tribber" is what you say to the fairies when you want them to give you a cup of tea,' it emerged one day.

Barrie was pleased, but advised that 'it is not so easy as it looks, for all the 'r's should be pronounced as 'w's.'

'What would you say,' George asked him, 'if you wanted them to turn you into a hollyhock?' He thought the ease with which they can turn you into things their most engaging quality. The answer is 'Fairy me lukka'.

'Fairy me bola' means 'Turn me back again', and George's discovery made Barrie uncomfortable, for he knew he had hitherto kept his distance from the fairies, mainly because of a feeling that their conversions are permanent.

Forsaking the realm of fairyland for a while, and indicating a change of subject by exposing his peculiarly large head to the elements, Barrie would gravely and reverently tell of some great explorer. Gallant tales of the search for the Northwest Passage, expeditions to the Arctic, the Antarctic, the exotic Orient and the dark continent of Africa provided a steady stream of adventure. On the little party a stillness would fall as all the time he spoke 'as one fresh to the world before ever he had time to breathe upon the glass', and they listened, spellbound.

George would trail around after him, Jack sometimes tagging along, while Peter was not out of his pram and was a long way from realising that 'Mr Barrie', as he later put it, 'became a unique influence in the lives of all of us, one that was to affect our destinies in ways as yet unknown.'

Nanny, being Nanny, feared this from the start and became less and less keen the more the boys were 'taken over by this strange little man'. Walks with the children became 'less pleasurable', she told her family in Kirkby Lonsdale and later came to look upon Barrie as an intrusion.

Chapter Five

1897: Barrie Comes Out

THE BARRIES MET Sylvia and Arthur at a high society dinner hosted by the leading London solicitor Sir George and Lady Lewis at their mansion at 88 Portland Place W1, on New Year's Eve, 1897.

Before his death the previous October, du Maurier had been a regular guest of the Lewises since at least the 1860s; he was among their oldest friends. Sometimes hundreds would be invited to the Lewis parties, a mixture of peers of the realm and celebrities from the world of the arts. Occasionally there would be a much more select, high-profile evening, involving royalty. Party lists show, for example, that in March 1885 the Prince of Wales (Albert Edward, later Edward VII) was the principal guest, and du Maurier and his wife Emma attended with only a dozen or so others.

Barrie's inclusion on party lists was singular and more recent – they show only one invitation earlier that same year (1897). At thirty-seven he was one of the most talked of figures in the literary world, with money pouring in from books and plays, in that very year to include a play based on his novel *The Little Minister* which it has been said earned him as much as £80,000, the equivalent of millions today. His invitation to the Lewises had seemed inevitable at some point.

But it was less inevitably to be accepted, for Barrie could be gauche in company. He and Mary by this time had begun to give little dinner-parties of their own at No. 133, so that their circle of friends was expanding all the time beyond the almost exclusively male band of friends that Barrie had enjoyed – mostly journalists and writers – up to the time he was married.

But even these little soirées could be difficult affairs, as very often Mrs Barrie was the only one who spoke.

Her husband's prolonged silences were deafening. They defined him more completely than any feature other than his small stature, strong Scottish accent and persistent smoker's cough. Said the writer Jerome K. Jerome:

Barrie could easily be the most silent man I have ever met. Sometimes he would sit through the whole of a dinner without ever speaking. Then, when all but the last one or two guests had gone – or even later – he would put his hands behind his back and, bummeling up and down the room, talk for maybe an hour straight on end. Once a beautiful but nervous young lady was handed over to his care. With the sole au gratin Barrie broke the silence:

'Have you ever been to Egypt?'

The young lady was too startled to answer immediately. It was necessary for her to collect herself. While waiting for the entrée she turned to him.

'No,' she answered.

Barrie made no comment. He went on with his dinner. At the end of the chicken en casserole, curiosity overcoming her awe, she turned to him again.

'Have you?' she asked.

A far-away expression came into Barrie's great deep eyes.

'No,' he answered.

After that they both lapsed into silence.

On an earlier occasion, before he was married, a great lady had invited him to her castle in the country. 'The house party was a large one,' recalled Jerome. 'There were peers and potentates, millionaires and magnates … Barrie did not say anything, but in the morning he was gone. No one had seen him leave, and the doors were still bolted. He had packed his bag and climbed out of the window.'

Increasingly, Mary Ansell found the situation difficult to bear, for he was as silent with her as in company. At first she assumed that all husbands were the same. 'Those silent meals. Haven't most of us experienced them? When the mind of your man is elsewhere, lord knows where, but nowhere in your direction.'

At such times she thanked God for Porthos.

Just when the silence is becoming unbearable, your dog steps in and attracts your attention. He lays his head on your knee, or he presses your hand, as it is in the act of conveying a succulent morsel to your mouth. 'Merely asking for food,' you interrupt. Quite true. But to be asked for *anything* is a relief.

Barrie's male friends saw his silences as 'full of unthinkable knowledge and unthinkable force'[11] – a quirky aspect of a uniquely fascinating individual, whose equally sudden, radiant, garrulous form was worth waiting for.

Of people meeting him for the first time, some took his silences as shyness or uneasiness on his part. Others interpreted them as a sneering aloofness or presumptuous superiority. Yet others were not a little intimidated, as if he was someone who set out to conquer by silence.

Barrie would have said that all were to some degree justified in holding these views and was the first to admit that 'my moods are as changeable as a hoary ocean. There are times I am the best of company, when my wit sparkles and cuts. At other times I walk in the shadows. Then let no one speak to me … for I am in a world of my own. Suppose I am ruminating with the mighty dead.'

It took a child to understand what that meant. 'He was made of silences,' Pamela Maude wrote in her autobiography *Worlds Away*. 'We did not find these strange, they were so much part of him … his silences spoke loudly. Mr Barrie did not talk and Mrs Barrie did not smile, and yet he was our companion.'

Children read his silences as detachment from the world of adults, a part of the magic aura he created around himself; as if he was off in another world, as Pamela recorded of a holiday she and her parents spent with Barrie in Scotland:

> In the evening, when the strange morning light had begun to change,
> Mr Barrie held out a hand to each of us in silence, and we slipped

---

11   D. H. Lawrence, who corresponded with Barrie, knew Mary Ansell, and met him at least once in London.

our own into his and walked still silently, into the beech-wood. We shuffled our feet through the leaves and listened, with Mr Barrie, for sudden sound made by birds and rabbits. One evening we saw a pea-pod lying in the hollow of a great tree-trunk, and we brought it to Mr Barrie.

There, inside, was a tiny letter, folded inside the pod, that a fairy had written. Mr Barrie said he could read fairy writing and read it to us. We received several more, in pea-pods, before the end of our visit...

At the Lewises on New Year's Eve 1897, there were no children present, but Barrie's increasing fascination with Sylvia's boys may be seen to have played a part in his decision to accept their invitation, even possibly to have moved it in the first place.

For if you wanted to meet du Maurier's daughter 'by chance', the best way to do so was to get yourself onto one of the Lewis party lists. The Lewises had not sent an invitation to Barrie cold. He had met one of their two young daughters at the house of a mutual friend and suggested she and her sister might like parts to play in the copyright performance of *The Little Minister*.[12] The casting led to his inclusion on a party list in February 1897.

In time, the Lewises would be among Barrie's greatest allies. Lady Lewis would be strong in her support of him. Barrie found special favour by contributing, even managing, the Lewises' entertainments, producing revues featuring satirical skits on some of their famous guests. Sir George's firm of solicitors, which gave Arthur his first briefs as a barrister, came to represent him. And a future head of the firm, Sir Reginald Poole, acted for his estate in a threatened conflict

---

12 A copyright performance was a pre-production performance of a new play, usually acted before an invited audience, and in this instance a number of friends, and friends of friends.

with Sylvia's boys, when three of them considered making a claim on it in 1937. But chiefly the Lewises earn their place in our story by playing matchmaker between Barrie and Sylvia in December 1897. Their names were next to one another on the seating plan.

That night, so he told the wife of Sylvia's son Peter years later, Barrie found himself sitting next to the most beautiful creature he had ever seen and was overwhelmed, but for once he did not remain silent.

Intrigued by the way Sylvia put aside some of the various sweets that were handed around, secreting them in her purse, he enquired of her why. She explained that she was keeping them for Peter.

'Peter?'

Sylvia told Barrie that Peter was her third son, born the previous February, who had been named after Peter Ibbetson, the hero and title of her father's first novel.

Barrie then revealed that he had named his St Bernard dog, Porthos, after Peter Ibbetson's St Bernard.

For Barrie this was unusually candid. He had not even told his wife that Porthos was named after Peter Ibbetson's dog. Mary imagined that he had been named after one of the three musketeers in Alexandre Dumas's famous novel. The nearest Barrie ever came to admitting publicly that the choice of name had anything to do with the dog in *Peter Ibbetson* was in a book he published in 1902,[13] where he admits, 'I think I cut him out of an old number of *Punch*.'

Porthos in *Peter Ibbetson* had itself been based on du Maurier's own St Bernard, named Chang after an eight-foot Chinese giant exhibited in the British Museum in the 1860s. Like other members of the du Maurier family, the St Bernard Chang appeared frequently

---

13   *The Little White Bird* (1902).

in his master's illustrations in *Punch*, so that when the dog died in 1883, his fans were stricken.

The four-legged Chang had sat at du Maurier's feet as he worked. The four-legged Porthos now sat at the feet of Barrie as he worked in the room above the front door at 133 Gloucester Road.

It is fair to say that George du Maurier had held a fascination for J. M. Barrie long before he met his grandchildren in Kensington Gardens. But for reasons that will fall clear he never liked to associate himself openly with the man.

Barrie had been electrified by *Peter Ibbetson*. In this he was far from alone. John Masefield, Poet Laureate in Britain from 1930, and sixteen years of age when the book was published, recalled the excitement of growing up at this time and how du Maurier delivered the era's most acute desire:

> Men were seeking to discover what limitations there were to the personal intellect; how far it could travel from its home, the personal brain; how deeply it could influence other minds at a distance from it, or near it; what limit, if any, there might be to an intense mental sympathy. This enquiry occupied many doctors and scientists in various ways. It interested many millions of men and women. It stirred George du Maurier ... to speculations which deeply delighted his generation.[14]

During his apprenticeship as a young artist in Paris, and later in Belgium, du Maurier had become adept at hypnotism, a practice widespread in the 1850s, particularly among artists whose life-models were required to hold their position in situ for hours at a time. His friend Felix Mocheles wrote about their hypnotic exploits together,

---

14   Introduction to *Peter Ibbetson* and *Trilby* (1947 edition).

which even extended to hypnotising at least one child that they had met in the street.[15]

In the course of his experiments, du Maurier developed a method of light trance or self-hypnotism, which he like to call 'dreaming-true', and it was his skill in this area that he wrote about in *Peter Ibbetson*.

Another friend, the artist Whistler, confirmed that

> [du Maurier] often used to talk about his dreams to me before *Peter Ibbetson* appeared … He used to say that when lying down he crossed his legs, put his hands behind his head, and then had all sorts of dreams at will. In fact, Peter Ibbetson who 'dreamt true' was partly taken from his own experience.

In the novel, Peter, a young architect, receives instruction from Mary Duchess of Towers – 'the duchess of dreams' – a woman who had learned the art of 'dreaming true' from her father. In the first instance, Peter focuses his mind on a memorable moment in his childhood:

> I lay straight on my back, with my feet crossed, and my hands clasped above my head in a symmetrical position; I would fix my will intently and persistently on a certain point in space and time that was within my memory – for instance, the avenue gate on a certain Christmas afternoon, when I remembered waiting for Le Major Duquesnois to go for a walk – at the same time never losing touch of my own present identity as Peter Ibbetson, architect, Wharton Street, Pentonville; all of which is not so easy to manage as one might think, although the dream duchess had said, 'Ce n'est que le premier pas qui coûte;'

---

15   *In Bohemia with George du Maurier* (1896).

and finally one night, instead of dreaming the ordinary dreams I had dreamed all my life, I had the rapture of waking up, the minute I was fairly asleep, by the avenue gate, and of seeing myself as a child sitting on one of the stone posts and looking up the snowy street for the major. Presently he jumped up to meet his old friend...'

In the course of his dream Peter becomes the boy he once was. With 'newly aroused self-consciousness at the intensity, the poignancy, the extremity of my bliss', he spends 'hours, enchanted hours' reliving his idyllic childhood in Passy, which was then 'a quiet village on the outskirts of Paris, facing the Bois de Boulogne'.

He rediscovers a long-forgotten friendship with a little girl called Mary Seraskier, known as Mimsey, a 'sick, ungainly child', full of gratitude and love that Peter should play with her. Peter is touchingly unaware that her little heart is so full of him that she would like to be his slave – she would, literally, die for Peter.

We also see him playing with two boys, pretending to be Athos, Porthos and Aramis in Dumas's *The Three Musketeers*, and Natty Bumppo in James Fenimore Cooper's famous frontiersman novels, rousing tales of adventure about American Indians and early pioneers of the American West. While alone he would engage in island fantasies, his favourite book being *Robinson Crusoe* and next favourite *The Swiss Family Robinson*.

But the real fun comes in the nearby Bois de Boulogne, not at all the pristine park it is now, and in particular beside a lake called the Mare d'Auteil, surrounded on three sides by 'a dense, wild wood ... The very name has a magic from all the associations that gathered round it at that time.'

How interesting, therefore, that Peter Ibbetson enjoyed boyish adventures in the park and the Mare d'Auteil just like du Maurier's grandchildren, Sylvia's boys, did with Barrie, in Kensington Gardens and by the Black Lake in Surrey. And islands are his delight.

More uncanny still, Peter Ibbetson even had an Uncle Jim figure in his life in the Bois de Boulogne, who captivated him with fairy tales.

Le Major Duquesnois lives on the edge of the park and befriends Peter: 'He took to me at once, in spite of my Englishness, and drilled me ... and told me a new fairy tale, I verily believe, every afternoon for seven years. Scheherazade could do no more for a Sultan, and to save her own neck from a bowstring!'

Again like Barrie, when he is tired of fairyland Duquesnois would tell Peter and his young French friends tales of adventure and high heroism (some of which he had, unlike Barrie, actually lived), 'of Brienne, of Marengo, and Austerlitz; of the farewells at Fontainebleau, and the Hundred Days – never of St Helena; he would not trust himself to speak to us of that! And gradually working his way to Waterloo, he would put his hat on, and demonstrate to us, by A+B, how, virtually, the English had lost the day, and why and wherefore.' On the little party of Duquesnois's followers, as on Barrie's young followers in Kensington Gardens, a solemn, awe-struck stillness would then fall.

At some point Sylvia will surely have recognised Barrie as the man in the park that George and Jack had told her about, the little man who would hypnotise with his eyebrows, enchant them with his fairy stories and amuse them boxing with his St Bernard dog. And because she knew the story of Peter Ibbetson well, she may even have addressed Barrie as Le Major Duquesnois that very night.

But she wouldn't have exposed him. It was in Sylvia's nature only to have mocked him gently. She would have loved that he was so ardent a fan of her father's dreamland. That *Peter Ibbetson* was Barrie's source remained their little secret.

Chapter Six

1897–99: Lost Boy

AFTER THEIR FIRST meeting the two families began to see a great deal of one another, though mainly when Arthur was out at work. Everyone knew of the association and began to speak of the Barries and the Davieses in the same breath. Barrie and his wife would walk the boys home from the park almost every day, Mary Ansell befriending Sylvia while her husband continued his fun and games with the boys upstairs in the nursery.

At the start Sylvia seems to have treated him a bit like a useful second nanny, who would keep her children amused for hours on end. As for Mary, Sylvia enjoyed her company at first. There was a shared interest in interior design, and there is no doubt that the friendship helped pave the way for what happened next. But it is clear that Mary knew nothing about *Peter Ibbetson*, and it is likely that Barrie didn't at first appreciate just how deeply Sylvia herself was caught up in *Peter Ibbetson*. This came out between them over the ensuing months and strengthened their bond considerably.

Sylvia had been her father's model for the Duchess of Towers. Indeed, she had a spiritual life that owed everything to her father's psychic ability and to the close relationship they had enjoyed with one another.

When Sylvia's third son, Peter, was researching a history of the family he caught wind of this and wrote to Sylvia's close friend, Dolly, about it.

Dolly tried to guide Peter to it without betraying Sylvia's confidence: 'Always [Sylvia's] reserve about what she cared about was very strong. She had an inner life of her own, which is what gave her her great interest.'

This was typical of the du Mauriers. There was an unspoken rule in the family, where fun and laughter were paramount, never to tax people with anything too deep. 'One must never be *au serieux* about anything,' observed Sylvia's sister Trixy's husband, Charles Hoyer Millar. 'The family in general had a rooted dislike to serious topics of any kind, at all events in the presence of each other.' Deep thoughts were not avoided, however. On the contrary, there were special words for them in their vocabulary, like 'main talks' or 'psychological politics'. Deep thoughts were in fact at the heart of what the du Mauriers were about.

Chief among these were psychological and supernatural matters. Daphne couldn't keep quiet about them in her fiction, and once spelled them out in her non-fiction, writing in *The Rebecca Notebook*:

There is a faculty among the myriad threads of our inheritance that, unlike the chemicals in our bodies and in our brains, has not yet been pinpointed by science, or even fully examined. I like to call this faculty 'the sixth sense'. It is a sort of seeing, a sort of hearing, something between perception and intuition, an indefinable grasp of things unknown ... The phenomena of precognition, of telepathy, of dreaming true, all depend upon this sixth sense, and the therapeutic value of hypnosis, still in its infancy, depends upon it too.

It was almost all too much for Dolly not to mention in her diary something about her paranormal beliefs and skills, though characteristically they had been told to her in absolute confidence: 'Sylvia couldn't talk about things she really felt to those who were not very close to her. She had an inner life of her own, & was to me always interesting.' The entry for Sunday 15 October 1892 reads: 'Talked a good deal with sweet Sylvia, who told me a good deal about her family etc.' There then follows instructions about how to hypnotise someone, clearly copied down after Sylvia had described the process to her:

Place yourself before the subject with your thoughts concentrated on the effect you wish to produce, you tell him to look at you steadily and think only of sleep. Raise your hands with the palms towards him, over the crown of head and before the forehead where you keep them for one or 2 minutes, & move them slowly down to the pit of stomach, without touching subject, at a distance of one or 2 inches from body, as soon as hands reach lowest part of the stroke you carry them again in a wide sweep with outspread arms over subject's head. Repeat same movements for 10 minutes.

The truth was that Sylvia's secret inner life made her who she was, the Sylvia she shows us in the dreamy photographs that Barrie took, her undemonstrative moments, as if she was away in another world, which she was when the mood took her.

Wrote her son, Peter, 'People of both sexes told of the indelible impression she left with them of something rarer than mere charm, and deeper than mere beauty.' Arthur's brother, Crompton, 'as a rule pretty reticent, once, shortly before his death, tried to talk about her to [Peter's wife] and me; and it was as if he spoke of a being of more than earthly loveliness'.

It was this 'more than earthly' aura that Peter was referring to when he wrote that he suspected Sylvia inherited 'a good deal' from her father, which made her anything but ordinary like her mother (du Maurier's wife, Emma, had done everything in her power to dissuade her husband from meddling in the paranormal).

This, Sylvia's most beguiling feature, brought her ever closer to Barrie as bit by bit it emerged how bound up she and her father were together, both in life and in the writing of du Maurier's books.

The physical similarity between Sylvia and the dream duchess in *Peter Ibbetson* is striking, and although the hypnotic heroine of du Maurier's second novel, *Trilby*, had been loosely based on a seventeen-year-old girl named 'Carry' who had been hypnotised on many an occasion by du Maurier as a young man, Sylvia had modelled for the illustrations of Trilby in the book.

Barrie became fascinated by the way du Maurier had captured Sylvia in book form as an artist might capture his subject on canvas. And, in his desire to win her over, he now captured Sylvia in an autobiographical novel he was writing.

Before they met, the two main characters in his novel *Tommy and Grizel* had been based on himself and his wife, Mary Ansell. After meeting Sylvia he had been so affected that he'd floundered

with the writing of it and made the decision to follow du Maurier
and model Grizel on Sylvia instead.

When Bernard Partridge came to illustrate the characters in *Tommy
and Grizel* for publication in *Scribner's Magazine*, Barrie told him he
could give him a real-life model for one of them. 'Mrs Llewelyn
Davies, whom she is meant to be a bit like is willing to sit to you for
this and she has some idea of the dressing too. If you like this idea
would you communicate with her about it?'

The physical similarity of Sylvia and Grizel is clear in the text.
Just as du Maurier gave Sylvia's nose to Mimsey in *Peter Ibbetson* and described it as 'rather tilted at the tip', so now Grizel has
Sylvia's 'tilted nose'. Grizel's gray eyes are also Sylvia's – 'unusually
far apart, [which] let you look straight into them and never quiv-
ered, they were such clear, gray, searching eyes, they seemed always
to be asking for the truth'. Diana Farr observed that 'perhaps Sylvia's
most remarkable feature' was her 'eyes, set wide apart'. Meanwhile,
Dolly wrote at this moment in her diary, 'Sylvia has got one of the
most delightful, brilliantly sparkling faces I have ever seen. Her nose
turns round the corner – also turns right up. Her mouth is quite
crooked.' In *Tommy and Grizel* Barrie gives Sylvia's characteristic
mouth to Grizel too:

> She had an adorable mouth. In repose it was perhaps hard because
> it shut so decisively, but often it screwed up provokingly at one side,
> as when she smiled or was sorry or for no particular reason, for she
> seemed unable to control this vagary, which was perhaps a little bit
> of babyhood that had forgotten to grow up with the rest of her.

Not to have grown up completely was the greatest thing – for the
time of childhood is the unforgettable emblem of the bliss to which

Peter Ibbetson aspired when dreaming true. Childhood is a time when what is dammed up later flows off without restraint, when things 'go of themselves', when there is no need to do this thing or that thing or find a way, or achieve a result.

And it was the little bit of the child left in Sylvia which soon crystallised in Barrie's mind his most famous idea. 'Genius is the power to be a boy again,' Tommy announces in the novel. Tommy had made up his mind. He was going to write a book of his own about a boy –

> a reverie about a little boy who was lost. His parents find him in a wood singing joyfully to himself because he thinks he can now be a boy for ever; and he fears that if they catch him they will compel him to grow into a man, so he runs farther from them into the wood and is running still, singing to himself because he is *always* to be a boy...

The moment he conceived the idea he knew that it was the idea for him.

So much a feature of the lives of Sylvia and her boys was Mr Barrie now that in the summer of 1899 he thought nothing of showing up uninvited at Rustington-on-Sea on the Sussex coast where Sylvia, Arthur and the boys were holidaying. Dolly Parry's family owned the Mill House there, which was really no more than a cottage, but right on the shore, 'an enchanted place,' Peter Davies recalled, 'with the windmill in working order and lofts and sacks of flour to play about among.' For the past eight years, this had been a more or less regular occurrence.

Barrie took his camera with him and turned out to be quite the little photographer, taking pictures on the beach of the boys as they changed from their bathing costumes, with Sylvia – towels swirling around her in the wind – drying and dressing them.

Chapter Seven

1900: Peter and Michael Break Through

OCCASIONALLY IN HER travels through her children's minds Sylvia would find things she could not understand, and of these quite the most perplexing, so Barrie tells us, was the word 'Peter'.

It is the nightly custom of every good mother after her children are asleep to rummage in their minds and put things straight for next morning. When you wake in the morning, the naughtinesses and evil passions with which you went to bed have been folded up small and placed at the bottom of your mind; and on the top, beautifully aired, are spread out your prettier thoughts, ready for you to put on.

I don't know whether you have ever seen a map of a person's mind. There are zigzag lines on it, just like your temperature on a card, and these are probably roads in the island; for the Neverland is always more or less an island, with astonishing splashes of colour here and there, and coral reefs and rakish-looking craft in the offing, and savages and lonely lairs, and gnomes who are mostly tailors, and caves through which a river runs, and princes with six elder brothers, and a hut fast going to decay, and one very small old lady with a hooked nose … On these magic shores children at play are for ever beaching their coracles. We too have been there; we can still hear the sound of the surf, though we shall land no more.

On the night we speak of the children were in bed. All were looking so safe and cosy that Sylvia sat down tranquilly by the fire to sew.

The fire was warm, however, and the nursery dimly lit by three nightlights, and presently the sewing lay on her lap. Then her head nodded, oh, so gracefully. She was asleep.

While she slept she had a dream. She dreamt that the Neverland had come too near and that a strange boy had broken through from it. He did not alarm her. But in her dream he had rent the film that obscures the Neverland, and she saw … Michael … peeping through the gap.

The dream by itself would have been a trifle, but while she was dreaming the window of the nursery blew open, and a boy did drop on the floor. He was accompanied by a strange light, no bigger than your fist, which darted about the room like a living thing; and I think it must have been this light that wakened her. She started up with a cry, and saw the boy, and somehow she knew at once that he was Peter Pan.

He was a lovely boy, clad in skeleton leaves and the juices that ooze out of trees; but the most entrancing thing about him was that he had all his first teeth. When he saw she was a grown-up, he gnashed the little pearls at her.[16]

Peter Pan had first entered her children's minds one sunny, autumnal day in the gardens, around the same time as Michael was conceived. The boys were standing on the banks of the Serpentine when Barrie pointed to a drowned forest at the bottom of it. Peering over the edge, they could see trees growing upside down. At night, so Barrie told them, there were also drowned stars in it. And beyond the bridge nearby, which crosses the Serpentine into Hyde Park, there is the island on which all the birds are born that become baby boys and girls, the island where lives wise old Solomon Caw.

'No one,' Barrie said, 'no one who is human can land on that island, except of course Peter Pan (and he is only half human).'

'Of course you may write to him on a piece of paper,' Barrie told them, 'and then twist it into the shape of a boat and slip it into the water, and it will reach Peter's island after dark.'

By the time they were home and the paper boats were well on their way to the island, George, Jack and Peter were rapt with wonder at Barrie's tale of how Peter Pan had got there.

For all of one week of his life, he had been a boy just like them. But then one night, looking out of the open bedroom window he had seen trees far away, which were doubtless the Kensington Gardens, and the moment he saw them he entirely forgot that he was now a little boy in a nightgown, and away he flew, right over the houses to the Gardens, eventually to find his way onto the island. It is wonderful that he could fly without wings, but the place itched tremendously, and perhaps we could all fly if we

16   J. M. Barrie, *Peter and Wendy* (1911).

were as dead-confident-sure of our capacity to do it, as was bold
Peter Pan that evening.

At first, George had not been so sure about this and was unable
to remember ever wanting to escape the nursery and return to the
Gardens. But Barrie told him to think back hard, pressing his hands
to his temples as usual, and when he had done this hard, and even
harder, George did distinctly remember a youthful desire to return
to the tree-tops, and with that memory came others, as that he had
lain in bed planning to escape as soon as his mother was asleep,
and how she had once caught him half-way up the chimney. It was
quite natural that Peter had been a little wild yet, having been a
bird before he was human, and, as George added, being still very
itchy at the shoulders, where his wings used to be.

Over the ensuing days, weeks, months and years, the story of
Peter grew and grew between them.

> Most of the time Peter's heart was so glad that he felt he must sing all
> day, just as the birds sing for joy, but, being partly human, he needed an
> instrument, so he made a pipe of reeds, and he used to sit by the shore
> of the island of an evening, practising the sough of the wind and the
> ripple of the water, and catching handfuls of the shine of the moon, and
> he put them all in his pipe and played them so beautifully that even the
> birds were deceived, and they would say to each other, 'Was that a fish
> leaping in the water or was it Peter playing leaping fish on his pipe?'
>
> Now he knew he could never be a real human again, and scarcely
> wanted to be one, but oh! how he longed to play as other children
> play! Wistful tears would start in Peter's eyes when he began to think
> like this…

To play as other children play he would have to leave the island, but Solomon warned him there is no second chance for a boy who flies away to the island of dreams. And now that he had lost faith, he found he could fly no longer. That was when the poet Shelley came to the rescue.

All true poets are half-and-halfs like Peter Pan – 'They are never exactly grown up,' Barrie wrote. 'They are people who despise money except what you need for today, and Shelley had all that and five pounds over. So, when he was walking in Kensington Gardens he made a paper boat of his banknote, and sent it sailing on the Serpentine. It reached the island at night: and the lookout brought it to Solomon Caw.'[17]

Shelley's five-pound note persuaded the thrushes to build Peter a boat in which he contrived to leave the island. It took many months during which Peter paid all the thrushes sixpence a day, but eventually he launched the boat and sailed to the Gardens, and with the help of the fairies there, flew home. This was not in the end a wise thing to have done, but at least it confirmed his destiny.

As for Michael, on the day he finally did break through the film that obscures the Neverland, Barrie was with George on the coast of Patagonia, whither they had gone to shoot the Great Sloth, known to be the largest of animals, though they found his size to have been underestimated.

Besides George (seven), Barrie and the sloths, there were George's father (Arthur) and mother (Sylvia) and nanny (Mary Hodgson). It made for quite a party, as Barrie recalled:

> George, his father and I had flung our limbs upon the beach and were having a last pipe before turning in, while Sylvia, attired in barbaric

17 Barrie in *The Little White Bird* (1902).

splendour, danced before us. It was a lovely evening, and we lolled man-like, gazing, well content, at the pretty creature.

The night was absolutely still, save for the roaring of the Sloths in the distance.

By and by Mary came to the entrance of our cave, where by the light of her torch we could see her exploring a shark that had been harpooned by George earlier in the day.

Everything conduced to repose, and a feeling of gentle peace crept over us, from which we were roused by a shrill cry. It was uttered by Mary, who came speeding to us, bearing certain articles, a watch, a pair of boots, a newspaper, which she had discovered in the interior of the shark. What was our surprise to find in the newspaper intelligence of the utmost importance to all of us! It was nothing less than this, the birth of a new baby in London to Sylvia.

How strange a method had Solomon chosen of sending us the news!

Mary's bald announcement plunged us into a fever of excitement, and next morning we set sail from Patagonia for England. Soon we came within sight of the white cliffs of Albion. Sylvia could not sit down for a moment, so hot was she to see her child. She paced the deck in uncontrollable agitation.

'So did I!' cried George, when I had reached this point in the story. On arriving at the docks we immediately hailed a cab.

'Never, George,' I said, 'shall I forget your mother's excitement. She kept putting her head out of the window and calling to the cabby to go quicker, quicker. How he lashed his horse! At last he drew up at your house, and then your mother, springing out, flew up the steps and beat with her hands upon the door.'

George was quite carried away by the reality of it. 'Father has the key!' he screamed.

'He opened the door,' I said grandly, 'and your mother rushed in, and next moment her Michael was in her arms.'

There was a pause.

'Margaret,' corrected George.

'Michael,' said I doggedly.

'Is that a girl's name?'

'No, it's a boy's name.'

'But mother wants a girl,' he said, very much shaken.

'Just like her presumption,' I replied testily. 'It is to be a boy, George, and you can tell her I said so.'

George, Jack and Peter had known for some time that a baby was expected and Sylvia had prepared them by telling them they must be good or the baby wouldn't be. Agitated about what they should give him, they settled on their Methuen button, memento of Field Marshal Paul Methuen's exploits in the Boer War. Sylvia was pleased, though she didn't appreciate the sacrifice they were making. Otherwise, *all* the talk had been whether it would be a boy or a girl.

In his notebook[18] Barrie suggests that George, Jack and Peter, now going on seven, six and three, wanted a boy and he sent them a jeering message – 'One girl is more use than twenty boys!' – which is what Peter Pan says to Wendy in the Peter Pan play. Sylvia admitted, 'I'm wanting a girl.' But she was so good at boys, so a boy it was.

Michael turned out to be the most beautiful and happiest baby of all, so beautiful he could have been a girl. Sylvia fell in love with him at first sight, as did everyone, and he kept his baby curls until he was at least seven.

---

18   Barrie's notebook was his constant companion – in successive editions he scribbled anything that caught his interest and might be used in a story.

A few days later Sylvia let Barrie know that Solomon had selected well and Uncle Jim responded with a present of a rocking horse and a letter.

My dear Jocelyn,

It is very sweet and kind of you to write me from the throne, which is what I take your residence to be. He is a gorgeous boy, is Delight, which was your own original name for him in the far back days of last week or thereabouts when you used to hug Peter with such sudden vehemence that I am sure he wondered whether you were up to anything.

I don't see how we could have expected him to be a girl; you are so good at boys, and this you know is the age of specialists. And you were very very nearly being a boy yourself.

May he always be a dear delight to you and may all your dreams about all of them come true.

Ever yours,
J. M. B.

'Jocelyn' was now Barrie's pet name for Sylvia. It had a special significance. Before du Maurier died he speculated that his extra-sensory receptivity would be inherited by someone in the family, conjuring the idea that 'a little live spark' of his own 'individual consciousness' might be handed down as it were genetically. This posthumous inheritance became the subject of his third and final novel, *The Martian*, published in 1896, the year of his death. In it, he appeared to be suggesting that Sylvia was to be a mediator. Her father called the hero of the novel (who is a lightly disguised version of himself) Barty Jocelyn. Jocelyn was Sylvia's second name.

His legacy would thus be inherited by someone *in the Jocelyn line*. In June 1900 it was one reason to look with singular optimism upon Michael's birth.

If Sylvia felt that it was down to her now to take her father's legacy into the next generation, in Barrie she found an ally to help her, and so he had taken to addressing her in letters 'Dear Jocelyn'. Soon she was signing her letters to him, 'Your Jocelyn'.

From Barrie it was praise indeed that Sylvia had been 'very very nearly a boy' herself. To be a boy was the highest compliment he could have paid her. Not only was genius 'the power to be a boy again', as he'd said, but also the line was straight out of her father's novel, *Trilby*, which because it was applied to the artist's model Trilby O'Ferrall herself, was a reference whimsical enough to amuse Sylvia that she was falling under his spell, as Trilby did under Svengali's.[19]

---

19 Artist's model Trilby O'Ferrall, who falls under the spell of the hypnotist Svengali, 'would have made a singularly handsome boy', and 'it was a real pity she wasn't a boy, she would have made a jolly nice one'.

Chapter Eight

1901–03: Island Games

ONE MONTH AFTER Michael was born, George Llewelyn Davies turned seven, and one afternoon in Kensington Gardens his friend, Oliver Bailey, a year or so older and about to graduate to a preparatory school known as Wilkinson's, told him that when you went to Wilkinson's you didn't talk about fairies any longer.

Named after its headmaster, Herbert 'Milky' Wilkinson, and located at Nos. 10 and 11 Orme Square, this was an independent day school for boys with a fine academic reputation. All the Davies boys would eventually attend it. Pupils – Peter and Michael included – regularly won scholarships to leading public schools. From a very early age the boys could remember watching them walking in a crocodile through Kensington Gardens.

As soon as he heard what Oliver had been saying, Barrie knew what was coming. 'On attaining the age of eight, or thereabout,' he wrote, 'children fly away from the Gardens, and never come back. When next you meet them they are ladies and gentlemen holding up their umbrellas to hail a hansom.'

The problem was, he scribbled to himself, 'children know such a lot now, they soon don't believe in fairies, but every time a child says, "I don't believe in fairies," there is a fairy somewhere that falls down dead'.

He realised he had to act, and once again drew upon Peter Ibbetson's example, graduating from fairies to boys' adventure.

I reconsidered my weapons, and I fought Oliver and beat him. With wrecked islands I turned him. I began in the most unpretentious way by telling them a story which might last an hour, and favoured by many an unexpected wind it lasted eighteen months.

It started as the wreck of the simple Swiss family [*Swiss Family Robinson* by Johann Weiss]. But soon a glorious inspiration of the night turned it into the wreck of George and Oliver Bailey.

At first it was what they were to do when they were wrecked, but imperceptibly it became what *they had done*. I spent much of my time staring reflectively at the titles of the boys' stories in the booksellers' windows [and] found the titles even more helpful than the stories. We wrecked everybody of note, including all Homer's characters and the hero of *Paradise Lost*. But we suffered them not to land. We stripped them of what we wanted, and left them to wander the high seas naked of adventure. And all this was merely the beginning.

Before long *I* had been cast upon the island. It was not my own proposal … They found me among the breakers with a large dog, which had kept me afloat throughout that terrible night. I was the sole survivor of the ill-fated *Anna Pink*. So exhausted was I that they had to carry me to their hut, and great was my gratitude when on opening my eyes I found myself in that romantic edifice instead of in Davy Jones's locker. As we walked in the Gardens I told them of the hut they had built; and they were inflated but not surprised. On the other hand they looked for surprise from me.

'Did we tell you about the eggs we found in the sand?' asked Oliver, reverting to deeds of theirs of which I had previously told them.

'You did.'

'Who found them?' demanded George, not as one who needed information, but after the manner of a schoolmaster...

'They were found,' I said, 'by George, the younger of the two youths.'

'Who stabbed the wild pig?' asked the older of the two youths.

'Oliver Bailey,' I replied.

'Was it Oliver,' asked George sharply, 'that found the cocoa-nut tree first?'

'On the contrary,' I answered, 'it was first observed by George, who immediately climbed it, remarking, "This is certainly the *cocos nucifera*, for, see, dear Oliver, the slender columns supporting the crown of leaves, which fall with a grace that no art can imitate."'

'That's what I said,' remarked George with a wave of his hand.

'I said things like that too,' Oliver insisted.

'No, you didn't then,' said George.

'Yes, I did so.'

'No, you didn't so.'

'Shut up.'

'Well, then, let's hear one you said.'

Oliver looked appealingly at me. 'The following,' I announced, 'is one that Oliver said: "Truly, dear comrade, though the perils of these happenings are great, and our privations calculated to break the stoutest heart, yet to be rewarded by such fair sights I would endure still greater trials, and still rejoice even as the bird on yonder bough.'"

'That's one I said !' crowed Oliver.

'I shot the bird,' said George instantly.

'What bird?'

'The yonder bird.'

'No, you didn't.'

'Did I not shoot the bird?'

'It was George who shot the bird,' I said, 'but it was Oliver who saw by its multi-coloured plumage that it was one of the Psittacidae, an excellent substitute for partridge.'

'You didn't see that,' said Oliver, rather swollen.

'Yes, I did.'

'What did you see?'

'I saw that?'

'What?'

'You shut up.'

'George shot it,' I summed up, 'and Oliver knew its name, but I ate it. Do you remember how hungry I was?'

'Rather!' said George.

'I cooked it,' said Oliver.

'It was served up on toast,' I reminded them.

'I toasted it,' said George.

'Toast from the bread-fruit tree,' I said, 'which (as you both remarked simultaneously) bears two and sometimes three crops in a year, and also affords a serviceable gum for the pitching of canoes.'

'I pitched mine best,' said Oliver.

'I pitched mine farthest,' said George.

'And when I had finished my repast,' said I, 'you amazed me by handing me a cigar from the tobacco-plant.'

'I handed it,' said Oliver.

'I snicked off the end,' said George.

'And then,' said I, 'you gave me a light.'

'Which of us?' they cried together.

'Both of you,' I said. 'Never shall I forget my amazement when I saw you get that light by striking two stones together.'

At this they waggled their heads. 'You couldn't have done it!' said George.

'No, George,' I admitted, 'I can't do it, but of course I know that all wrecked boys do it quite easily. Show me how you did it.'

But after consulting apart they agreed not to show me. I was not shown everything.

George was now firmly convinced that he had once been wrecked on an island, while Oliver passed his days in dubiety. They used to argue it out together, and among their friends. As I unfolded the story Oliver listened with an open knife in his hand, and George, who was not allowed to have a knife, wore a pirate-string round his waist.

Mary Hodgson, as usual, objected to the open knife and Barrie was all for defying her, but George convinced him to let her in and 'she proved a great success and recognised the *Yucca filamentosa* by its long narrow leaves the very day she joined us. Thereafter we had no more scoffing from Nanny Hodgson, who listened to the story as hotly as anybody.'

The Swiss Family Robinson had been one of the earliest books Barrie read as a child, but intuitively he knew that his island challenges with the boys would not be so easily solved as theirs were. So he turned to his real favourite, *The Coral Island*, which tells of three ship's boys – Ralph, Jack and Peterkin – wrecked on a South Sea coral island. They build their own house, make fires, gather fruits, build boats to explore neighbouring islands, and settle down to an idyllic life, until the war canoes arrive full of cannibals…

R. M. Ballantyne's spell never left him from when he was a child, and now in the very year of Michael's birth he encouraged his wife to buy Black Lake Cottage, a rural retreat a couple of miles south of Farnham on the Tilford Road in Surrey. It was here that he found the ideal base from which to indulge his island and wrecking fantasies with Sylvia's boys.

First he journeyed with them to the Reform Club in London, surely the oddest place to learn to make a fire as Jack made it in *Coral Island*. Their teacher was a learned American by name of Seton-Thompson:

> It is a few years ago and I am in a solemn London Club, there to meet a learned American who had vowed that he would show me how to make a fire. We adjourned to the library (where we knew we were not likely to be disturbed) and there from concealed places about his person, he produced Jack's implements, a rough bow and a rougher arrow, pointed at both ends. Then he ordered a pat of butter (the waiter must be wondering still), and, like Jack, he twisted the arrow around the string of the bow and began to saw, placing the end of the arrow against his chest, which was protected from its point by a chip of wood; the other point he placed against a bit of tinder. Jack had no butter, but we had no bit of tinder. The result, however, was the same. In half a minute, my friend had made a fire, at which we lit our cigars and smoked to the memory of Ballantyne and *The Coral Island*.

Then it was down to Black Lake Cottage, where Peter Pan made the transition from Kensington Gardens, and Michael's formal initiation took place just six weeks into his young life.

In those days the salmon-coloured trains of the South-Western Railway took one peacefully down from Waterloo to alight at Farnham. Then you cycled or drove for two miles down the Tilford Road behind a horse…

> until presently, to the right of the dusty, yellow road, there was a sudden clearing in the trees. Here, in still unspoilt Surrey and the very depths, as it seemed, of the country, the little two-storey cottage stood. On three sides the dark woods came right up to the edge of the garden, and as you climbed the rising ground at the back there were glimpses and then a wide prospect through the tall, straight trunks of acres of tree-tops laid out below. No other house, in those days, was within sight or sound. And though under grey skies there was something a little forbidding about the way that Black Lake Cottage was shut in, the summer poured plenty of sunlight through its windows and over the long, level lawn.[20]

Denis Mackail's description, written in 1940, catches the atmosphere well. Today there may be more houses, but they are not intrusive. The 'cottage' is now considerably more than a cottage, there is even a new house built behind it, within the old grounds, which once included 'four acres of garden with carefully planned zig-zagging paths [which] led to secret bowers, rockeries, a Japanese garden and a pond with lizards and goldfish. There was a little tea-house lit on summer nights by Chinese lanterns,'[21] and still plenty of room for a cricket pitch and a place to play golf croquet.

The Tilford Road follows the line of one of those ancient sunken

---

20   Denis Mackail, *The Story of J. M. Barrie* (1941).

21   Diana Farr, *Gilbert Cannan: A Georgian Prodigy* (1978).

lanes for which rural Britain was once famous, and still the house is almost hidden from view by trees. On the north side, a broad-leaved haven where once Sylvia's boys let rip with their bows and arrows, is even open to the public, though it can surely only be locals who know. Across the road lies the massive, scented, impossibly tall perpendicular forestation of pine surrounding the Black Lake itself, soon to become a South Seas lagoon.

It is to the letter Peter Ibbetson's secluded pocket of dreams, cut-off from the wide world on three sides by trees, as described by du Maurier:

> An Eden where one might gather and eat of the fruit of the Tree of Knowledge without fear, and learn lovingly the ways of life without losing one's innocence; a forest that had remade for itself a new virginity, and become primeval once more; where beautiful Nature had reasserted her own sweet will, and massed and tangled everything together.

With George and Oliver challenging his belief in fairies, Barrie feared 'I was losing my grip.' But here at Black Lake he restored it by recreating Peter's childhood paradise, even using the same mystical terminology as du Maurier – 'the Tree of Knowledge':

> One by one as you swung monkey-wise from branch to branch in the wood of make-believe you reached the Tree of Knowledge. Sometimes you swung back into the wood, as the unthinking may at a cross-road take a familiar path that no longer leads to home; or you perched ostentatiously on its boughs to please me, pretending that you still belonged: soon you knew it only as the vanished wood, for it vanishes if one needs to look for it.

A time came when I saw that No. 1 [George], the most gallant of you all, ceased to believe that he was ploughing woods incarnadine, and with an apologetic eye for me derided the lingering faith of No. 2 [Jack]; when even No. 3 [Peter] questioned gloomily whether he did not really spend his nights in bed. There were still two who knew no better [Michael and Nico, the latter born in 1903], but their day was dawning.

The Black Lake experience was an extraordinary fillip to the whole fantastic Neverland adventure, just as the Mare d'Auteil had clung to the young du Maurier's mind in the Bois de Boulogne. Perhaps it was so effective because Barrie was returning the boys to the du Maurier collective unconscious as expressed in the family myth.

For that is what *Peter Ibbetson* became for the family, a kind of source-myth, and not limited to the blissful experience of the lost joy of childhood. In the novel it emerges that Mary, Duchess of Towers, *is* Mimsey Seraskier, the little girl who was besotted with Peter in their childhood – she is 'the one survivor of that sweet time'. They fall in love. She shows him how they can dream true together, Mary's 'warm life-current mixing' with his, a telepathic union offering rapture unadulterated by the physical world. Peter is overwhelmed with the joy they experience together: 'Was there ever … ever since the world began, such ecstasy as I feel now?'

Du Maurier, it seemed to readers at the time, had found a way into a timeless 'other world' just out of reach, tinkering with the idea that our terrestrial, mundane life is a mere front for true mystical being. He was a Romantic through and through and had an exquisite, spiritual sense of beauty. And now he had found a way to induce in himself a state that could replicate 'such as moves in sweet melodies, such as entrances in Chopin's Ètudes, and in Schubert's Romances'.

When John Masefield wrote that du Maurier's 'effect upon that generation was profound – I can think of no book which so startled and delighted the questing mind', he gave *Peter Ibbetson*'s public reception its proper context. In the milieu of the family, du Maurier had an even stronger influence. 'He affected us all greatly,' admitted Daphne, who owed her success to it from the moment in Alexandria when she dreamt she went to Manderley again and 'was possessed of a sudden with supernatural powers...' (*Rebecca*, 1938)

Although the first notes for the play of *Peter Pan* did not appear in Barrie's notebook until the spring of 1903, the adventures that informed so much of the action unfolded here at the Black Lake: 'I have no recollection of writing the play of *Peter Pan*,' Barrie confessed to the boys years later.

> You had played it until you tired of it, and tossed it in the air and gored it and left it derelict in the mud and went on your way singing other songs; and then I stole back and sewed some of the gory fragments together with a pen-nib. That is what must have happened, but I cannot remember doing it ... The play of Peter is streaky with you still ... A score of Acts had to be left out, and you were in them all.

Out of Black Lake, characters and episodes fell onto the page. When Peter Pan, Wendy, John and Michael arrive in the Neverland 'the chief forces of the island', which emerged from the games, are introduced. '[They] were disposed as follows. The lost boys were out looking for Peter, the pirates were out looking for the lost boys, the redskins were out looking for the pirates, and the beasts were out looking for the redskins.

'The lost boys are the children who fall out of their perambulators when the nurse is looking the other way. If they are not claimed in seven days they are sent far away to the Neverland to defray expenses. I'm captain,' says Peter.

The central conflict in the play between Captain Hook (initially called Captain Swarthy in the games) and Peter Pan – 'Most of all I want their captain, Peter Pan. 'Twas he cut off my arm.' – was also formed here. Barrie took the role of Captain Swarthy and Porthos played the pirate's dog (or a tiger in a papier-mâché mask).

Hook – a 'dark and sinister' man – is deemed 'by those in the know', as Barrie also confessed, 'to be autobiographical'. He is his doppelgänger, a strange mix of menace and 'a touch of the feminine', he admitted, adding with disarming wit: 'it sometimes gave him intuitions'.

'No. 4 [Michael] rested so much at this period that he was merely an honorary member of the band,' wrote Barrie to the boys, 'waving his foot to you for luck when you set off with bow and arrow to shoot his dinner for him; and one may rummage in vain for any trace of No. 5.'

Nico, still three years away from being born, would miss out on Black Lake altogether and his character would be utterly different to those of the others. He was never to penetrate the Neverland on this side of the curtain.

But Barrie lost no time in involving Michael wherever and whenever he could. In the area of the Black Lake that Barrie dubbed 'the haunted groves of Waverley' (with reference to the nearby ruins of the twelfth-century Cistercian abbey), Michael became the agent for the reintroduction of certain fairy tale elements into the proceedings. Here, in the midst of the most adventurous of games, 'we cassocked our first fairies (all little friends of St Benedict) in white violets'.

Long before Michael could even walk he was credited with

discovering Tinkerbell: 'It was one evening when we climbed the wood carrying No. 4 to show him what the trail was like by twilight,' recalled Barrie.

> As our lanterns twinkled among the leaves he saw a twinkle stand still for a moment and he waved his foot gaily to it, thus creating Tink. It must not be thought, however, that there were any other sentimental passages between No. 4 and Tink; indeed, as he got to know her better he suspected her of frequenting the hut to see what we had been having for supper, and to partake of the same, and he pursued her with malignancy.

On that first Black Lake holiday in the summer of 1900, the boys stayed with their parents a dozen or so miles hence in the village of Burpham, and it was here that Michael's formal initiation into the Pan cult took place.

'Do you remember a garden at Burpham,' Barrie wrote to the grown-up boys more than twenty years later, 'and the initiation there of No. 4 when he was six weeks old, and the three of you grudged letting him in so young?'

Michael was *in* all right. He had never been out.

Chapter Nine

1901–03: Unrest Within the Family

PERHAPS IT WAS actually watching Sylvia *mother* her new baby that first made Michael Barrie's favourite, or that she and Barrie secretly hoped that he would show signs of having inherited the du Maurier 'spark'. Certainly, Barrie feted Sylvia as a mother. Enacting the transmutation of Sylvia into Grizel, as one of Barrie's notebooks reveals, Sylvia was to him 'a woman who will always look glorious as a mother … a woman to confide in (no sex, we feel it in man or woman). All secrets of womanhood you felt behind those calm eyes.' One can imagine what this meant to a woman who bore five sons in ten years.

Barrie's reverence for the mother in Mrs Davies irritated Mary

Ansell, who disliked children. In a letter to No. 3 son Peter, many years later, she blamed the absence of children in their own family on Barrie's impotence, but we should also harken to Pamela Maude's view of her and Mary's confession that she didn't like them.

One is inclined to close both eyes and ears and seek sanctuary in the undeniable truth that Barrie was happiest when being a child in the company of other children. As Tommy in the novel, remembering that all children were birds once, he says as much to Grizel:

> 'Any feathers left, do you think, Grizel?' he asked jocularly and turned his shoulders to her for examination.
>
> 'A great many, sir,' she said, 'and I am glad. I used to want to pull them all out, but now I like to know that they are still there, for it means that you remain among the facts not because you can't fly but because you won't.'
>
> 'I still have my little fights with myself,' he blurted out boyishly, though it was a thing he had never meant to tell her, and Grizel pressed his hand for telling her what she already knew so well.

However, Barrie's games produced their own pressures, which as yet went unnoticed by the boys, who were dancing to a different tune to the grown-ups, who themselves were divided as to where their position should be on the issue.

Sylvia, who already shared the wild, free spirit of a boy, was all for the Black Lake experience, particularly as the first holiday followed hard on the birth of Michael and she needed all the rest she could get.

But Arthur, the father, was not so sure. He looked forward to spending time with his boys when he wasn't at work, and found it irksome that he almost always found them at play with 'Uncle Jim'.

Arthur began picking holes in Barrie's plans, drawing attention to hidden dangers of boys playing with bows and arrows and so on. But how could he complain, so happy were they in Barrie's company?

Nevertheless, Barrie must have been aware of the tension his presence was creating.

The following Easter, Arthur and Sylvia holidayed with the three eldest boys in the Isle of Wight, leaving Michael with a cold in the care of Nanny Hodgson at home. This was the first of many illnesses: health concerns for the boy perpetuated throughout his childhood. On a later occasion it would become so serious that TB was feared and Michael was transferred to Ramsgate for six months, to the seaside home of du Maurier's widow, Emma, in East Kent.

At the end of July 1901 the whole family made it down to Black Lake, this time staying at a farmhouse in Tilford for about six weeks. This was far closer than they'd been at Burpham and the boys were at Barrie's cottage every day, the distance made easier by his purchase of a steam-car, until eventually a Lanchester, the first of its sort coming out that very year, and a new chauffeur called Frederick, took over.

If Edwardian England was one long hot summer before the First World War engulfed it and almost destroyed a generation, 1901 was when it began, and was surely the most memorable part of it for the boy castaways of Black Lake Island. Happy and carefree they went naked most of the time 'that strange and terrible summer', as Barrie referred to it. He took scores of photographs and made an elaborate, illustrated book with extended captions and called it after them: *The Boy Castaways of Black Lake Island*.

Two copies only were hand-printed and bound, specifically for

Michael's benefit, so Barrie wrote in the preface – 'If it teaches him by example lessons in fortitude and manly endurance we shall consider that we were not wrecked in vain.'

One of the two was given to Arthur to read and he left it on a train. This was Arthur's role, it sometimes seemed.

The last piece of news that year was bad, the death of Porthos. He was replaced by a black and white Newfoundland, Luath, dull and apathetic of nature but no less a character. He began by catching hedgehogs in the garden of Black Lake and bringing them to the boys as if to announce he wanted to be part of the games. In time he became the model for Nana in the play of *Peter Pan*, crossing gender for the purpose.

Barrie liked to point to a particular picture of Luath nannying the boys at Black Lake, a clear forecast of his role in the fictional Darling nursery, captioning it: 'We trained the dog to watch over us while we slept.' In it Luath is sleeping in a position that is a careful copy of his charges. 'Indeed,' wrote Barrie, 'any trouble we had with him was because, once he knew he was in a story, he thought his safest course was to imitate you [the boys] in everything you did.'

How anxious he was to show that he understood the game … He became so used to living in the world of Pretend that when we reached the hut of a morning he was often there waiting for us, looking, it is true, rather idiotic, but with a new bark he had invented which puzzled us until we decided that he was demanding the password. He was always willing to do any extra jobs, such as becoming the tiger in mask, and when after a fierce engagement you carried home that mask in triumph, he joined in the procession proudly and never let on that the trophy had ever been part of him.

Long afterwards he saw the play from a box in the theatre, and as familiar scenes were unrolled before his eyes I have never seen a dog so bothered. At one matinee we even let him for a moment take the place of the actor who played Nana, and I don't know that any members of the audience ever noticed the change, though he introduced some 'business' that was new to them but old to you and me. In after years when the actor who was Nana had to go to the wars he first taught his wife how to take his place as the dog till he came back, and I am glad that I see nothing funny in this; it seems to me to belong to the play. I offer this obtuseness on my part as my first proof that I am the author. .

In London that same year the Barries moved closer to the Davieses, an address on Leinster Terrace at the corner of the Bayswater Road, situated on the north side of the Kensington Gardens and looking over the park.

Leinster Corner, as the house became known, was a two-storey, semi-detached building with a small garden in front and a larger one behind, with formal pond and fountain and at the far end a building where Barrie would write *Peter Pan*.

Mary Ansell saw their move and the death of Porthos as the beginning of the end: 'Buried with Porthos,' she wrote, 'was the first seven years of my marriage.' And Leinster Corner was walking distance to the Davieses, which made her husband's 'philanderings' (her word) with the boys ever more easy. The Davieses had in fact also moved, but only across the street to No. 23 Kensington Park Gardens.

Mary's heart pained further when in November Barrie took Sylvia and Michael on holiday to Paris, leaving both her and Arthur at home. This was to be a trend into the future, and it devastated Arthur:

2, Garden Court, Temple, E.C.

Nov. 28, 1902

Dearest Father

I don't know what your arrangements are for Christmas, nor if you
are likely to have the vicarage very full. I should like to come, if possible, bringing one boy or perhaps two. It is just possible that Sylvia
may be induced to come too, but that is not likely…

Sylvia is at present on a trip to Paris with her friends the Barries,
by way of celebration of the huge success of Barrie's new plays and
new book. The party is completed by another novelist, Mason,[22] and
they seem to be living in great splendour and enjoying themselves
very much. They left on Monday and return tomorrow [Saturday].
Barrie's new book, *The Little White Bird*, is largely taken up with Kensington Gardens and our and similar children…

My work is moderately prosperous but no more…

Your affect. son,

A. Ll. D.

Arthur's letter makes pathetic reading. His purpose in writing to his
father had been to discuss Christmas, and clearly, by 1902, there
was doubt that Sylvia and Arthur would be spending it together.

Forty-four years later, Peter, compiling the family record, read the
letter and wrote to Nanny Hodgson for her opinion, 'Did JMB's entry

---

22   A. E. W. Mason, remembered best for his 'heroic' novel *The Four Feathers*, published that
      year, 1902. For a single term from 1906 Mason was also a Liberal Member of Parliament,
      and since they met in 1898 he had been an intimate of Barrie, indeed one of his closest
      circle.

into the scheme of things occasionally cause ill-feeling or quarrel-ling between father and mother?'

Nanny replied with devotion, diplomacy and a commendable lack of clarity: 'What was of value to the One had little or no value to the Other. Your Father's attitude at all times was as "one Gen-tleman (in the true sense) to Another." Any difference of opinion was *never* "Public Property" – in the Home.'

Would Barrie wake up and acknowledge that his dream was intrud-ing on the reality of Arthur and Sylvia's marriage and threatening it? Or was their marriage not the reality? No one was quite sure any more where the fantasy began and reality ended.

Cousin Daphne wrote to Peter that Arthur could not have been hurt deeply by Barrie taking Sylvia off, that it was normal in those days for a married woman to enjoy the attentions of an admirer without the relationship becoming intimate.

But how often was that extended to going on holiday together?

It is a significant matter because, as it augured badly for the mar-riage, the tensions would have found their way in to the minds of the children, even if only subconsciously. A 'state of tension' was already being felt between Sylvia and her sister Trixy over Barrie's interference in their lives, as a number of letters show.

The feeling was that Barrie had insinuated his way into Sylvia's affections against Arthur's wishes and that she had encouraged him, and that Arthur had bottled up his feelings, perhaps to the detri-ment ultimately of his own health.

But that is to ignore what was plainly also on the table, namely Sylvia's wild, free personality, which she had never been one to hide and which Arthur knew about before they married, and indeed must have been part of what attracted him to her.

Peter recognised this and commented that his mother's 'wit

and individual attraction owed something to her heritage from
Mary Anne Clarke, the memory of which survived'. Mary Anne
Clarke was the boys' 'naughty great-great-grandmother', later to
be the subject of a novel by the boys' cousin Daphne. She was the
nineteenth-century kiss-and-tell mistress of the Duke of York, a
flirt and a bitch of the first order, whose fortune she owed to her
betrayal of the Duke.

Another analysis came from Dolly:

> I suppose [Sylvia] liked the admiration of men – if that is considered
> a fault – but as she was free from any sort of jealousy – or desire to be
> the centre of things – which may be the characteristic of those who
> love men – they naturally felt her attraction very strongly … Her
> love of admiration was less than in most attractive women, I should
> say. She was full of fun & gaiety with men – but not the true flirt, as
> she was too light in hand & in her treatment of them – to induce a
> feeling that she really liked them.

The boys were devoted to their mother and only her second son Jack
saw the situation with Barrie in less than positive terms:

> I couldn't at all agree that father did anything but most cordially dis-
> like [Barrie]. I felt again & again that father's remarks & letters simply
> blazoned the fact that he was doing all he could poor man to put up
> a smoke screen & leave Mother a little less sad…

By 1903 George and Jack were attending Wilkinson's. In March
Sylvia became pregnant with her fifth son, Nicholas (known as
Nico), who would be born on 24 November.

Peter (six) and Michael (three) became main participants in the

Kensington Garden games and Michael in particular began making up for lost time.

'At three,' Peter reminded Dolly years later, 'Michael was one of the most lovable people in the world. And he was the world to Uncle Jim.' As soon as he was able he was off with Barrie in the Gardens, picking up all the stories and mythical topography that was ingrained in the minds of the two eldest brothers.

On 11 May, Barrie wrote to both Peter and Michael a thank-you letter after Sylvia had arranged for them to give him a birthday present:

Leinster Corner, Lancaster Gate W.

11 May, 1903

Dear Petermikle,

i thank u 2 very much 4 your birth day presents and i have putt your portraitgrafs on mi wall and yourselves in my hart and your honey lower down.

i am
your friend,
J. M. Barrie

Barrie was now pinning photographs of the boys on his wall at home and confessing his love for them. Then in August the whole family were down again to Tilford. 'New and old stories for them. New and old games. Other visitors coming and going at the Cottage, expeditions in the Lanchester, or still sometimes on bicycles, to friends in the neighbourhood; and Barrie, whatever else he was doing, thinking more and more of the play,' as Mackail wrote.

One of the trips out in the car was to see Dolly, who had by this time herself married an Arthur, a diplomat and later Liberal and then Labour Member of Parliament, eventually to become a Labour Lord – 1st Baron Ponsonby of Shulbrede, a beautiful twelfth-century Augustine Priory.

It was to this thoroughly English home-county jewel, a distance of about ten miles, that Barrie brought Sylvia and Michael one afternoon in the summer of 1903. Dolly, now mother of two-year-old Elizabeth, known as 'Girly', was expecting them for tea. It was a sunny afternoon at the end of a week of incessant rain. The idyllic picture was captured in Dolly's diary.

> Jim Barry [*sic*] with a child clinging to each hand at once went & sat in the dining room chimney corner & looked so characteristic & like one of his own books. Elizabeth petrified at all the company sat refusing to eat her tea. Sylvia beautiful & satisfying – loving the house & appealing to 'Jimmy' [Barrie] about it … It was very charming to see Girly give her hand to Jimmy & with Michael [who was three] on one side & her on the other they walked down the garden path into the field – his devotion & genius-like understanding of children is beautiful & touching beyond words – as he has none himself.

Barrie with his faraway look and hand-held children: one can imagine nothing but beauty and goodness coming of it. But a darker side was also apparent. For Dolly reported that Sylvia had 'a sort of morbidness about her'. She interpreted this as 'a sort of premonition'.

When she began to say something critical about Barrie in the presence of three-year-old Michael, 'I remember [Sylvia] saying "Ssh" when I burst out with [it] … looking at Michael [in case he heard], and I felt quite ashamed.' Dolly referred to this as Sylvia's 'apprehensive imagination'.

Mackail wrote of Barrie at this time that his 'gifts' could be 'turned on to hypnotise almost anyone'. It was Svengali and Trilby all over again.

Chapter Ten

1903–04:
The Real Play

BARRIE STARTED WRITING *Peter Pan* on 23 November 1903. Its original title, *The Happy Boy*, changed to *Fairy*, then *Peter and Wendy*, later still *The Great White Father*, and latterly, before settling as *Peter Pan*, it was *Anon – A Play*. He claimed the first hand-scripted draft to have been mislaid, but in fact he had given it to Maude Adams, the first actress to play Peter in America. On page two he wrote a note vertically down the page from the top left-hand corner – 'To Maude Adams this the M. S. of Peter Pan from his humble servant and affectionate friend J. M. Barrie.' The manuscript, all handwritten and containing many second thoughts by Barrie, is now safely in the Library of Indiana University.

From it we see that the original cast list comprised: Mrs Darling; Peter Pan; John Frederick Darling; Alexander Roger Darling; Tootles; Nibs; Slightly; Curly; First Twin; Second Twin; Captain Hook; Starkey; Mr Darling; Nannna; Tiger Lily; Tippy (the Last Fairy); Wendy Maria Elizabeth Darling; Pirates; Redskins; Beautiful Mothers etc; a crocodile; a lion; a jaguar; and a Bunch of Wolves.

No Michael. His role was taken at this stage by 'Alex' or 'Alexander', possibly on account of the growing unease at home about Barrie's increasingly close friendship with him. Barrie had never used the true names of any of the boys in a work before. However, that would be corrected on the cast list the following year, when Michael was very much in evidence.

No Smee either, no Noodles, Mullins, Jukes, etc. Nanna was spelled with three 'n's (later two), and Tinkerbell went under the name of Tippy. That would change with Tink being 'quite a common girl, you know. She is called Tinker Bell because she mends the fairy pots and kettles.'

In Barrie's hometown Kirriemuir in Scotland, these sort of good fairies were known as brownies, which during the day hid in out-of-the-way corners of the house, but at night would make themselves useful in some onerous or pressing housework.

The production wasn't plain sailing. Beerbohm Tree, the famous Shakespearian actor/producer at His Majesty's Theatre, rejected the play, even suggesting that Barrie had gone quite mad. But he sold the idea to American impresario Charles Frohman over dinner at the Garrick Club, and so began one of the most fruitful associations in the history of theatre.

By the spring of 1904 the play was in production and the costumes for the lost boys were modelled on the berets, blouses and breeches Barrie first saw George and Jack wearing in Kensington Gardens in

1897. Sylvia had provided a basketful, along with photographs and a sketch of Michael. On 20 November, he wrote to her:

> My dear Jocelyn,
>
> It seems almost profanation to turn your pretty ideas about babies to stage account, but I am giving the basketful of them to those people nonetheless, and the pictures too, and may they treat them with reverence. You know Michael so well that though you didn't dare trust yourself to drawing his head (you adore him so), the rest is so like him that he could be picked out as the kings of the castle from among a million boys. He is so beautiful that the loveliest bit of him is almost as pretty as the plainest bit of his mother...
>
> Your loving
> J. M. B.

Barrie arranged for Sylvia and the boys to attend a rehearsal after the school term finished in late December. They were introduced to members of the cast as the real authors of the play and allowed to fly about the stage.

The original script commenced, as future scripts, with the famous scene in the Darling nursery at night – which could just as well be the boys' nursery on the top floor of 23 Kensington Park Gardens. We have the antics of the children at bedtime, amusing but almost too true characterisations of Arthur and Sylvia as Mr and Mrs Darling, and of Nana of course, based on Luath. Mr and Mrs Darling leave for a dinner engagement. Peter Pan appears at the window looking for his shadow (left behind on an earlier appearance), meets Wendy, who sews back his shadow and offers Peter a kiss, which becomes confused with a thimble because, being motherless, he doesn't know what a kiss is. Wendy gives him a kiss (a thimble) and Peter returns the favour by giving her an acorn button.

Tink is also discovered and redefines herself as not at all the brownie of Scottish folklore, rather a tricksy, even malignant creature who is in love with Peter (he, innocent of all matters of the heart), and has Wendy jealously in her sights. Wendy, on the other hand, is appalled to learn that Tinkerbell is the only fairy left.

We learn from Peter that 'any time a child says, "I don't believe in fairies" there is a fairy somewhere that falls down dead. They just crumple up like that [bending a finger].' Barrie returns us to this thought towards the end of the play when Tink, whose personality has been transformed, drinks Peter's medicine (poisoned by Hook) in order to save him, and appears to be dying. 'Her light is growing faint,' says Peter, 'and if it goes out, that means she is dead!' She does, however, manage to whisper to Peter that she thinks she might survive if children's belief in fairies was somehow affirmed.

Peter rises and throws out his arms – 'he knows not to whom' and implores 'She's going to die unless we do something. Do you believe in fairies? Clap your hands! Clap your hands and say, "I believe in fairies!"'

On opening night at the Duke of York's Theatre – 27 December 1904 – the cast held their breath. This was the crux. For if the audience booed and said 'No!' (as a few nasties did in later performances), Barrie was sunk.

He needn't have worried and probably didn't personally. As one, the audience, which included more grown-ups than children, shouted that they *did* believe and put their hands together and clapped.

Tink's light rose to the applause, amounting to affirmation that unless we do believe in a world of the spirit, the real world can be no more than banal.

Some reviewers celebrated this deeper significance of the play and Mark Twain wrote to Maude Adams, who would play the lead role in America, that *Peter Pan* was 'a great and refining and uplifting benefaction to this sordid and money-mad age'.

Barrie's skilful handling of the audience's emotions was matched only by the mechanical engineering for the flying. The Kirby Flying Ballet Company had filed a patent for a drum-and-shaft-based system in 1898, and produced a highly successful refined version for Barrie in 1904.

'Flying' was of course the big test. If you could fly like Peter Pan you could leave the real world behind and enter the Neverland, like du Maurier in *Peter Ibbetson*, but in a kind of children's nursery sort of way.

Not unlike the *deus ex machina* of Greek tragedy, the machine used to convey actors playing gods onto the stage, for Barrie Kirby's machine would affirm and realise the children's belief in Peter Pan.

In the original script Wendy is nervous, she's prepared to be taught how to fly but 'though I learn, mind, I won't go away with you … I don't think there's the least chance of my going.'

Peter replies: 'You won't be able to help it.'

She doesn't understand that in order to fly you have to let go. Michael, who 'looked as sharp as a knife with six blades and a saw', was the first of the boys to do so – and once you've let go you are already in the Neverland.

So successful was this aspect of the play that children were having accidents at home trying to fly, and the Prince of Wales was supposed to have had to be restrained from flying out of the Royal Box. So Barrie added a line about having to be sprinkled with fairy dust before the flying instructions would work.

Chapter Eleven

1904–05: Arthur's Retreat

I N THE SPRING of 1904, as first rehearsals began, Arthur moved the whole family out of London. It would do him no good, however, for already Barrie held the emotional balance of the family fast in his hand.

He made a symbolic gesture that underlined that his involvement with them would not be stymied by distance – he made Sylvia a gift of a horse and cart and continued writing to her and the boys, signing himself to Sylvia as 'Your loving J. M. B.'

Certainly it did nothing to curtail the separate holidays. And although visits to Kensington Gardens would be less regular and there'd be no more summer holidays at Black Lake on the scale of previous years, the move would not stop Barrie and Michael continuing to explore both, and in greater depth than before.

Also, according to Mackail, over the next few years Barrie visited them over a hundred times – 'for the day, for the night, or for the week-end'.

The new home, Egerton House in Berkhamsted, Hertfordshire, was a two-storey Elizabethan mansion on the High Street. Berkhamsted was a commuter town thirty-three miles north-west of London. The boys loved it. When the house was sold at auction in 1895, the property had comprised three sitting rooms, a dining room, a billiards room, a conservatory, four bedrooms, four box rooms and stables, and the garden with orchard was extensive enough for Black Lake Cottage never to be a justifiable draw in the following summers.

Dolly Ponsonby tells what Sylvia made of it when, on 13 February the following year, she stayed there as Sylvia's guest:

> There are huge nurseries & a schoolroom with mullioned windows which occupy the whole length of the rooms – odd-shaped bedrooms with beams & sloping floors – & all so charmingly done as only Sylvia can do things, with harmonious chinzes & lovely bits of Chippendale furniture … Spent a day with Sylvia, who is as dear as ever she was. I like to see her at luncheon at the head of her long table in the beautiful Hall with its huge windows & great 16th century chimney piece – serving food to 4 beautiful boys who all have perfect manners & are most agreeable companions, especially George [by this stage eleven going on twelve]. Arthur came down in the evening, looking handsome and severe.

It happened at this time that the writer A. E. W. Mason, a dedicated bachelor who was a firm friend of Barrie, introduced him to Captain Robert Falcon Scott. They took to one another 'instantaneously', according to Mackail – 'something more than a response on both sides. Here, for Barrie, was the bravest and manliest sailor in the world. There, from Scott, was such instant admiration – spurred on by all the tricks and all the spells – that he was captured and appropriated at once.'

Barrie described their first meeting in an Introduction to *The Personal Journals of Captain R. F. Scott, RN, CVO, on his Journey to the South Pole*, which he edited after the explorer's death in 1912.

> On the night when my friendship with Scott began he was but lately home from his first adventure into the Antarctic, and I well remember how, having found the entrancing man, I was unable to leave him. In vain he escorted me through the streets of London to my home, for when he had said good-night I then escorted him to his, and so it went on I know not for how long through the small hours. Our talk was largely a comparison of the life of action (which he pooh-poohed) with the loathly life of those who sit at home (which I scorned); but I also remember that he assured me he was of Scots extraction … According to [family traditions] his great-great-grandfather was the Scott of Brownhead whose estates were sequestered after the '45…

The Black Lake holidays had coincided with Scott's first, heroic and widely publicised expedition to the Antarctic (1901–03). Throughout the country, patriotic fervour permeated all levels of society in hopes that the Union Jack should wave first at the South Pole. Indeed, Scott became a focus for patriotism leading up to the 1914–18 war, such that 6,000–8,000 eager young men applied, as for a modern pop idol competition, for a place on his 1911 expedition.

Reports of his heroic exploits had added spice to the games, and now Barrie began to court him (there is no better word). He confessed himself 'intoxicated' by Scott's two-volume record of his first

Antarctic expedition, *The Voyage of the Discovery*, which he 'fell on [and] raced through' before flying with his new friend to a rehearsal of *Peter Pan*, which left Scott 'exhilarated and impressed'. He next took him to Black Lake Cottage, and mounted an accelerated re-run of the Castaway games. From this time his letters to Scott were signed, 'Your loving … J. M. Barrie'.

Soon he would invite him into the inner sanctum, his 'family' – and introduce him to Sylvia and the boys. What this meant to Michael was that he and Nico would join the two men after lock-out at Kensington Gardens for what Barrie referred to as 'our Antarctic exploits'.

These involved a race to reach the Pole 'in advance of our friend Captain Scott and cut our initials in it,' wrote Barrie in 1924. 'It was a strange foreshadowing of what was really to happen.' Presumably then Barrie and Michael's team won, for 'what was really to happen' was the fatal 1911 expedition when Scott was beaten to the South Pole by the Norwegian, Roald Amundsen, and died in his tent only a handful of miles away from safety, after Captain Oates trudged to his frozen grave with the immortal words, 'I am just going outside and may be some time.'

During the Easter holidays of 1905, Sylvia travelled with Barrie to Normandy, taking Michael. Peter described Michael at five as 'just about at his most beautiful', his curls and dress such that he would almost certainly been taken as a girl. He was accompanied by his more rumbustious brother Jack (ten), while Arthur, George and Peter went north to Kirkby Lonsdale. 'It has always seemed to me, looking back,' wrote Peter, 'that this arrangement can hardly have been come to without a good deal of argument and protest; and Mackail evidently takes that view. But who can say with any certainty? I have no letters referring to the episode…'

The party stayed at L'Hostellerie de Guillaume Conquérant in

Dives, the town in Northern France where William the Conqueror set sail with his fleet to conquer England in 1066.

One afternoon Barrie bought Michael a costume and had him reciting Romeo's call to Juliet, who was played by Sylvia leaning over the balcony of the hotel.

In the evenings he took Sylvia to the casino at Trouville, always the frivolous painted lady of this area. We learn from Barrie's notebook that 'Sylvia gambles – loses – gambles children.' Not literally of course, but there was a ticklish shard of truth in it.

Sylvia was nothing if not honest. She would love to have money – 'I should like to have gold stays and a scented bed and real lace pillows,' she once wrote to Arthur's sister. Now Barrie was so rich that he could afford anything she might want. 'After he made the boys famous,' said Jack, 'she [Sylvia] wore her children as other women wear pearls or fox-furs.'

While he loved his mother dearly, Jack alone of the boys recognised that the various strengths of his parents were not in any traditional Edwardian sense evenly distributed. For example 'if one of the boys was ill, it was never Sylvia who held their heads or took their temperatures – it was always Arthur who did that kind of thing.' Interesting how at odds this view was with Barrie's about Sylvia's motherliness.

His attitude set Jack apart from his brothers. 'Jack sort of took against Uncle Jim,' remembered Nico. 'Jack, who worshipped our father and mother, couldn't stand the thought of this little man thinking he could take Father's place.'

After the Paris trip, while Mary was motoring in France, Barrie invited Sylvia and Michael to Black Lake Cottage, because, he said, he needed Michael's company to inspire him in his writing, the seminal scene already described in Chapter One.

Although cricket wasn't the main point of the invitation, Black Lake Cottage had from the start been an important venue for an annual cricket festival for Barrie's team, the Allahakbarries, by then well-known.

Barrie was himself a good cricketer, and the team had formed around some of his earliest friends after coming to London in the mid-1880s. His early years in London had been a lonely time. He had shared rooms with Thomas Gilmour, a constant support emotionally who also helped him organise his finances. Money was never of interest to Barrie, nor did he wish it to be.

Beyond Gilmour he'd met a few fellow writers in the offices of a magazine called *Home Chimes*, which operated from a tiny office up two flights of stairs in a narrow lane off Paternoster Row in the City. Among them was Jerome K. Jerome, who found fame with *Three Men in a Boat*.

'We were an odd collection of about a dozen,' Jerome recalled. 'We dined together at the fixed price of two shillings a head, and most of us drank Chianti at one and fourpence the half flask.'

On other days of the week, according to Joseph Connolly in his biography of Jerome, 'Cosy evenings were quite the norm. George Wingrave and Car Hentschel would be typical company, with possibly J. M. Barrie or one or two others dropping in.'

More often, however, Barrie spent the evening alone, writing and then lying awake while Gilmour slept – which meant that Gilmour would get more work done during the day than Barrie, who having slept badly would have to take a nap on the sofa during the afternoon, his brain tired out.

Cricket bound the men into a team with a common purpose, undertaken with wit but nonetheless serious intent. Barrie loved to play games. It was the one aspect of true boyishness that he never lost, and he had a way of enthusing others to play with him. His favourites always involved a 'dead eye'. As a boy it had been spyo, smuggle bools, kickbonnety, peeries, the preens, suckers, pilly, buttony, palaulays, and fivey … On coming to London his skill at tiddleywinks was outstanding. He was amazing and une-qualled at throwing cards into a hat. There was also a trick with a penny and a stamp. He'd lick the stamp, place it face down on the penny, then flick it through the air towards the ceiling in such a way that the penny would deposit the stamp on the ceiling. 'Bar-rie was almost infallible at this,' a friend recalled. For years, there was one of these stamps stuck to the ceiling of the hall at Chequers following a weekend there with Prime Minister Stanley Baldwin and his wife in 1927.

Later, he espoused shuffleboard, where you sent a metal disc scud-ding down the deck of a long table to end up as near as possible at the end beyond two lines without dropping off the end into a tray. Or for less of a score you made the disc stop between the two lines.

'For left-handed JMB, with his wrist and its rare judgment,' wrote Denis Mackail, 'these were naturally challenges that must be met at once. Night after night, either as a guest or presently as a tenant and host, he exhibited the same skill, the same cunning, and the same insatiable eagerness for one more game.'

But of all the games he played, cricket was without doubt the fin-est – the game of the gods, as far as he was concerned. Barrie was a gifted, quirky, left-handed bowler of spin, but also a useful right-handed batsman.

'Barrie was no novice,' the writer Arthur Conan Doyle, who played for his team, once wrote. 'He bowled an insidious, left-hand good length ball coming from leg which was always likely to get a wicket.'

Wrote Mackail:

> His right-handed batting – for in games where both arms are employed
> he was always a right-hander – was almost uniformly successful. But
> perhaps his greatest distinction was the astounding courage with which
> he faced the fastest or most incalculable ball. For in those matches …
> he never flinched. He hardly troubled to dodge. His calm was spectac-
> ular, and no violent or unexpected blow was ever seen to disturb it.
> It was the others who gasped, yelled, or shuddered, but never Barrie.
> Indomitable; there can be no other epithet to sum up the cricketing
> spirit in that small and fragile frame.

It was his interest in cricket more than any other game that extended
his all-male circle. The idea of a team occurred in 1887 at Shere, a
village in Surrey where Jerome had a cottage that summer.

> It was a little old-world village in those days. There was lonely coun-
> try round it: wide-stretching heaths, where the road would dwindle
> to a cart track and finally disappear. One might drive for miles before
> meeting a living soul of whom to ask the way: and ten to one he
> didn't know. Barrie had got us together. He was a good captain. It was
> to have been Married v. Single. But the wife of one of the Married
> had run away with one of the Singles a few days before. So to keep
> our minds off a painful subject, we called it Literature v. Journalism.

On the way down from London in the train, realising that they
hadn't much hope of winning, Barrie asked his friend the explorer
Joseph Thomson what the African for 'Heaven help us' was. The
answer came, 'Allahakbar', so the club became the Allahakbars and
later the Allahakbarries.

Against Shere they were all out for eleven runs, but the Alla-hakbarries became a famous institution, with village and country house fixtures and an annual game first with the famous artistic community in the beautiful village of Broadway in Worcestershire, and then from 1900 in the large flat garden at Black Lake Cottage.

A match would be followed by all the games Barrie could imagine including golf-croquet, and cricket with the men playing left-handed to the ladies. 'The new variant [of golf] that some inspired charac-ter had recently given to the world,' wrote Mackail, 'had instantly become a mania [for Barrie] only second to cricket, and he must have played it thousands of times during the next thirty-odd years.'

No one ever had such an eye, or no one at any rate combined it with such astonishing luck … In tactics he was incomparable. The game never had a greater or more devoted exponent.

As the game then had no governing body or association, Barrie made up his own rules: one was that nobody, male or female, must ever swing the mallet between their own feet. Others, perhaps, were less surprising, but whatever they were, you must always accept what you were told. There was no appeal, and it was quite useless to say that you had played differently elsewhere.

[The impresario] Charles Frohman, for whom even this amount of exercise was against all precedent, would find himself playing golf-croquet at Black Lake. And because it was Barrie who made him do it, he was fascinated. Insisted on installing hoops, pegs, and all the rest of it at the retreat which he shared with another manager, Charles Dillingham, outside New York. Amazement of all onlookers, and, alas, disillusionment for C F. Even with other English playwrights it just wasn't the same game. It wasn't funny, or exciting, and there was no magic. Barrie, he discovered again, had got to be there for that.

By the time it was all over Barrie's friends wouldn't believe how they had been so led into the childish follies in which they became involved.

In 1905, when Sylvia and Michael came down to Black Lake Cottage, Michael was recruited as the team's mascot and photographed on the lawn being presented with the match ball by E. V. Lucas, there with his wife Elizabeth and daughter Audrey,[23] Michael looking 'like he could be either a girl or a boy with his long hair and loose-fitting smock: an ideal Peter Pan', according to Kevin Telfer.[24]

But far and away the more significant event occurred after the Allahakbarries dispersed, and Barrie and Michael discovered that death by drowning in the mermaid's pool could be an awfully big adventure.

---

23 E. V. Lucas was a prolific and well-known writer with reputedly the largest collection of pornography in England. Audrey, just two years older than Michael, would remain a friend of his for life.

24 Kevin Telfer, *Peter Pan's First XI* (2010).

Chapter Twelve

1905–07:
Death Takes a Hand

FROM THIS MOMENT the definition of 'boy' changed: 'To be a real boy' was to pass over to the other side. It was a turning point. Henceforth, Peter Pan had one foot in the afterlife, a Neverland altogether more profound than Barrie had given the play's original audiences to imagine. The inspiration for it brought Peter's story to its third arena. After Kensington Gardens in London and the Black Lake in Surrey came the Highlands and islands of Scotland.

In the same year as Michael played Peter on the point of drowning in the mermaid's lagoon, 1905, Barrie wrote in his notebook: 'Hogg's Queen's Wake – a sort of Rip van Winkle.' Hogg is James

Hogg, the Scots shepherd, born in Ettrick in 1770, who imbibed the great oral tradition of the supernatural at his mother's knee and was at his poetic best writing poems of the vernacular patterned on the old minstrelsy, such as 'The Witch of Fife'.

As a young man with an ink-horn slung around his neck, Hogg had wandered the hills of Scotland's Arcadia, teaching himself to write and discovering a genius for poems that gave the whole world of Fairyland and floating thought, witchcraft and necromancy, a permanent substantial form.

Being spirited away to 'the other world' is the main force of Hogg's poem 'Queen's Wake', which Barrie had noted as the basis of a play. Embedded in it is the poem or ballad of *Kilmeny*.

Hogg is said to have fallen asleep one day out on the hills and dreamed the dream of Kilmeny, about a girl of poetic nature, a lover of solitude, who, wandering alone at twilight, is spirited away into the 'land of thought' and disappears into the wild among the hills. Her friends look for her, their cries echoing around the glen. Their search is in vain, but long years later she returns to find a place in the land of living, and can remember nothing of where she has been:

> For Kilmeny had been she knew not where,
> And Kilmeny had seen what she could not declare.
> Kilmeny had been where the cock never crew,
> Where the rain never fell, and the wind never blew;
> But it seemed as the harp of the sky had rung,
> And the airs of heaven played round her tongue,
> When she spake of the lovely forms she had seen,
> And a land where sin had never been,—
> A land of love, and a land of light,
> Withouten sun or moon or night;

Where the river swa'd a living stream,
And the light a pure celestial beam:
The land of vision it would seem,
A still, an everlasting dream.

Kilmeny, now too good and pure for this world, must inevitably return to 'that silent shadow-world that marches a hand's breadth from our own'.[25]

Hogg carried Kilmeny's image in his mind's eye until the day he died. And the legend became a touchstone for Barrie. He alluded to it in various books, and often, as we shall see, in his relationship with Michael, and in the play *Mary Rose*, which many see as Barrie's best and which is still produced today, more faithfully than any production to be seen of *Peter Pan*.

There are countless instances of men as well as women vanishing in the hill country of Scotland and then returning when all hope of their being seen again has disappeared. They haven't aged and they remember nothing. The fairies have taken them and then, perhaps having tired of them, returned them with all memory of the episode wiped from their minds, to the spot where they first disappeared.

As early as 1902 in *The Little White Bird* Barrie had rehearsed the possibility of dead young mothers returning as ghosts to see how their children fare. 'There is no other inducement great enough', he wrote, 'to bring the departed back.'

By April 1906, Barrie was writing to his close friend, the author and academic Sir Arthur Quiller-Couch, known as 'Q': 'I do strongly believe in the return from the dead as a strong dramatic motive.'

---

25 Daphne du Maurier, *The du Mauriers* (1937). Daphne, another of Barrie's prodigies at this time, picked up on his preoccupation with the passage 'between two worlds' as surely as Michael would.

In January 1906, he invited Sylvia and Michael to Paris again, but Sylvia declined, saying Michael was ill. Illness had also apparently prevented the boy from attending the first of the annual revivals of *Peter Pan*.

By now it was obvious to everyone that Barrie and Michael had a special relationship. No. 5 son Nico would say that Barrie was in love with him, 'as he was in love with my mother'.

Barrie was a self-made man of forty-six, a big name as an author and playwright. In 1906 alone he made £44,000, the equivalent of £3.5 million today (the Prime Minister, as First Lord of the Treasury, was paid one-tenth of that). He wrote about his fabulous wealth in a play, *The Accursed Thing* (1907), but, however accursed, it played a significant part in his main business, his relationship with Michael, which needed Sylvia's compliance.

He was, wrote Mackail,

> a man of power, a man who had got what he wanted – or at any rate what he had set out to get – a man whose gifts could be turned on to hypnotise almost anyone, who had gone his own way as an author and yet brought the world to his feet. A man who had left Scotland with twelve pounds in his purse, and was now so rich that only Gilmour, as a matter of fact, had the faintest idea what his fortune was worth.

Michael's illness was not going to stand in the way of his seeing him when he wanted to. Barrie commanded Frohman, now one of the most, if not *the* most, powerful impresario on Broadway and in London's West End, to transport *Peter Pan* to Michael's bedside in Berkhamsted. 'Frohman waved his own wand, had dresses and properties packed up, and sent some of the company down to Egerton House to act scenes from the play in Michael's nursery,' wrote Mackail, noting also that no one else on the planet could have got Frohman to do such a thing.

Barrie wrote of the event,

> We took the play to his nursery, far away in the country, an array of vehicles almost as glorious as a travelling circus; the leading parts were played by the youngest children in the London company, and No. 4, aged five, looked on solemnly at the performance from his bed and never smiled once.

In May, Barrie repeated his invitation for Sylvia and Michael to accompany him to Paris. And she accepted.

The whole magical, emotional, ridiculous charabanc was careering out of control, perhaps looking unconsciously for an escape route from major upset.

Arthur provided one. Later the same month he noticed a slight swelling on the side of his face. He had taken himself to the dentist, and the dentist had made him an appointment with 'an expert in cheek and jaw'.

Then another Arthur had shot himself. Barrie's agent, Arthur Addison Bright, had been caught diverting money from his clients' accounts into his. In Barrie's case, it amounted to £16,000. He hadn't even noticed the shortfall and argued for clemency.

This, besides causing great dismay for everyone concerned, meant that Sylvia and Michael would not now be accompanying Barrie to Paris. It was just as well. On 2 June, Arthur wrote to his sister, Margaret:

Dearest Margaret,

I am sorry to say I have bad news. The swelling in my face turns out on investigation not to be an abscess, as was hoped, but a growth. It is of a very serious kind, called sarcoma, and requires an operation…

Your affect. brother,
A. Ll. D.

The operation involved the removal of Arthur's upper jaw and the roof of his mouth. Barrie dropped everything and put himself at Sylvia and Arthur's disposal, standing sentinel over Arthur in his decline, playing, as Peter put it, 'the leading part in the grand manner'. While Arthur scribbled notes of what he was thinking about – his sons, 'S's blue dress', Porthgwarra (where he and Sylvia honeymooned in 1892', etc. – Barrie made notes for a prospective work: 'The 1,000 Nightingales: A hero who is dying. "Poor devil, he'll be dead in six months."'

Barrie saw to it that he had the best possible treatment, and in October wrote to Dolly a little tersely after she expressed concern about Arthur's treatment:

Oct 10, 1906

Dear Mrs Ponsonby,

Dr Rendel and the local doctor are attending Arthur mainly to do certain necessary things that any medical man can do. They have not and never have had in any way this case in their charge, that

is [surgeon] Mr Roughton's, from whom they have their instructions. He is in touch with Sir Frederick Treves [also a surgeon …
who said] that everything that could be done for a human being
was being done.

Yours sincerely,
J. M. Barrie

Dolly might have been reassured to know that Treves was the surgeon who treated Joseph Merrick, the man known as the Elephant
Man who had such severe facial and other deformities that he was
exhibited in a penny gaff shop on the Whitechapel Road in London's East End, where Treves met him.

Thank goodness for Nanny, who was keeping everything on an
even keel at home. While Sylvia was at Arthur's bedside at the nursing home at 12 Beaumont Street (next to where the King Edward
VII Hospital for Officers is today), Michael's sixth birthday was
approaching:

For June 16th

My Michael's birthday

I am coming to see you and I will bring my present to you my dear
darling. I want to tell you about Father, who is so brave & you will
be so proud that you are his little boy.

I don't like being away from you on your dear birthday but I shall see
you in a few hours. Oh my little Michael won't it be nice when we are
all together again. Father does so want to be back with his sons. He is
sleeping now, & I am being very still & writing this letter by his bed.

Mr Barrie is our fairy prince, much the best fairy prince that was ever born because he is real.

Loving Mother

Barrie had been buying the boys presents to keep them happy. Sylvia, aware now that she really couldn't do without Barrie, felt the need to draw a clear line between reality and fantasy for Michael. But the difference between Michael and the other boys was that they knew the Neverland was make-believe, while to Michael make-believe and true were the same.

On the same day Arthur wrote *his* birthday letter to Michael:

My very dear birthday boy Michael,

How I wish I could see you with my own eyes on your birthday, when you are really 6 years old. But I can only wish you many happy returns by a letter, and send you my dear love, and a pencil as a little birthday present for you … Perhaps when I am well enough to come back you will take me to see some cricket matches. I am going to have quite a long holiday, and shall be able you take you to school every morning…

Now goodbye my dearest 6 year-old boy, and I hope you will have a very very very jolly birthday.

From your affectionate Father

Barrie ensured that he would. He ordered William Nicholson, the designer responsible for the costumes in *Peter Pan* to run up a Pan costume for Michael and get it down to Egerton House. As any six-year-old would have been, Michael was knocked out by the gift and wasn't out of it for days.

Eleven days later, Arthur announced he was coming home.

My dear Michael,

Here is my last letter of all before coming home to Berkhamsted and my boys. We are coming all the way in Mr Barrie's motor car, if it is fine, and we shall arrive in good time for tea. I want very much to see your motor car and Peter's stone roach [fishing gear], as well as Nico's musical wheel-barrow. And I wonder whether there will be any good songs to be heard which I have never heard before. If there are it will be altogether a fine homecoming for Mother and me. After tea tomorrow you will take me carefully for a walk all round the garden, and show me all the flowers which have come up since we went away?

I wonder whether I shall be able to read to you when we have come back. You know that I cannot speak very plainly just now but if you can understand what I say well enough, I shall have plenty of time to go on reading Biblia to you right on to the end. Or perhaps you will now be able to read aloud to me as well as sing songs to me.

Goodbye now, my dear boy. My love to all my boys, not forgetting dear Nicko.

From your affectionate Father

Arthur had an artificial jaw fitted and was wearing a black eye patch, and it is unlikely that reading Biblia in his distorted voice to Michael (presumably some sort of bible study) will have been anything other than disturbing.

The reactions of the boys go unrecorded, other than Peter's, who referred to the artificial jaw as 'the most dreadful element in the whole sad story … a nightmare … it so soon became impossible to wear'.

In August, Barrie accompanied the family to Rustington. Arthur, Sylvia and 'Jimmy', as Arthur began to refer to him, made 'as odd a variation of the *mènage à trois* as ever there was', as Peter had to admit.

Granny Emma du Maurier had called the family together and rented Cudlow House, a large detached dwelling with plenty of privacy, occupied by Sir Hubert Parry before his family had moved to Knightscroft House on the opposite side of Sea Road.

In Arthur's words, the boys played 'endless cricket and lawn tennis in the garden', Sylvia and Barrie too, though his underhand serve, while reputedly treacherous, demanded little of most opponents. And it was on this holiday that Barrie took the now famous photographs of Michael in costume as Peter Pan. In time they would be used as a reference for the sculptor commissioned to create the statue of Pan still to be seen in Kensington Gardens today.

It was on this holiday, too, following the one-to-one sessions between Barrie and Michael at the Black Lake, that it first became clear that Michael had developed an unnatural terror of water. Nightmares had also ensued. His sleep was full not so much of dreams as of 'strange scenes of inexplicable reminiscence, all vague and incoherent, but which had something to do with the number seven'.[26]

Barrie's method of captivating a child was to tell him a story in which both he and the child figured, consuming the child's interest with a narrative often full of menace, and the session at the mermaid's lagoon would have been no exception. We may legitimately wonder whether Michael was indeed placed on a rock in the Black Lake, probably naked as the boys often were there, with the waters

---

26   J. M. Barrie, *Neil and Tintinnabulum* (1925), largely based on his relationship with Michael.

apparently rising around him, in order to plumb the situation for Michael's imaginative response. There is a photograph of Barrie and Michael in the Peter Pan costume, with Barrie playing Hook wrestling menacingly with Michael's Peter Pan, a situation that Nico – while looking at the photograph – much later described as 'very typical [of their interaction] and unusual'.[27]

Whatever did happen, not even Sylvia could entice Michael into the sea now, and as Nanny didn't swim, Barrie arranged for the housekeeper of Black Lake Cottage, one Mabel Llewelyn, to come down for three weeks to teach him, but it did no good.

In fact, Michael would never be able to swim more than twenty yards in spite of developing into perhaps the most sporty of all the boys and making great efforts to overcome his fear. His brothers, on the other hand, were all fine swimmers.

Barrie never holidayed by choice at the seaside, which he regarded as a dull experience – all you can do is 'wander along the weary beach, fling pebbles at the sea and wonder how long it will be until dinner time'. So, towards the end of their stay he repaired to Scotland and invited the family to take another holiday as his guests at Fortingall, just a few miles west of Strathtay.

Arthur wrote to Margaret on 6 September:

> We are just at the end of our stay here, having failed to get an extra week for which we asked. We have succumbed to an invitation to go to Scotland with Jimmy for the close of the holidays.
>
> First the scheme was to take George and Jack only, then we were unwilling to abandon Peter, and lastly Michael has, inevitably, been included. Nicholas [at three] so far remains out of the cast. We are to

---

27   Letter to Andrew Birkin.

stay at a small village called Fortingal, in Glen Lyon, Two and a half
miles from Loch Tay among high mountains … and surrounded by
burns in which the boys will fish. They are all prodigiously excited
at the prospect … The holiday [at Rustington] has altogether been
entirely successful.

Arthur barely disguised his true feelings. He had 'succumbed' to
the invitation, and the inevitability of Michael being in the party
seems laced with not a little cynicism. It would of course have
been unthinkable for Barrie to invite the family anywhere without
Michael. Nevertheless, Arthur committed to going with all but
Nico in attendance.

'Dear Jimmy,' he wrote after it was all over,

You have done wonderful things for us since the beginning of June
– most, of course, during June and also in the last week – but at
Rustington also you made all the difference to the success and pleas-
antness of the holiday.

We all hope to see you soon and often,

Yours,
A. Ll. D.

Chapter Thirteen

1906: Barrie's Scotland

BARRIE'S SCOTTISH HERITAGE ran deep. He was an Ogilvy by virtue of his mother, Margaret, who was the dominant force in the family, but modestly born. The Ogilvies are one of the most distinguished families in Scotland. Oglilvy lands are in Angus, a county in eastern Scotland located between the mighty Grampians to the north and the city of Dundee on the Tay estuary to the south. Running through its high central plain in the lea of this mighty mountain range is the South Esk River, which channels many a Grampian torrent into the sea at Montrose to the east. 'Ogilvy' (in Gaelic, 'Ocel-fa') actually means high plain, so clan identity is hewn out of the very landscape over which it held sway for many years, on and off, since Pictish times (as early as 100 BC) into which Barrie was born.

In the first century AD the Ogilvy line supplied one of the earliest recorded Mormaers (regional leaders in medieval Scotland), by name 'Dubacan of Angus'. A descendant of his, one Gilchrist, became the first Earl of Angus in about 1115 AD, the highest position in the nobility after the feudal system was adopted under King David, and of course hereditary.

In the fourteenth and fifteenth centuries the Ogilvies also became hereditary sheriffs in the county. In the 1430s Sir Patrick Ogilvy commanded the Scottish forces fighting with Joan of Arc against the English. In 1425 Sir Walter Ogilvy was appointed Lord High Treasurer of Scotland under James I. In 1430, he was an ambassador to England, and four years later attended Princess Margaret on her marriage to the Dauphin, heir of the throne of France. From Sir Walter's son, Sir John Ogilvy, descend the Ogilvies of Airlie – in 1459 Sir John received a charter to Airlie Castle, four miles to the south-east of Kirriemuir. In 1473 the family also acquired Cortachy Castle, four miles to the north of Kirriemuir. And so on, the line continuing and still based at Cortachy to the present day.

So, students of Barrie used to thinking of him as a poor weaver's son from Kirriemuir, which is a burgh in Angus, should also remember that he had Ogilvy blood in him, and the clan was all around him. Membership offered certain advantages. With the coming of power looms to the weaving industry in Kirriemuir, Barrie's father David had left to become an accounts clerk in nearby Forfar, but returned home when Messrs Ogilvy opened a big factory on the banks of the little Gairie, where David was instantly in line for the better position of principal clerk.

Ogilvy exploits also formed a significant part of Jamie Barrie's early cultural education. Kirriemuir lies on the west side of the high plain that gave the clan their name, then Forfar and finally Brechin on the east side. Along the way lies a miscellany of little villages, such as Careston, Fern, Glenquiech, Memus, Shielhill, Inverquharity and Glamis, all heavy with stories, legends and folklore – stories which seem to define the landscape more perfectly than any map and in their telling project the spirit of the local people and the magical world they took for granted.

Nico wrote of how the boys would listen 'with bated breath while he told us magic stories', not only as they walked through Kensington Gardens but now in Scotland – 'through Dhivach [above Loch Ness, which they would visit in 1907 for the first time] or through the Trossachs'.

Next to telling stories was his love of walking and fishing. In his schooldays Barrie was so famed for walking his native landscape that his maths master formulated a special problem for his class: 'If two boys walk from Dumfries to Carlisle, a distance of thirty-three miles, in eight-and-a-half hours, how long would one boy take to cover the same distance walking at the same pace?' Barrie would say, in gloomily self-deprecating fashion, how this 'floored one youth repeatedly – and he may be at it still'.

Meanwhile his appetite for fishing was first filed in his notebook when he was sixteen. It includes his 'Fishing and Walking Statistics' for the holidays of that year and the next. He lists 'Distance Gone Over', 'Catch', 'Name of the Stream', 'Name of Companions' – most often only one, James Robb, who would become an ironmonger and remain a friend for ever. The tallies are often amazing and the recording pernickety, for example: 'Fished 12 times. Caught average of 2 doz & 6 in all 30 doz. Walked 18 times. Average of 13 11/18 in all 245 miles. J. M. Barrie [signature]. holidays. 1876.' Again: 'Fished six times. Caught average of 2 doz & 6 in all 15 doz. Walked in 1 six times average of 13 5/6 in all 83 miles. J. M. Barrie [sig.]. holidays. 1877.'

From the moment Arthur Davies fell terminally ill with cancer of the jaw, Barrie's Scotland became the big new influence on the lives of the boys, and particularly, eventually, on Michael's life, for Barrie would soon be bringing him to Scotland annually, often for two or more months at a time. The mountains and lochs would open to Michael more readily than to any of the boys. Here he would find his own 'island', and in spiritual and aesthetic terms climb to the top of a mountain that Barrie would never reach.

The Highlands had become the holiday choice of the rich English, and some great Scottish estates were now opening their doors, rivers and wildlife habitats to them. The popularity of the novels of Sir Walter Scott, the English artist J. M. W. Turner's Romantic vision of the magnificence of nature and the violence of the elements, Edmund Burke's philosophical appreciation of the concept of the Sublime and the poetic interpretation of elemental forces in nature by such as Byron, Shelley and Wordsworth prepared the way. But it was royalty's adoption of Balmoral Castle (Queen Victoria first leasing it in 1842 and Prince Albert buying it for his wife as a Highland residence in 1852), that led to sporting lodges, ghillies' bothies, housing for stalkers and other attendants, as the gentry made the summer school holidays and parliamentary recess a time to come to Scotland, fish the rivers, rent a boat.

Barrie's choice of Fortingall for the Davieses' first foray was far from arbitrary. The place still abounds today in stories close to his heart.

About fifty miles west of Kirriemuir, the village lies in Glen Lyon, the long, narrow, winding glen in Highland Perthshire through which the River Lyon flows west to east, through a narrow pass where the mountains rise straight up from its banks, into the Tay.

At Fortingall the glen widens into level fields and the village occupies a quite beautiful location that has been occupied since time immemorial. Its church, dedicated to Coeddi, Bishop of Iona, was founded circa 700 AD, while recent archaeological investigations suggest that this was one of the earliest monasteries in Britain. Iona was the fount of Christianity in Scotland. Fortingall was in there at the very advent of it in Britain.

But this is only the surface picture. Finely carved cross-slabs put the site at the very changeover from pagan times, and there is much evidence that takes us back further into history.

At the head of Glenlyon stands a tiny pagan shrine called Tigh-nam-bodach, which means 'the old woman's glen'. The old woman refers to the witch, or goddess source of all rivers. Her 'family' are said to live within the shrine in winter but outside in summer. These are in fact water-worn stones, many of which have been purloined to stand sentry on the gateposts of local houses to ward off evil spirits. 'Lyon', you will soon discover over a drink at the local pub, is the Gaelic word for 'grinder', which refers to the action of the river on these stones, which are said to be moulded by the river witch into their unusual shapes. Between two of them is said to run the most prominent ley-line[28] through the glen.

Pulling us further back in time are three groups of three standing stones between 6,000 and 3,000 years old. They can be seen in a field to the east of the village, and to the south of them lies Duneaves.

'Duneaves' derives from the Gaelic 'Tigh Neimhidh', meaning 'House of the Nemed' ('House of the Spirits', a pagan meeting-place). But this pagan meeting place must have been special, because it lies in the shadow of Schiehallion, Gaelic for *Sìdh Chailleann*, which translates as 'Fairy Hill of the Caledonians'.

---

28 Ley-lines are supposed to form a network of energy highways of historical and mystical significance on the earth's surface. Alfred Watkins, 1921.

Schiehallion, the bold, brooding mountain that rises high above Fortingall to the north (and more immediately behind the grim castle of the Stewarts of Garth), was indeed the epicentre of the sacred in the Scottish Highlands, and is still regarded as such today.

All this rather strange history is brought together into a living whole today by a 5,000-year-old yew tree, quite possibly the oldest living thing on earth, which sits in its own place beside the church. Today's New Age pagan people have decorated it with coloured strings carrying a small white skeleton, wool from sheep or goat and other animal parts.

It is clear from all that one discovers of Fortingall that from the beginning the lairds of Glenlyon's knowledge of the magic arts and apparent ability to 'summon spirits from the vasty deep'[29] characterised the culture here right into the nineteenth century and continues to do so today. One is not surprised to hear that the creator of Harry Potter chose it as her habitat. J. K. Rowling has the Killiechassie estate just eight miles away.

Heroic medieval and later stories of clan conflict also abound, signalled by place names such as MacGregor's Leap. In 1565, high up on the road which leads west and northwards out of the village, following the line of the Lyon which cascades forcefully down a series of falls and dark, tranquil pools here, Gregor MacGregor of Glenstrae, local MacGregor chieftain but also foster son and son-in-law of one of the early Campbell chiefs of Glenlyon, leapt to safety across the roaring torrent to evade those Campbells who would take him for avenging the murder of two of his clan.

Turner painted the Leap. The Laird of Glenlyon whom Barrie knew – Sir Donald Currie (1825–1909), a shipping magnate from

---

Greenock who became MP for Perthshire and in 1885 purchased the Glenlyon Estate, including the village of Fortingall – had a large collection of Turners.

When the Davies family arrived in September 1906 they stayed not at the Fortingall hotel, an eye-catching building which, along with most of the village was redesigned in 1891 by Arts & Crafts architect James MacLaren, but in the Laird's own Glenlyon House on the western fringe of the village. Glenlyon House is reputed to have been the home of Robert Campbell of Glenlyon, infamous for his part in the massacre of the MacDonalds at Glencoe.

All of this must have been an exciting prospect for the boys, particularly as the whole supernatural culture was a rather different one to the delicate, joyous, pretty little fairies of middle-class Edwardian England, and it was Barrie's birthright.

In Scotland, dour gloom regularly attends its supernatural beliefs and legends, even if all summer long the young folk were having fun up in the sheilings. The national psyche of Scotland has a sense of its own fate or *doom*, a sense of the cruelty of the mystery of life and death and of the darkness that enshrouds the whole. A gloom so tangible that even 'to praise a babe upon the nurse's arm was to incur suspicion of wishing to bring down ill upon its head', wrote Sir George Douglas in 1901.

Kirriemuir and neighbouring Forfar became famous for the practice of witchcraft. Many of the older buildings have a 'witches stane' built in to ward off evil. This is a hard grey stone set into the local red sandstone, which the buildings were built from.

In Scotland in the 1660s, some 300 women were executed as witches. Names such as Isobel Shyrie, Jane Howatt, Helen Guthrie, Janet Galloway and Elspet Alexander, the last two of which participated in the Kirriemuir coven, are still known in the area today.

Helen was strangled by the executioner on 14 November 1662, and her body incinerated in a barrel of tar. This was the usual method of execution for a witch, although tar was not the only means used to burn the body.

The Auld Licht, a fiercely puritanical Protestant sect and 'the keenest heresy hunters' in the Presbyterian Church, which Barrie wrote about in the three novels that first made him famous,[30] was the organisation behind the trials and executions of hundreds of witches in Scotland, having laboured strenuously to stir the civil authorities to inflict the death penalty.

We read of Barrie's maternal grandfather, 'a stoop' of the Auld Licht, going to the local kirk with

> his mouth very firm now as if there were a case of discipline to face, but on his way home he is bowed with pity. Perhaps his little daughter who saw him so stern an hour ago does not understand why he wrestles so long in prayer tonight, or why when he rises from his knees he presses her to him with unwonted tenderness.

In fact, the Auld Licht did nothing to stamp out superstition, it simply drove it underground. Even Church ministers preached against them, while watching their backs the whole time.

The effect exercised upon popular superstition by the ruling passion of Calvinistic religion is one of the most striking features of Scottish folklore. Pamphlets and articles written by ministers show their acceptance of the idea of fairies and the phenomenon of second

---

30   *Auld Licht Idylls, A Window on Thrums* and *The Little Minister*.

sight, and there are cases in which ministers join with parishioners to recover women who have been spirited away.[31]

Barrie's mother may have been born a member of the Auld Licht, but she had left it of her own volition long before her son Jamie was born. He grew up saturated with the supernatural superstitions of previous generations. In his time there were still people interested in the way witches exercised their domination over the minds of those they would control. Only the methods were changing – from casting a spell to playing mind games; from sticking pins in a tiny human effigy to pegging a fictional character on a person and re-writing their destiny in a story.

The effect was the same. It was all about creating 'a secret sympathy' with a life and then dominating and manipulating it. In his novel *Tommy and Grizel* Barrie explained how it was done: to re-write Grizel's destiny was to explore the possibility that the fictional effigy he was creating of her might intrude on the reality, 'as a wheel may revolve for a moment after the spring breaks'. What was being undertaken was the same today as yesterday, only now it was being described in psychological rather than supernatural terms. Barrie lived right on the cusp of the two interpretations.

Barrie himself used the language of spiritualism in analysis of the 'unruly sinister' side of himself which he admitted lay beyond the more witty, whimsical exterior:

> Did I never tell you of my little gods? I so often emerged triumphant from my troubles, and so undeservedly, that I thought I was especially looked after by certain tricky spirits in return for the entertainment I gave them. My little gods I called them, and we had quite a bowing

---

31   Sir George Douglas, *Scottish Fairy & Folk Tales* (1900).

acquaintance. But you see, at the critical moment they flew away laughing.

This is identical to the spiritualists' belief that people are inhabited by immortal spirits, which may be beneficent or malevolent. In Barrie's novel *Tommy and Grizel*, his little gods are bad devils that enjoy the cruel games he plays with Grizel's heart, and when he is about to offer poor Grizel marriage, 'Tommy heard the voices of his little gods screaming to him to draw back.'

In 1898, Barrie's interest in spiritualism had brought him to Strathtay with his wife and close friend Arthur Conan Doyle, a member of the Society for Psychical Research (SPR) since 1893. Their purpose was to look into the haunting of Ballechin House, which had made the pages of *The Times* in August 1896 and led to a decision by the SPR to begin a long-term investigation, the first of its kind anywhere in the world.

Barrie's interest also led to a friendship with the writer Marie Corelli, who had a house not far from Strathtay, at Killiekrankie. Corelli was a highly successful occult novelist and Queen Victoria's favourite author. Barrie would stay at her house with Michael in the summer of 1913.

Millions of people were spiritualists in Britain at this time. Members of the SPR included Prime Minister Arthur Balfour; philosopher William James, the brother of novelist Henry James; naturalist Alfred Russell Wallace; and scientists William Crookes and Oliver Lodge.

There were all sorts of tricksy and malevolent figures in the superstitious culture of the area of Barrie's childhood, such as the Kelpie, whose appearances were generally timed either to give warning of death by drowning, or to lure men to a watery grave, and tales of 'ghaists' or wraiths of the sort reported at Ballechin House at Strath-tay: 'These are the ghosts that go wailing about old houses,' wrote Barrie, who before long would be writing about them in plays such as A *Well-Remembered Voice* and *Mary Rose*.

Small wonder then, as he was developing an idea about the dead returning to move among the living, that he had chosen as the boys' introduction to Scotland the very fount of the supernatural in Fortingall.

Michael, who will have enjoyed Barrie's magical and heroic tales of the region as much as his brothers, felt immediately at home for another reason, however.

At Fortingall he was for the first time really in the wild. The contrast with London and even rural Surrey and Sussex-by-the-sea was immense. The first sight of highland Scotland must have moved him even at six, as it had Pamela Maude a few years earlier:

Late at night a private bus pulled by two horses took us in darkness to a great station [King's Cross, London]. There was a load of trunks and bicycles with us, a fishing rod ... We saw the fitful lights of the streets and then the station; smelt the puffing smoke and heard whistles and shouts through a haze of drowsiness. Suddenly we were awake form [sic] a deep sleep and sitting up in our bunks. Someone had pulled up a blind and said: 'Look children! You're in Scotland!'

It was soon after dawn and the light was strange to us. We looked through the carriage window and saw a new world below, great moors of heather stretching far and lonely into the distance. The sound of the train was different now and its pace slower; it climbed over the purple moorland as though it were looking about it. We saw rivers that swirled and thundered against great boulders of stone, with foam and spray like smoke from a witch's cauldron, and we saw lochs lying still and small. All day long, in Scotland, the light seemed to be the same – that of the early morning.

When one of the party lowered the train window never before had such freshness blown in their faces. With Rannoch Moor to the north and Breadalbane to the south, Fortingall was on the doorstep of the Scotland of one of Barrie's favourite correspondents,[32] the Scotland of 'huts and peat smoke and brown swirling rivers and wet clothes and whisky, and the romance of the past, and the indescribable bite of the whole thing at a man's heart which is, or rather lies, at the bottom of a story'. How Robert Louis Stevenson would have loved to entertain the boys here.

Nature was all around them. For the first time they felt free, truly liberated. No demands, no human habitation in sight. Michael's appreciation of natural beauty and enchantment was with him from the start, but it was at Fortingall that he first participated in primitive beauty, fishing it like the native hunter gatherers had in Fortingall thousands of years earlier.

Over the next fourteen years the Highlands of Scotland became Michael's Neverland. Yet this was no land of dreams, it was reality. Here were the waters with which his boyhood feelings first *truly* engaged, the Lyon and the Tay. People have always fished these rivers because they love the places of beauty where trout and salmon feed, but as the poet said, 'the only real experiences in life [are] those lived with a virgin sensibility ... All life is an echo of our first sensations, and we build up our consciousness, our whole mental life, by variations and combinations of these elementary sensations.'[33]

---

32   Until his death in 1894.

33   Herbert Read, *The Innocent Eye* (1933).

Four boys under fourteen and Barrie and Sylvia (who proved herself an intuitive fisher, as so many women do) participated with rod and line. The Lyon in particular was fun because it was a short walk from the house to the well-named Peter's Pool. Here Michael first saw salmon rising.

Fishing was not yet the solitary occupation it would become for him. As often as not, he fished sitting astride Barrie's shoulders, the master 'knee-deep in the stream', while Arthur watched from the bank through his dreadful death mask.

We do not know that he was watching from the bank; no photographs were taken of him anywhere. Perhaps he was sitting reading in the beautiful garden enclosure of Glenlyon House, with its stair tower, octagonal dovecote on the farm steading and views of the mountains.

What we do know is that this was the last holiday he would ever have, and that Michael will have been deeply distressed by the presence of the man who had left for hospital as his father and returned from a nursing home with a failing, artificial jaw and a voice that carried no consonants at all.

No doubt Arthur will have been distressed too that Michael resisted sitting on his knee to listen to him reading the Biblia.

Chapter Fourteen

1907: The Widow Sylvia

SIX IS YOUNG for a child to lose his father, let alone to a death so diabolical and lingering as this. For Michael it was not the first time he had thought deeply about death. Barrie had opened the innings with their creative session down by the mermaids' lagoon, with Peter Pan excited about death being an awfully big adventure. Now his own father was actually dying in a way that couldn't look less of an adventure.

We know from notes written by Arthur to his sister Margaret that Barrie had advised Arthur to tell the oldest boy, George, everything. So Arthur had told George that 'probably' he was going to die, 'tho' always a chance' not, and it hadn't gone well. George was thirteen.

Margaret gave her advice – 'better talk to G of other things', she told him. He turned to Peter. He did not think of death as a glorious thing, rather it 'was the end of a glorious thing, Life'. No. 3 son Peter said that he did see this.

Jack, it seems, had not been invited to give his opinion at all, having been reduced to floods of tears when his father had told him he was off for the big operation – 'I remember very clearly indeed father walking me up and down the right hand (looking up the garden) path & telling me more or less what he was in for,' he told Peter. 'He drove me to tears – an easy matter!' Michael wasn't told that his father was about to die either – he hadn't needed to be. When Arthur asked him 'what gift [the boys] would like best', his answer was simply: 'Not to die.'

Barrie chose the holiday to address Jack's future. He announced that he had received a letter from Captain Scott, telling him that he was thinking about another expedition to the Antarctic and asking him if he knew of a boy who could fill a vacancy at Osborne Naval College, the 'under' college in the grounds of Osborne House on the Isle of Wight where naval cadets spent two years before joining the Royal Naval College, Dartmouth.

Barrie replied on 6 September, 'My dear Scott, I know the right boy so well that it is as if I had been waiting for your letter.' He had then pursued the project with gusto, recommending Jack to Scott for his heroic qualities, as 'a fine, intelligent, quick boy with the open fearless face that attracts at first sight'. Thus was Jack, the only one to voice concern at Barrie's increasing control over the family – Jack who adored his mother and, as Peter wrote, 'loved and worshipped his father' – removed from the scene. He endured a terrible time at Osborne – 'The ragging and the bullying that went on was intolerably horrible,' his wife later told the film maker Andrew Birkin, 'and a little boy who had never been away from home was easy meat.'

Barrie's arrangement effectively put Jack out of the family from 1907. He would always holiday at different times to his brothers – no holiday at Easter, one week at Christmas, six at the end of summer was the order at Osborne – so that they were rarely all together. His four brothers trod a different path – Eton and Oxford. And that cultural difference also left its mark – Jack matured earlier than the others and was always a little the outsider of the family.

The way did seem to be increasingly clear for Barrie, what with Arthur dying and Jack on the Isle of Wight. No one now stood in his way. Only the du Mauriers could have done, and other than Emma, none of them did.

The du Mauriers kept out of the picture all through the period in which Arthur was ill and dying – 'I fear because it was "their side",' as Daphne wrote to Peter in 1963, meaning the Llewelyn Davies side, 'so they did not feel responsible … I have a disquieting feeling that Daddy [Sylvia's brother Gerald du M] mocked at them. Why? Some old resentment? Obviously the two families were never close.'

Did it matter much? Possibly not emotionally at the time. Half the problem for children in such a situation is being the centre of excessive attention. A child of a parent with a terminal disease is invariably the focus of endless activities and kindnesses, which can make the burden almost heavier to bear. What you want is the impossible return to normality.

While for Arthur,

[Sylvia] & all the boys were never so desirable to me as now, & it is hard if I have to leave them … But whatever comes after death,

> whether anything or nothing, to die & leave them is not like what
> it would be if I were away from them in life, conscious that I could
> not see them or talk to them or help them,

as he wrote to his father towards the end of September.

In early November there was one rare moment – real hope for remission, some new-fangled electrical treatment – and Barrie brought fireworks down to Egerton House to celebrate Guy Fawkes' Night on the 5th.

But it was a mirage in the desert landscape of Arthur's final days. The cancer spread.

Barrie was in almost constant attendance now, 'lurking in the background' as Dolly put it, and his notebook entries benefited: 'A dying man's fears of breaking down at the end', 'his wish for a second chance', '*The Widow's Mite* (Little man's devotion to widow)' … and so on. We shouldn't be surprised. Writing was what he did. All life was his inspiration. Although Peter, as family historian and the first after Barrie to read all his notebooks, must have wondered at the extent to which his family had been used by him as material.

In February, Arthur suffered a serious haemorrhage, but rallied. Barrie repeatedly assured him that he would look after his family financially, an incredible commitment when one considers that four of the five would be seen through Eton College, the famous English public school. But of course the money kept pouring in, with new plays and *Peter Pan* repeating every Christmas season, and soon he would be single again.

At Easter, Jack, Peter and Michael, who again was suffering from a cold, were taken to Ramsgate to stay with Granny Emma, where before long Michael received a letter from his father:

Egerton House, Berkhamsted
April 15, 1907

My dearest Michael

My letters from my boys are indeed a pleasure to me when they arrive in the morning. I hope my boys are getting lots of happiness out of other people's kindness to them and their own kindness to other people every day. It would be fine to have a magic carpet and go first to London, across from Euston to Holborn Viaduct or Victoria, & on to Ramsgate, and find what is going on at Royal Viaduct and all the other jolly places at Ramsgate. I expect you are having penny of fun and very fine weather, but that we are getting more flowers, especially primroses. My nurse is very good at finding primroses and violets.

Your affectionate Father

It was the last letter of Arthur's life; he died three days later, aged forty-four. It was the du Maurier family's unlucky number. Curiously, the telephone number of the clinic where he died was 4444.

It is unclear when Michael realised that his father had died. A few hours after the death he received a letter from Sylvia.

18 April 1907

Darling son Michael,

I hope your cold is not bad – get it quite well quickly for my sake. Here are some silkworm eggs from papa Gibbs – I don't know what you do with them, but I've no doubt Mary [Nanny] will know … George is just going to Mr Timson to have his knickerbockers mended, but they look almost too bad to mend. What a pity it is that you all have to wear things – how much better if you could go about like Mowgli – then perhaps you would never have any colds.

Goodbye now darling – write to me soon
Mother

Papa Gibbs was the local chemist in Berkhamsted. Peter described how first Jack (twelve) and then he (ten) was informed of Arthur's death by Granny Emma, who was sitting up in her bed with a lace nightcap on her head. The news was delivered

very simply, without circumlocution or excessive emotion … It was, as I remember it, a dull and windy day, and I recollect wandering up to the night nursery and staring out of the window for long minutes in vague wretchedness and gloom, at the grey sea and the distant Gull lightship … as likely as not I was digging on the sands as usual the next morning.

The strain on Sylvia after a whole year of Arthur in suffering and turmoil must have been considerable. As was the way, she went into mourning, dressing in black with a hat and lace veil over her face. Photographs show her despair. She was prescribed a sedative by the family physician, Dr Rendell. Two weeks later she had regained control over the conflict of emotion she will have been feeling to write plausibly enough to Dolly:

Dear darling Dolly,

I think of you so often & I know how you love Arthur and me & that helps me in my sorrow – you will love me always won't you – and help me to live through these long years. How shall I do it I wonder – it seems to me impossible. We were so utterly and altogether happy & that happiness is the most precious thing on earth. We were not going to part. I must be terribly brave now & I know our boys will help me. They only keep me alive & I shall live for them and as always what Arthur wd most like in them. How he loved us all & he has been taken from us.

Kind Hugh Macnaghten – a dear friend of Arthur's is going to have George in his house at Eton in September. This was a promise made by Arthur to Hugh some time ago & I am so grateful to Hugh for his love and generosity. I am grateful to many many friends. I will show it one day I hope, but just now I am full of deadly pain & sorrow & I often wonder I am alive. The five boys are loving & thoughtful & I always sleep with my George now – & it comforts more than I can say to touch him & I feel Arthur must know. He will live again in them I feel & that must be my dear comfort until I go to him at last. We longed to grow old together – oh my dear friend it is all so utterly impossible to understand.

My Jack is at Osborne [naval college] now & writes happy letters to me – I am going to pay him a visit when I am strong enough – I miss him very much – but they have all got to be men & love me & for Arthur's sake I must fight that fight too.

I shall come to London later on – we are trying to let the house – it is too big for me and too full of pain & sorrow. I think of him almost always now as he was before the tragic illness & God gave him the finest face in the world.

Lovingly
I am Sylvia

The letter is remarkable in that Barrie's name is absent from every context in which he made a significant contribution.

According to Mackail, Arthur left virtually no money at all. Egerton House was leased, there would have been next to nothing to finance Eton for George, who had sat for a scholarship and failed to win one. Again, Barrie's plan was for Sylvia and the boys to move from the leased house in Berkhamsted to 23 Campden Hill Square, a three-storey terraced house a short walk from Kensington Palace, a very good address. The house currently has a value in excess of £8 million and even at 1907 prices would have been out of the question for Sylvia without serious financial input from the millionaire Barrie.

Yet she never mentions his name to Dolly in her letter, knowing her concern about Sylvia's friendship with Barrie. Knowing that Dolly might think that it should be a matter of concern was an added burden for someone whose mind was already swimming with sorrow, self-recrimination and loss.

In these difficult circumstances Barrie did the best thing to settle everything down. He took the family to Scotland. From 23 July until September he rented Dhivach Lodge near Drumnadrochit, Invernesshire. Drumnadrochit lies many miles farther into the Highlands than Fortingall, between Fort Augustus and Inverness in the wooded hills high above Loch Ness.

Dhivach couldn't have been a better choice – all wooded glades and becks and rushing falls, and magical gates leading to who knows where – vignettes which were always going to return in the boys' dreams. To all except Nico, that is, for Nico never got beyond the perimeter of the magic wood: 'When one – I at any rate – gets on to dreams, one is in a world of lovely non-comprehension,' he wrote, though as it turned out Nico was the only one of the boys really to return, with great nostalgia, to the Scottish haunts as an adult.

Among Barrie's many guests during the two months here in 1907 was George Skelton, whom he had come across in 1876 when he was writing plays to put on at school and Skelton was a young actor at the Dumfries Theatre nearby. Now he played Smee, Captain Hook's bosun in *Peter Pan*, the human side of pirating – 'a man who stabbed without offence', as Barrie put it.

Also the actress Lilian McCarthy and her husband, playwright Harley Granville Barker, whose play *Waste* had been refused a licence by the Censor, which had made Barrie so furious he'd helped establish a committee to abolish the office. And Captain Scott, whose rousing conversation about a new expedition to Antarctica led Barrie to draft notes for a play about 'the North or South Pole' about an explorer returning to Antarctica in old age and dying in the snow: 'We see his dream – succeeding ages represented by individuals getting nearer & nearer Pole, always having to turn back & die.' All oddly predictive.

During the day and in spite of a great deal of rain, the boys did enjoy themselves hugely, 'sometimes still chasing butterflies but fishing madly with worms most of the time in every burn within walking distance', as Peter recalled. Barrie wrote to the actress Hilda Trevelyan on 26 August, 'I do nothing up here but fish & fish & fish, and we ought all to be fishes to feel at home in this weather.'

Barrie made a note that 'Michael coming to me cried one tear at Dhivach – I picture it remorsefully alone among hills & streams – Send his laugh to be friends to it & gay together.'

The boy now had a rod of his own and photographs show him dressed for the part – glengarry on head, trout basket slung around his shoulder, thigh-high waders and Harris Tweed jacket. In fact Barrie, with his guest list constantly on the turn, did much other than fish, leaving Michael to spend hours at a time fishing on his own, enjoying being apart from the world of death and distress in an activity which came naturally to him and was fun.

The main river forms the boundary on the eastern edge of the Lodge. One day Luath was swept into it and would have drowned, had not Sylvia run along the bank and got hold of him before he whirled past.

Next to the Lodge was a field with two donkeys, called Togo and Dewet, which the boys would ride, and sometimes they'd attach one to a donkey cart and drive down through the gorge at the back of the house covered with a magnificent, ancient woodland of oak and birch and dissected by a 30-metre high waterfall cascading into the river below. Otherwise, there were games of cricket and stories. 'Michael, seven now, was at the best age for listening,' records Mackail, especially when the stories were about a particular character that Barrie had started to call Michael Pan.

There were also outings to the Beauly, a river rising near the village of Struy and spilling into the sea a few miles west of Inverness beyond the town that gives it its name. Naturally, Barrie and the boys came here to fish. On a still, sunny day in July sitting on the banks of the Beauly at Eskadale you could believe you were 1,000 miles away on the Helford Estuary in Cornwall – wooded banks, blue water, undisturbed, here is enchantment of a gentle sort and would have appealed to the du Maurier soul in Michael for sure.

Barrie's memory was of a different sort.

> We had one exciting day with – the cows. I may tell you that up there they are terrific. They had been separated from their calves a few days before and the glens were full of their moanings and stampings. On this day I was watching a fisherman when the cows got beyond all control and swam the river – a roaring torrent in which no man could live – one hundred or more of them, then formed in battle array and

thundered down the glen after their calves, which were some miles
away. I leapt into a tree ... It was as wild as though they had been
Highland men rushing to the standard of Prince Charlie.

At last, maybe because it was the end of an era, what with George
and Jack bound for Eton and Osborne Naval College respectively,
all the boys carved their initials on a tree in 'the arbour', which is
still there today.

But that was not the whole story of course, because the shadow of
Arthur's death remained over them, with Sylvia appearing in some
of the photographs still in mourning. For all the fun and games,
Peter Davies wrote that 'the whole pattern of the Dhivach holiday
seems to me to have had something rather deplorable about it'. The
years 1907–10 he referred to as the seat of all his later neuroses. He
was to commit suicide sixty years later by throwing himself under a
train at Sloane Square tube station in London.

Seven-year-old Michael was further troubled now by his mother's distress, the full depths of which may have been unfathomable
to an adult, but were etched on her face as clearly to him as if she
had written them down.

He started to react badly. 'It was always the same nameless enemy
he was seeking,' wrote Barrie of his nightmares, 'and he stole about
in various parts of the house in search of it, probing fiercely for it
in cupboards, or standing at the top of the stairs pouring out invec-
tive and shouting challenges to it to come up.'

The nightmares would become worse in his early teens, when
Michael's cousin Daphne would overhear her nanny saying to Mary
Hodgson: 'Michael has bad nightmares. He dreams of ghosts com-
ing through the window.' (*The Rebecca Notebook*, 1981)

But back in 1907 they proved useful to Barrie who, following

Arthur's death, was already making numerous entries about the boy in his notebook for a new work – story or play – provisionally entitled 'Michael Pan' to be written about Peter's brother.

The work never came to anything, but the material didn't go to waste, for Barrie had begun to incorporate Michael into Peter Pan himself as he developed the novel *Peter and Wendy*:

> Sometimes … [Peter Pan] had dreams, and they were more painful than the dreams of other boys. For hours he could not be separated from these dreams, though he wailed piteously in them. They had to do, I think, with the riddle of his existence. At such times it had been Wendy's custom to take him out of bed and sit with him on her lap, soothing him in dear ways of her own invention, and when he grew calmer to put him back to bed before he quite woke up, so that he should not know of the indignity to which she had subjected him.

More unsettling is another notebook entry, perhaps because it suggests his view that children, on account of their remoteness from the world, are not as vulnerable to negative emotional experience as adults (hence his earlier suggestion that they should be told about their father's impending death): 'Children have the strangest adventures without being troubled by them. For instance, they may remember to mention, a week after the event happened, that when they were in the wood they met their dead father and had a game with him.' This sort of suggestion, whether dreamed up by Michael or by Barrie, shows a level of unrest less than healthy.

Barrie would write that there was 'a horror looking for Michael in his childhood'. Neither of them thought it might have anything to do with Barrie.

Dhivach Lodge was followed by a break for Sylvia and the boys with Emma du Maurier in Ramsgate, where Michael continued to fish. On 8 October he wrote to Barrie:

DEAR MR BARRIE
I hope you are quite well.
I HAVE SENT YOU A
Pictures of a Pirate he has
GOT PLENTY OF WEAPONS
and looks very fierce. Please
COME SOON TO FISH
from Michael with Love
FROM NIC-O THE END

Chapter Fifteen

1908: Dependence and Uncertainty

THEN CAME THE move back to London, to 23 Campden Hill Square, which was made ready for them by Christmas 1907. The boys were ecstatic to find on the first floor, in what became known as the schoolroom, a long table which when flipped over was transformed into a three-quarter-sized billiard table. Billiards became of fanatical interest, particularly for Michael and Barrie, whose games on this table would be scored on a board and photographed for posterity. Of course, as with other games, Barrie developed his own versions. There was one called Slosh, a cross between billiards and pool, and another called the Cue Game, which involved four cues and a rest being placed across the table and what Nico described as 'a mysterious game when the table was covered with books'. Later came puff-billiards where each player had a hand-held puffer and squeezed it frantically to blow the lightweight ball into an opponent's goal, though this was a long time in the future.

They loved every minute of it. They were all by nature good games players, Nico judging Michael both as the 'the best all-rounder as he was very good at all games', particularly cricket in the years to follow.

The point is that, when he wasn't drawing them into his work psychologically and emotionally, and when he wasn't making Arthur sad and splitting the camp as it were, which of course he couldn't any longer, Barrie was almost everything the boys wanted. He was in his element now that he had them in 'his' house, which naturally sported one of his stamps on the dining room ceiling from the very first day.

The rest of the layout of the house had Sylvia's bedroom next to the schoolroom on the first floor, the nursery and night-nursery on the second where Michael, Nico and Nanny Hodgson slept. The third floor had Peter's room, a two-bed servants room and a two-bed room for George and Jack for when they came home from Eton and Osborne, though their visits coincided infrequently.

At this stage Barrie appears not to have had a room of his own even for occasional use, though that would change. For now he was still married and living with Mary at Leinster Corner.

Shortly after Arthur's death, Sylvia had made notes for a will. If anything happened to her she would like Florence Gay, a family friend, to look after them, along with Nanny Hodgson ('I hope she will stay with them always'), calling upon Arthur's sister Margaret, Barrie, and her own sisters and brother Gerald to give advice. But she ended the document, 'Of one thing I am certain – that

J. M. Barrie (the best friend in the whole world) will always be ready to advise out of his love for…'

Sylvia was now completely dependent on Barrie, but one might say that he was also dependent on her, or at least on her boys – life without them was unimaginable, Michael in particular.

Dolly remarked in her diary, 'it is extraordinary to see how [the boys] fill his life & supply all his human interest'.

Sylvia never finished the last sentence of her draft will, but the missing word had to have been 'Michael', for he was, as all agreed, the focus of Barrie's love more than any other. He was 'The One', as Nico had said.

The boys had all been attending day school in Berkhamsted. In September George had started at Eton and Jack at Osborne Naval College, both boarding. Now, in the New Year of 1908, following the move to London in December, Michael and Nico started together at Norland Place, the primary or pre-prep school that George and Jack had attended before the family moved to Berkhamsted. Norland Place was a short walk with Nanny from Campden Hill Square to Holland Park Avenue.

Occasionally Sylvia did put in an appearance, her rather sad presence remembered by a fellow pupil, Betty Macleod, and recorded in the school's 1976 centenary magazine: 'On Visitors' day, twice, we noticed, watching drill [marching to a brass band was a core tradition of many a school in those days] – a lady with two really beautiful little boys. She had one of the saddest expressions on her face we had ever seen.'

Enquiring who she was, Betty learned that she was a friend of J. M. Barrie, who had based Peter Pan on one of her boys. But how sad a picture of Sylvia, so very different to Dolly's picture of 'the extraordinary charm, and beauty, and grace, and wit, and sense of humour, which she possessed as a girl and in early married life'. Michael turned eight on 16 June. Barrie was in Paris at the time, staying at the Hotel d'Albe with Frohman, presenting *Peter Pan* for a summer run at the Théatre du Vaudeville. He sent Michael a letter and an American Indian outfit, complete with wigwam, bow and arrows, and peace pipe. The letter read:

My dear Michael,

Paris is looking very excited today and all the people think it is because there were races yesterday, but I know it is because tomorrow it is your birthday. I wish I could be with you and your candles. You can look at me as one of your candles, the one still burning. I am Michael's candle. I wish I could see you putting on the redskin's clothes for the first time. Won't your mother be frightened. Nick will hide beneath the bed and Peter will go for the police.

Dear Michael I am very fond of you. But don't tell anybody.

The End
J. M. Barrie

Then back to London and Black Lake Cottage, where he learned some news that took him aback. The sculptor Kathleen Bruce, who had been staying there with a friend, suddenly announced that she was engaged to Captain Scott. Barrie had been unaware that Bruce had been seeing both Scott and Gilbert Cannan, who was Secretary of Barrie's committee to abolish the Censor, its headquarters at Black Lake Cottage, and when some in the Black Lake party had expressed doubts that Scott would ever marry, she decided on the spur of the moment to make her announcement.

Barrie was startled and deeply upset when he discovered all this from Mason; and Scott had been so worried as to how he would react he had not dared approach him about it.

When Barrie and Scott first met in 1905, they had taken to one another 'instantaneously', according to Mackail – 'something more than a response on both sides'.

Barrie's interest in explorers had been there since he was a boy, but there was something special about Scott that magnetised Barrie. He had, like D. H. Lawrence's fictional explorer Gerald Crich in *Sons and Lovers*, 'a northern kind of beauty, like light refracted from snow … In his clear northern flesh and his fair hair was a glisten like sunshine refracted through crystals of ice. And he looked so new, unbroached, pure as an arctic thing.'

There is no evidence that Barrie was stirred by Scott sexually, but if not there was certainly a male bonding of a sort less common today. Whether Scott measured up to Barrie's view of him is unlikely, but that did not concern Barrie: 'I doubt if he brought out or even recognised (or wanted to) the true characteristrics [sic] of anyone he made much of,' Peter would write.

Scott did play up to the heroic fantasy that Barrie wove about him, no less in their intimate dealings than with Michael and Nico in Kensington Gardens. He was even a bit carried away by it, one reason perhaps why his expedition in 1911 would fail. Scott became such a slave to the heroic ideal that he insisted on the sleighs being dragged by his men not by dogs, irrational, unnecessary, an emotionally motivating ideal that turned out a fatal burden on his team.

'When Barrie was strongly attracted by people, he wanted at once to own them and to be dominated by them, whichever their sex,' wrote Peter, martialling all his evidence from mountains of papers appertaining to the man. Scott, though amiable, held command by force of personality, and had enjoyed Barrie's need to be dominated, their first conversation being 'largely a comparison of the life of action [Scott's] with the loathly life of those who sit at home [Barrie's],' as Barrie himself noted.

So, over the three years they had known one another Barrie and Scott had developed an almost heroic bond, in which Scott's force of personality was the venerated god. It wasn't a unique bond exactly, as deep relationships between men were a feature of the times. Nor did it need to be sexual. If they burned for each other inwardly they would never admit it. They were not going to be so unmanly and unnatural as to allow any sentimentality into it. But you could call it love nonetheless, as love between the old German knights, who used to make a wound in their arms, rub each other's blood into the cut and swear a *Blutbrüdershaft*.

In this context we can begin to see why, when so personal a departure as Scott's engagement to Kathleen Bruce became public knowledge, it seemed a betrayal to Barrie.

Scott realised he'd made a terrible mistake not telling him first. Kathleen advised him: 'Please write quite by return of post … As nice a letter as ever you can think of.'

But the deed had been done and was irretrievable. There would be bitterness between them even after the marriage the following September, only partly assuaged after the birth of their son, Peter (to become the famous naturalist), when Scott asked Barrie to be godfather and he accepted.

When Scott lay dying in his tent in Antarctica, his last action was to write a letter to Barrie, saying:

It hurt me grievously when you partially withdrew your friendship or seemed so to do – I want to tell you I never gave you cause … Give my memory back the friendship which you suspended – I never met a man in my life whom I admired and loved more than you but I never could show you how much your friendship meant to me, as you had much to give and I nothing.

The letter was found on Scott's body and posted to Kathleen, who sent it to Barrie in 1913.

As if all this wasn't enough, Barrie's relationship with Sylvia's actor brother Gerald also broke down in 1908. As with Scott, according to Nico, Barrie 'thought Gerald irresistible'. He first employed him in *The Admirable Crichton* in 1902, after he had come down to Black Lake Cottage and Barrie had enjoyed his 'gay, happy go lucky flair' and reputation as a practical joker.

That play made Gerald's name in the theatre. Barrie then cast him in *Peter Pan* as Captain Hook (Barrie's dark side) and Mr Darling (the 'Arthur LID' role). Gerald played them in the same production for a few years, and other roles besides.

So empathic did the relationship between actor and playwright become that, as Mackail put it, Gerald made Barrie's plays 'even more like Barrie-plays than they were already, though Gerald hated, or thought he hated, everything fanciful and whimsical, and swore by whisky and cold beef and golf'.

There was an almost perilous intimacy between them, which could as well be described as enmity as love. 'They thought they saw through each other, and then again they weren't at all sure that they weren't being seen through themselves,' commented Mackail. 'There was often a kind of jealousy, too, when each found himself wanting the other's more special and peculiar gifts – though of course as well as his own...'

The relationship reached its peak with Barrie's hit play *What*

Every Woman Knows, which opened on 3 September, the day after Scott's wedding, and is a lightly camouflaged representation of their relationship. It ran for 384 performances – for the actor a dreadful experience. Afterwards he decided on a long and complete break – Gerald did not act in another Barrie play until 1916.

Rejection for Barrie again. There was more to come.

During the same period he had seen little of Michael. Sylvia had opted to take the boys to the New Forest for their summer holiday. Barrie managed only 'a grand motor expedition to Bournemouth' part way through the New Forest trip, after which he dropped in on Dolly at Shulbrede Priory.

Barrie wasn't in the habit of dropping in on the Ponsonbys unless he had Sylvia and the boys with him. He was not on a one-to-one relationship with either Dolly or her husband Arthur. It must have been quite a surprise. Dolly noted a stiffening of his attitude, an ever-keener focus on the boys, and a hardening of resolve. On 12 August 1908, she wrote in her diary: 'Mr Barrie arrived in the evening … We talked a great deal of Sylvia's boys.' Dolly remarked particularly on his talkativeness and on his trenchant opinions about 'boys education and of the political world'. Arthur Ponsonby noted this in his diary too. It was almost as if Barrie was trying to impress Arthur with a serious side to what he was doing with Michael. But something about him triggered a wariness in Dolly: 'JMB does alarm me. I feel he absolutely sees right through one & just how stupid I am – but I hope also he sees my good intentions.'

But were Dolly's intentions 'good' from Barrie's point of view? It seems pretty clear whose side Dolly would be on – at no point did she recommend Barrie to Sylvia as a solution to her woes. And Barrie will have known her feelings, which is perhaps why he dropped round on the way back from speaking to Sylvia, and 'seen right through' her.

This was the other side to the game-playing, avuncular Barrie that the children loved. Mackail recalled that he would meet your conversation with an expression 'horribly like a sneer ... Oh, yes, we have suffered. No, don't let's remember ... the faint, Caledonian grunt with which our desperate observations are received.'

But what really got to people was a sense they had of something dark about him. Interviewd by Andrew Birkin in 1978, George and Jack's friend, Norma Douglas Henry, had this to say: 'I think one or two people were rather disturbed about Barrie, though of course it was never talked about openly. There was something sinister about him, rather shivery.'

Of course people in the family could feel intimidated and con-cerned about his relationship with Michael and stop short of talking about it openly because he was a phenomenally rich and generous man, and many owed a great deal to him, not least Sylvia.

It was now more than a year since Arthur Llewelyn Davies had died and if Barrie was to keep his hand on the tiller, the situation needed his attention.

His theatrical imagination took over. He invited everyone to Switzerland for Christmas at the Grand Hôtel in the Alpine resort of Caux, situated on the east side of Lake Geneva not far from Mon-treux, with wonderful views over the lake. The plan was to travel on Christmas Day – the ferry across the English Channel, then by train across Europe, to arrive on Boxing Day.

George took advice from housemaster Macnaghten at Eton and the message came home that the boys would need 'a knickerbocker change suit (a good warm one), sweaters and thick stockings'. No expense would be spared. Mary Ansell would come too and so would Gilbert Cannan.

On the train, while Barrie was learning from a sporting-work how to ski by crossing his right leg along the line A.B. and his left along C.D. (as in diagrams), Michael filled out a page in Barrie's 'Querist's Album', a book the like of which Barrie had himself been given by his mother when he was seventeen, a sort of confession as to what he was thinking at a particular moment in time, and signed at the bottom under the words, 'My Confession'.

It provides a sort of self-analytical snapshot of the eight-year-old Michael. We learn that in his view 'the highest characteristic in man' is 'Fun' and in a woman, 'Kindness'; that 'Decency' is Michael's own most esteemed virtue and 'Sylvia' is his most lovable name. That his favourite novelist is J. M. Barrie and his happiest employment reading; that Longfellow is his most admired poet, and Hereward the Wake and Joan of Arc his favourite historical heroes, while Peter Pan was his favourite fictional hero, fishing his favourite amusement, while his greatest misery continued to be – 'Nightmares'.

Fun, kindness and decency, Sylvia and J. M. Barrie, Peter Pan and fishing, yet the nightmares continued to invade his dreams.

How different were the five boys becoming now that they were growing up, even if as Nico, the youngest, pointed out in terms of 'fun to be with', they were 'dead level'.

Peter observed that George had a romantic character of mind, a fair share of du Maurier charm and 'a good leavening of sound, kind, sterling Davies' too; but also that he had a '*simplicity* which Barrie and Macnaghten saw in Arthur', which meant 'straightforward', ultimately 'limited', not the elegant simplicity of a seeking and discerning mind, which became Michael's.

Daphne remembered Jack as the one 'who could climb nearly to the top of the great cedar tree on the lawn of Slyfield House, near Stoke d'Abernon in Surrey, where her family was staying one summer, and she was down in awe of him: 'Had I known, at the age of

five, six, seven, how the Greeks felt about their Olympian gods,'
she recalled in *Myself When Young* (1977), 'I would have shared
their sentiments.' An attractive combination of adventurousness
and sensitivity made him a favourite of Sylvia, more or less equally
with Michael. He was her white knight and would become something of a womaniser, as Nico recalled in interview with Andrew
Birkin in the 1970s.

'He used to take me to such places as The Palace Theatre and thrill
me to the quick at his getting glorious smiles from the chorus girls.'

Intellectually sound Peter, as a child pale and indifferent, was
Dolly's favourite, while Nico was the practical one, the odd one
out. He didn't really like to see into things, and was lost in the face
of the artistic, spiritual or psychological. Although no fool, he was
occasionally the clown – 'the complete extrovert, completely happy',
as Jack's wife described him to Birkin.

Marching into the lobby of the Grand Hôtel, Caux, aged five,
one of the female guests caught sight of Nico and exclaimed: 'My
word, you *are* a lovely boy!' – 'So he was,' recalled Peter, 'but this
was the last way to curry favour with a young Davies, and Nico duly
retaliated with a face of fury and the comprehensive nursery repar-
tee: "Oh, ditto!"'

Caux was wonderful, deep in snow. The train had been hot and
stifling, but Barrie remembered how frozen with ice was the mountain train on their arrival. Then they drove from the station in an
open sledge and arrived exhilarated.

'The world here is given over to lugeing [sic],' wrote Barrie to the
Duchess of Sutherland on 9 January – he had almost a fetish for
duchesses now that he was successful enough to be able to handle
any company he wanted to handle. And where better to indulge a
bit of harmless snobbism than from a swish Swiss ski resort? 'I don't

know whether you have a luge, you have everything else. It's a little toboggan, and they glide down on it for ever and ever.'

What he didn't tell her was that when he fell, skiing, having crossed his right leg along the line A.B. and his left along C.D. he had lain on the snow helpless until he remembered how to rise 'by doing things with E, F and G'.

This was before the winter sports business had really got going, but luging was more of a success, 'We tobogganed often down to Glion from Caux and even all the way down to Montreux,' wrote Barrie.

But the real sport during the holiday was interpersonal. Included in the party were Mary Ansell and Barrie's Secretary to the Anti-Censor campaign, the young barrister and budding novelist Gilbert Cannan, now more often than not working with Ansell on the Censor business out of Black Lake Cottage. And they were having an affair.

Barrie, it seemed to everyone, was the only one not to be aware that something was going on. As usual, Jack among the boys was the one to wonder. 'Why is Mr Cannan always with Mrs Barrie?' he asked meaningfully.

Diana Farr wrote in her biography of Cannan that 'Sylvia encouraged and abetted Cannan's affair with Mary Barrie, making it easy for them to see each other unknown to Barrie.'[34] Farr's biography was published in 1978. Almost certainly she took the prompt from Denis Mackail's official biography of Barrie, which was published in 1941 and suggests that Sylvia saw how the situation could play into her hands – by clearing Mary out of the way and making her financially secure after Arthur's death, writing: 'Temptation here, as well as elsewhere. The money again.'

---

34   Diana Farr, *Gilbert Cannan: A Georgian Prodigy* (1978).

This is conjecture, as Mackail admits, and seems to overlook the complexity of Sylvia's situation. She didn't need to take a begging bowl to Barrie and had indeed managed not to see him very much throughout the previous year. What's more, Sylvia already had her line into Barrie's bank account and there was never a danger that it would be stopped. Michael was too important to him.

No doubt Sylvia did encourage the relationship between Cannan and Ansell, but only because to do so was absolutely in character. She would have thought the affair a real hoot. When Lady Ottoline Morrell met Ansell and Cannan not long after Caux she wrote of Cannan as

> that rather charming and gifted, but conceited novelist of whom we saw a great deal ... He had recently run off with Sir[35] James Barrie's wife, and perhaps I felt that people would be prejudiced against him on this account, and certainly on the outside it did not appear very honourable, as he had been one of Barrie's protégés. I believe Mary Ansell, however, had not found Barrie very satisfactory as a husband and she had become entranced with this young man, who indeed had the appearance of a rather vacant Sir Galahad, and whose mind was prolific, poetic and romantic. I never could understand why he could be tempted to run away with this lady, for she was double his age, and devoid of any atmosphere of romance, and certainly unable to run very far or very fast. But how can one divine the reasons for such foolish acts?

I certainly don't believe that Sylvia wanted to make her relationship

---

35   Morrell is writing some time into the future. Barrie wasn't a knight of the realm in 1909. In fact he always claimed he had turned down a knighthood that very year, but did accept a baronetcy in 1913.

legal with Barrie for the security of herself and her boys. It is more likely that Barrie would rather have had her boys to himself without Sylvia (which is what he ended up with). Sylvia knew that he would never withdraw from her boys. Granted, she would have been bound to imagine at some stage the possibility of becoming Barrie's wife. What woman would not turn it over in their mind given her situation, his involvement with her and her sons and the material ease with which they would henceforth live life. But Sylvia was never one to have found satisfaction in basic repulsion. Beauty was her star.

On reflection, it also seems unlikely that Barrie didn't know what was going on between his wife and Cannan. He, the great playwright, had set the scene in Caux, invited everyone along and was enjoying the 'play' into which he had cast them, as it promised some interesting turns. He would later write a play a bit like this called *Shall We Join The Ladies?* in which the cast were invited to dinner. Barrie was not himself part of the main plot at Caux, however, whereas he was the host in that. Instead, he and the boys starred in the fun-loving, low-life *sub*-plot, luging down the slopes, 'pranging' Nico's 'little bum' in a tobogganing accident, and (the crowning glory in this secondary narrative), Peter having the wool pulled over his eyes in a case of mistaken identity.

One evening at dusk Barrie invited eleven-year-old Peter up to his room. When he knocked at the door, Barrie's voice commanded him in a high-pitched Scottish wail to come in. Peter opened the door and saw Barrie sitting at the far end of the bedroom in semi-darkness. He made his way across the room towards him as Barrie, apparently in great discomfort, whined, 'Peter, something dreadful has happened to my feet.' Glancing down, Peter saw to his horror 'that his feet were bare and swollen to four or five times their natural size. For several seconds I was deceived, and have never since forgotten the terror that filled me, until I realised that the feet were artificial.' Barrie had bought the pink, waxy monstrosities at Hamleys, the famous toyshop on Regent's Street in London.

Aside from the sub-plot, in which Barrie alone of the adults was participant, there was, so Mackail wrote, 'something dreadfully ominous ... Something behind the laughter as cold and relentless as the Alps.'

There was, but it had nothing to do with Gilbert Cannan and Mary Ansell. Sylvia fell ill. She collapsed complaining of a terrible pain around her heart. The hotel staff informed Barrie that there was an English doctor among the guests, but he appears to have been as unhelpful as he could be, claiming invisibility because he was on holiday.

Chapter Sixteen

1909: Mind Games and Manoeuvres

SYLVIA'S RECOVERY WAS slow but it allowed her to return to London and her bed at Campden Hill Square. There were two reports of her fainting – in the hall of No. 23 and on the stairs between her bedroom and the lavatory up the next flight of stairs. X-ray images were taken, but showed nothing.

Barrie was a constant visitor – 'No jarring or suspected criticism here,' writes Mackail. It should be said that Mackail was writing his biography after Barrie's death in 1937 but under the fierce and eagle eye of Lady Cynthia Asquith, who had ended up with most of his money and power as executor over his works. She kept him on a tight rein. Any criticism was frowned upon, which is why one

gets from Mackail these simpering phrases like 'No jarring or suspected criticism here.' Why should we think there is any criticism
in Barrie visiting Sylvia constantly unless it was something Sylvia
found too much? The sentence ends: 'though the boys scarcely knew
what had happened and would sometimes start a fresh silence with
a thoughtless word'.

There were clearly tensions at No. 23 in January 1909, a year in
which Sylvia would spend a great deal of time with her mother in
Ramsgate, where she knew Barrie would not follow. For Emma du
Maurier made no bones about not liking the little man.

Why this should have been is not immediately clear. It is possible
that Emma simply viewed Barrie's friendship with Sylvia's family as
an intrusion. But it is also possible that there was a little animos-
ity between Barrie and the du Mauriers even before he met Sylvia.

Mackail writes that her husband George du Maurier and Barrie
must have met in the years leading up to du Maurier's death in 1896,
seeing as they had so many personal friends in common. Henry
James, du Maurier's closest friend, knew Barrie well. Other close
friends included the writers Thomas Hardy and George Meredith,
actors Henry Irving, Beerbohm Tree and J. L. Toole, editors W. D.
Nichols and W. E. Henley, and the artists Alma-Tadema, J. L. Toole,
Edwin Abbey, and the landscape painter Alfred Parsons, who knew
du Maurier intimately and was a member of Barrie's Allahakbarries.

In any case, du Maurier was the bestselling author of the day and
Barrie the rising star, who had been so smitten by *Peter Ibbetson* that
he changed the focus of his writing completely to follow du Maurier's line. Everyone knew everyone in literary London. There were
but half a dozen salons where such people met. How could it be that
these two literary lions did not meet? The answer, which is the same
conclusion that Mackail reached, is that they did.

The bedrock of Barrie's story is the collection of his notebooks, but uniquely the notebooks from June 1896, when he would have known du Maurier, to June 1898, by which time he had met Sylvia and the boys, are missing.

It is highly likely that the two men didn't get on. On the surface they had much in common, both diminutive and boyish, both with the same dry sense of humour and lugubrious way of expressing it, both satirical in their work. Yet beneath the surface no two men could have been more dissimilar. While du Maurier's satire was upbeat and palpably sincere, Barrie's, according to the writer Sir Walter Raleigh, chair of English Literature at Oxford, goes under the guise of sentimentality, often has a cruel side and doesn't quite come off. The critic Desmond MacCarthy agreed. Barrie's genius 'is a coquettish thing, with just a benevolent drop of acid in it sometimes'.

Also, du Maurier was a Romantic, he worshipped beauty; *feeling* was what he was all about, while Barrie confessed he was incapable of 'even a genuine feeling that wasn't merely sentiment', actively disliked music – ('I have no ear for it,' he admitted), and had no interest in art. According to Mackail, Barrie's insensitivity to art was the reason he 'could never, even spiritually, be one of the real or esoteric Broadway gang' – a reference to the cricket-playing artistic community in Worcestershire, where many of du Maurier's literary and artistic friends, including Henry James (who wrote about it), used to gather.

This difference is especially important when sensitivity to art, and music in particular, is the *sine qua non* of true existence in *Trilby*, for Trilby herself is tone deaf until Svengali hypnotises her, activating her sixth sense. So, Barrie is absolutely blind, deaf and dumb when it comes to the important things, as far as du Maurier is concerned.

Even the boys, Peter and Michael especially, noted and rued this state of affairs, Peter conceding that while Barrie 'gallantly accompanied' him to the opera…

> Being himself totally unmusical, he not only did not encourage such leanings, but in one way and another could not help discouraging them … One had also at the time a calf-love for the Russian ballet [Diaghilev], then an exciting novelty, and that was still more emphatically frowned on and ridiculed … The fact is that music and painting and poetry, and the part they may be supposed to play in making a civilised being, had a curiously small place in JMB's view of things.

We will see that this artistic, even spiritual, insensitivity is what ultimately lost him Michael. For while Michael, with a poet's eye, came to discern a spiritual dimension in the Scottish landscape, Barrie remained stuck in his gloomy supernatural heritage and in the 'Kailyard', or Cabbage-patch, school of cosy sentimentality to which his novels about Thrums (his name for Kirriemuir), *Auld Licht Idylls*, *A Window in Thrums* and *The Little Minister*, adhere.

Du Maurier would have scorned Barrie's lack of Romantic vision and excluded him for it, if for no other reason. It was something he was good at when a face didn't fit. And this was just the moment in Barrie's career when he would have benefited from being *in* rather than *out*. It makes his pursuit of du Maurier's daughter and her boys look rather strange, purposeful, anything but mere chance. In 1922, after it was all over, he admitted, as if it had been of critical significance to the direction his life took: 'I think an individual may have done me harm by thinking too little of me.'

Emma would have had no difficulty in recalling the period in the mid- to late 1890s when her husband would have met Barrie and when, much to her chagrin, du Maurier returned to a preoccupation with the occult and took a house in Bayswater, entertaining his friends and writing *Peter Ibbetson*, while still keeping the family home in Hampstead.

All might well have been revealed in Emma's very full correspondence with Sylvia in subsequent years after Barrie became a fixture in her life, for mother and daughter wrote to one another 'almost daily'.[36] But, again, the papers were destroyed, this correspondence was nowhere to be found among Barrie's effects after he died, which included everything else that Sylvia left.

The3rd of April 1909 found Barrie in Edinburgh receiving an honorary degree from his alma mater. All he could think of was Michael. 'If Michael had met me in a wood,' he wrote to Sylvia about his red and blue ceremonial gown, 'he would have tried to net me as a Scarlet Emperor.'

Barrie was dying to get together with Michael at Easter, eight days later, but Sylvia denied him. So, on the 11th, Barrie was spending Easter at Black Lake Cottage with Mason and other guests, including the actress Hilda Trevelyan (Wendy in *Peter Pan*), who was looking out of her bedroom window one morning when a vision appeared beneath the window of Barrie walking slowly down the garden in deep thought, apparently oblivious to the fact that Luath was following hard on his heels on two legs, his forepaws up on Barrie's shoulders. Trevelyan shook her head in disbelief and the vision passed on.

Probably Barrie had been composing his letter to Sylvia, written that day, in which he referred to a statue of Peter Pan modelled on Michael which he had commissioned from Sir George Frampton for display in due course in Kensington Gardens. He had given Frampton

---

36 Nanny Hodgson's testimony to Peter.

the photographs of Michael dressed in the Peter Pan costume that Barrie had given to the boy on his sixth birthday. 'Frampton was very taken with Mick's pictures,' he wrote, '& I had to leave them with him. He prefers the Peter clothes to a nude child … I don't feel gay, so no more at present, dear Jocelyn.'

No doubt Sylvia was relieved that Michael would not be appearing in Kensington Gardens in the nude. But still, by June he had not seen him and was driven to write:

Dearest Jocelyn,

…How I wish I were going down to see Michael and Nicholas. All the donkey boys and the fishermen and sailors [in Ramsgate] see them but I don't. I feel they are growing up without my looking on, when I grudge any blank day without them. I can't picture a summer day that does not have Michael skipping on in front. That is summer to me. And all the five know me as nobody does. The bland indifference with which they accept my tantrums is the most engaging thing in the world to me. They are quite sure that despite appearances I am all right. To be able to help them and you, that is my dear ambition, to do the best I can always and always, and my greatest pride is that you let me do it. I wish I did it so much better … I am so sorry about those pains in your head.

Your affectionate
J. M. B.

Clearly it is Michael that he is missing, but it is perfectly true that all of them, except Jack, did indeed love Uncle Jim with that natural, no-strings-love that children reserve for close family, Michael in particular. Barrie and Jack were poles apart, but as Jack's wife,

Geraldine Gibb, told Andrew Birkin later, 'Michael and Barrie spent so much time together. They were there with each other. It was almost bound to happen.'

Nor was the boys' love at root self-seeking, as the loving and respectful letters of George and Peter from the Front in the First World War will show. Barrie was always a favourite with them for his own sake, and now that Arthur was dead he did in many ways already play the role of father in their lives.

But that is where the problem lay for Sylvia. The relationship had started out almost as if he had been a second nanny, which is why Nanny Hodgson's nose was originally put out of joint. Barrie admitted there were 'many coldnesses and even bickerings between us … We were rivals.' Sylvia, with three sons under five, had been only too happy to have him take them off her hands. Barrie enjoyed being dominated by her, as Peter pointed out, and she rose to his wit and sense of humour, and, yes, increasingly to the money. Barrie was a year-on-year earning millionaire. *Peter Pan* had taken over and they all now lived within the Peter Pan cult. At school, George, Peter and Michael were ragged about it, and Peter of course suffered more in this way than the others on account of his name, so that even as a sixty-year-old he was bitter about it. Again, like the children at Norland Place, people pointed at Sylvia as the friend of J. M. Barrie and mother of Peter Pan.

Now, since Arthur's death, the *mènage à trois* had become a *mènage à deux*, yet the dynamic between Sylvia and Barrie was nowhere near being a 'partner' relationship. When Arthur was dying he was her 'fairy prince' and immediately afterwards he was 'the best friend in the whole world' because the need was there. Sylvia had been closest to Barrie when the chips were down. The need was still there for his financial support and, yes, the boys would miss him, but by now it was clear to both parties that there would be no marriage between the mother of all mothers and the fairy prince.

In July the second summer presentation of *Peter Pan* opened in Paris and somehow or other Barrie – there is no explanation of how he was conveyed – had managed to get Michael to join the party already there, which, besides Barrie, included Mary Ansell, Charles Frohman, Paulene Chase, who had replaced Dion Boucicault as Peter Pan in England, and Lord Esher's younger daughter.

There is a photograph of Michael driving a miniature electric hire car in Le Grand Trianons at Versailles, and there was some sort of row in which Frohman refused to participate in the fun at either of the Trianons and eventually insisted that 'his man' Herbert get the boy home to England.

No good would come of this potentially explosive state of affairs. Nor did it. Sylvia was dying. First Arthur, then Sylvia, both in their early forties, leaving Barrie with the family he wanted above all else. You couldn't write it. Except as a horror story. And that is what it was, a horror story. Which is why Michael was still having night-mares. No jarring or suspected criticism here.

If, during 1909, in which she spent a great deal of time with her mother, Sylvia kept her distance from Barrie, she was helped in this by events. Barrie was drawn into the affair between his wife and Gilbert Cannan when Mary Ansell's infidelity was officially made known to him by the gardener at Black Lake Cottage, a Mr Hunt. He had informed on Ansell in retaliation for her criticism of his gardening skills, we are to believe.

Barrie's lawyer, Sir George Lewis, advised him to avoid too much contact with Sylvia in case the prosecution implicated her in any way. The shame of divorce was one thing. To be named in a divorce could destroy your reputation.

So that summer of 1909 Barrie went to Switzerland with Gilmour and Mason, while Sylvia had a holiday with the boys at Postbridge, a far more ancient hamlet than the road of Roman origin that strikes through it, situated in the centre of Dartmoor in Devon beside the East River Dart, forded by a medieval clapper bridge. Here in summer purple shadows leap the rivers and chase across the heathered hills, while in winter Conan Doyle's hound of the Baskervilles can easily be imagined to break upon one out of a wall of fog.

How much the boys must have missed Barrie to bring it alive for them. Instead, he was writing a letter from Mason's London apartment in Stratton Street off Piccadilly, where he had taken refuge away from Leinster Corner, which 'it is always so painful to me to go to now'.

The letter, dated 12 August, is addressed to:

Dear Jocelyn,

I hope you are all settled down comfortably now, and that there is a bracing feeling in the air despite the heat. In this weather the boys need not expect to get as many trout as the waters will all be small and clear but after all the sun is better than trout and they will find lots of other things to do. I sent some gut, etc. and some fly hooks…

Yours ever
J. M. B.

The reduction from his usual 'Dearest Jocelyn' to 'Dear' matches the unusually restrained feel of Barrie's letter, possibly in reaction to the wide publicising of his impending divorce, which will have been anathema to him – as Peter notes, the letter was written a fortnight after the storm burst. And he signs himself with just the kind of neutrality Sir George would have advised, but it all makes a good fit too with the cooling of his relationship with Sylvia.

There is a sad photograph of Sylvia fishing the river in full mourning dress, including hat and veil, but in fact she seldom ventured more than a few hundred yards from the house. It was all butterfly chasing, bug hunting and line-and-hook worm fishing for the boys. Jack followed Barrie's advice and found something better to do. Going on fifteen, but more mature than his older, Etonian brother George, he found amusement with the daughter of a local farmer.

A fortnight later Barrie confirmed that he was travelling to Zermatt at the end of August, where he would be staying with Gilmour and Mason at the Monte Rosa, a hotel frequented by the Alpine Club, including Edward Whymper who made the first ascent of the Matterhorn in 1865. They actually met the great man, which raised Barrie's spirits and will have fascinated the boys when he wrote to them about it, but his own attempts at climbing met with abject failure. He resented the guide's instructions and he soon called it a day, going walking instead with Gilmour while Mason climbed. At the end of September they moved on to Lausanne.

By this time Michael had joined Peter at Wilkinson's in Orme Square and suffered the indignity of having tea with Milky and his wife at home in their rural retreat, a cottage close to E. V. Lucas's place – Kingson Manor House – in Sussex. Audrey described Milky as a most genial man, but when Peter and Michael happened to be staying and were invited with Audrey to tea 'a marked change came over their demeanour. They were positively subdued and never, in spite of Mrs Wilkinson's cakes, quite natural again until we were well out in the road with the front door shut behind us.'

Entering Wilkinson's had meant cutting off Michael's long wavy tresses, the shearing seeming to add Samsonian proportion to the moment of childhood loss already associated with graduation to the school.

But Michael would never lose the aura of mysterious innocence, open countenance and unconscious awareness that characterised his original state, even after Eton and the tragedies that were heaped upon of him – it was what Barrie loved about him and identified him as that innocent spark of Peter Pan, that betwixt-and-between boy, which Barrie had lost to shrewdness and canniness and old age. 'He strikes me as more than old,' said Cynthia Asquith who knew Barrie intimately, 'in fact I doubt whether he ever was a boy.'

Losing his locks meant nothing to Michael, but Barrie was distraught to have missed the moment of matriculation and wrote a piece fantasising that he had indeed been there.

> When he was nine I took him to his preparatory, he prancing in the glories of the unknown until the hour came for me to go, 'the hour between the dog and the wolf,' and then he was afraid. I said that in the holidays all would be just as it had been before, but the newly-wise one shook his head; and on my return home, when I wandered out unmanned to look at his tool-shed, I found these smashing words in his writing pinned to the door:
>
> THIS ESTABLISHMENT is NOW PRERMANENTLY [sic] CLOSED.
>
> I went white as I saw that [Michael] already understood life better than I did.[37]

In fact, Barrie had not returned from Switzerland until the beginning of October, long after the winter term at Wilkinson's had begun.

---

37 J. M. Barrie, *Neil and Tintinnabulum* (1925).

The date of his return was determined rather by the divorce hearing on the 13th.

Mary wrote to H. G. Wells that Barrie 'came out badly in court. Three lies.' First, that Mary had said the affair with Cannan was the only one she had had; it was not, nor had she said that it was. Second, that Black Lake Cottage was his property, when it had been Mary's name on the lease, not his. Third, that he had lived happily with his wife.

Mary retreated to Black Lake Cottage. Barrie stayed with Mason at No. 17 Stratton Street: 'Walking up and down when his friend set off for the House [of Commons], and still walking up and down when he returns. The silences are as long and overpowering as ever. And Mason, though the burden grows no lighter, is endlessly patient.'[38]

After six weeks of this, Lady Lewis found Barrie a flat at 3 Adelphi Terrace House in Robert Street just off the Strand, on a bend of the Thames affording a view of five bridges. Barrie slept there for the first time on 20 November: 'I am in and it is all so comfortable and beautiful & all owing to you.' Five months later, in better fettle, he wrote to Lady Lewis, describing the awesome feeling of looking out through the wide expanse of window across the Thames:

> I feel I am writing on board the good ship Adelphi, 1200 tons. The wind is blowing so hard. The skipper has lashed himself to the wheel. Down in the terrace a bicycle has just been blown across the street. Mr Shaw has just made a gallant attempt to reach the pillar box. His beard is well in front of him. I feel I ought to open my portal and fling him a life-buoy. See if he does not have a column about this in tomorrow's *Times*.

---

38   Denis Mackail, *The Story of J. M. Barrie* (1941).

Some years later Barrie wrote to Thomas Hardy's wife that Turner 'when very young used to come to 8 Adelphi Terrace and paint panoramas of the river'.

Everything then seemed more settled, until, after a visit to the Lucases in their new home near Lewes, in Sussex, Sylvia collapsed again.

Chapter Seventeen

1910: No Idle Steer

IN HINDSIGHT, IT was then that the countdown began. Occasionally she might summon the energy to walk from the house to the green in Campden Square and watch Barrie play cricket with Michael and Nico, but generally Sylvia was in bed, and the doctors were becoming increasingly concerned, although in the absence of any record, diagnosis, treatment or post-mortem, thirty years later Peter was baffled about what exactly was wrong with her.

'While, thanks to the letters I know all about father's illness I am strangely ignorant about mother's. Can you tell me where the disease attacked her?'

Nanny replied only that it was too near the heart to operate, and when Peter pressed her further, she didn't respond to the question.

Christmas 1909 was a low-key affair. Barrie was now in attendance, as he had been for Arthur. No arguments now as to his presence. The need was there, as in this case, where Barrie was despatched to pick up Peter from Eton where he had just sat the scholarship examination and was about to join George there (thanks again to Barrie) whether or not he won an award:

July 6, 1910

Dear J,

Would you do something for me. I want 11/2 doz. White collars (George wears the shape) for Peter & 2 doz. white ties (also like George), as they are best bought at Eton. The shop is called New & Lingwood. Ask for collars for tails & Peter will know what size & can try one on if wanted. He must bring them home with him…

Affec:
S.

Michael sat with his mother in her darkened room whenever he could. It was also he who sat on the end of her bath chair on a rare trip to Kensington Gardens, guiding it while a helper pushed it from behind. On a visit to see his sister, Gerald du Maurier entered her room to find Michael sitting at a small desk in the corner doing his homework, tears flowing down his cheeks. As with his father, he didn't need to be told.

But it wasn't all tears. When Peter was informed that he had won a scholarship to Eton he was playing corridor cricket with his brothers. The joy this news gave Sylvia was very welcome, particularly as

Peter's academic success lit up a link to Arthur's side of the family, for Arthur was still sorely missed.

Sylvia had to be carried to bed now and was under 24-hour-a-day care by one Nurse Loosemore, who was suddenly faced with an extraordinary plan to deliver Sylvia to Ashdon Farm on Exmoor, on the borders of Somerset and North Devon.

To say that the farm, which is still there today, is remote and isolated is understatement. It lies alone in the valley of the River Oare, close to where John Ridd emerged in R. D. Blackmore's *Lorna Doone*, the novel that tells of the savage deeds of the Doone family who terrorised the country round about and escaped with their booty across the wild hills of Exmoor precisely where Sylvia now found herself.

The area is indeed beautiful. Francis Kilvert writes in his *Diaries* of Lynton, a small town six or so miles distant as 'one of the loveliest nooks in the Paradise of this world'. But the journey from London – almost five hours on the train followed by a dozen or so miles in a car across what was then a poor moorland road – would have been exhausting for Sylvia.

Where did the idea come from? Nurse Loosemore couldn't believe that Barrie and Dr Rendel, the doctor who had supervised the last days of Arthur, had agreed to such a crazy idea. Barrie had booked the farm for the whole summer.

Having delivered Sylvia and Nurse Loosemore to the farm he then left, returning for the odd weekend until the boys' school holidays began. When the main force arrived, Nurse Loosemore warned Nanny Hodgson to make herself and the boys scarce 'as *anything* might happen'!

It wasn't long before Emma du Maurier herself appeared, to find out what was going on. Barrie took Peter in a car to pick her up at

Minehead station and after delivering her to her daughter beat a hasty retreat to Brendon, a hamlet a few miles away, where he took rooms. Emma was appalled to find Sylvia weakening rapidly.

A local doctor had been called, who asked fruitless questions and knew nothing of the history of the patient or her condition. Emma immediately insisted that Dr Rendell be telegraphed to send a replacement.

On 1 August Emma wrote to Sylvia's younger sister May, 'It is terrible to think of Sylvia so far from doctors … It is a nice house but hill all round, even from the lawn to the garden is quite a hill. This ought never to have been taken.'

While writing the letter a Dr Spicer arrived from London, the Rendell recommendation, his advent serving only to convince Sylvia that she must be very ill indeed. No one, not even the doctors, seemed to know what was wrong with her.

A month earlier, on 2 July, Emma had written to May imply-ing that one of the doctors consulted had denied that Sylvia was as seriously ill as she had been said to be by the others, including Rendel. As late as that, there was no sense that Sylvia was suffer-ing from a fatal disease.

Now, Emma was troubled, very troubled indeed. If it had been known by Barrie and/or Rendell that she had a terminal disease, would they have brought her to so isolated a spot? Yet that was what was done, and four weeks later she was dead.

The boys meanwhile were off almost every day walking with Barrie, watching buzzards circling high above the valley of the Lynn, eating huge teas of Devonshire cream and jam at Lynton, or fish-ing the Doone valley and bringing their catch back to Sylvia at tea time; then to her delight playing in the garden within sight of her room. She found she wanted to watch them rather than interact with them now. Nico's clowning around was simply too much for her in her little room.

Arthur's brother Crompton also booked rooms in Brendon for a few days and took them climbing to the top of Dunkery Beacon, the highest point of Exmoor. The only other visitor was Maude Adams, the actress who played Peter Pan in America. She was invited by Barrie to meet Sylvia and the boys. Sylvia was barely able to raise a smile.

Shortly afterwards came the day, 26 August, on the morning of which she died. She called for a hand mirror and gave orders that her boys should no longer be brought in to see her. Dr Rendel, Barrie, Nurse Loosemore and Emma du Maurier were the only ones present at the end.

Barrie then told the children, one by one. He related later that Michael (ten), had broken into a rage and stamped his foot in fury, a credible response – the unfairness of losing the person he loved more than any other, the unfairness of it being so soon after the death of his father. Anger, too. All a common enough response from a child of his age to the loss of both parents.

Sylvia dying turned this already introspective child further inside himself, but not depressively. He was fast developing a way of dealing with life. The story of Michael's life reads like a series of tests, which ultimately developed within himself an adamantine grasp of who he was and how much of himself he was prepared to share with the world.

Michael's increasing retreat from the world that caused him so much distress was enhancing the aura of detachment which had set him apart from the start, and would impress many and make genius expected of him by some who described him as 'gifted' long before ever he produced anything of note. Barrie encouraged this by electing to discuss his own ideas with Michael (the *only* person with whom he did this), seeking his approval even and discarding anything he didn't like.

It was in this way that Barrie gave his heart to Michael, proud when he took the lead, happy when he could describe Michael as 'the dark and dour and impenetrable', which he often did, almost as if he liked to think he had met his match.

On the Saturday, the morning after Sylvia died, George (seventeen) walked in an atmosphere of gloom with Peter to the nearest village Post Office carrying a sheaf of telegrams for despatch to members of the family and close friends. Then George observed to his younger brother that after all things were considered, they had managed that morning to get up, wash, get dressed and have breakfast in spite of the great tragedy that had befallen them. It was *not* the end of the world. All four of George's brothers looked to him as leader and Peter took his point, though years later he was

> a little surprised, and rather disgusted too, to find, on the evidence of old letters and the memories they recall, how little I can have felt *at the time*, thanks to dwelling in the selfish and separate world of childhood. The delayed effect those events had on me is another matter.

Jack's feelings were not to be influenced by George, however much all the boys looked up to the eldest as leader. Barrie had told Jack that Sylvia agreed on her deathbed to marry him: 'I was taken into a room where [Barrie] was alone and he told me, which angered me even then, that Mother had promised to marry him and wore his ring. Even then I thought if it was true it must be because she knew she was dying.' To Jack, the thought of Barrie marrying his mother 'was intolerable, even monstrous', wrote Peter, who doubted that Sylvia had ever agreed to it.

The question now was what should happen to the boys, and Emma didn't know what to think. 'At a quarter to two [Nurse Loosemore] called me,' she wrote to May, her youngest daughter, of Sylvia's death,

> And the doctor was holding dear Sylvia's hands and asked me to fan her, but I didn't know the end was so near. She was breathing with great difficulty and I couldn't bear to look at her, then they called in Mr Barrie and I saw what it was and it was all over in about a quarter of an hour. It was her breathing that was exhausted, not heart failure…

Henry James, in Chocorua, New Hampshire, burying his brother William, who had died there on the same day, wrote at once to Emma on hearing of Sylvia's death from a neighbour of his in England.

Henry had known the family intimately since the early 1880s, when Sylvia was fifteen, so fiery and uncontrollable that she was nicknamed 'the blizzard'. Sylvia had insisted Henry join in the family fun and games. No one had ever invited this 'benign, indulgent but grave' man, 'not often unbending beyond a genial chuckle'[39] to do such a thing before. With the du Mauriers he had come alive.

'My dear dear Mrs du Maurier,' he wrote on 11 September.

> It moves me to the deepest pity and sympathy that you should have had helplessly to watch the dreadful process of her going, and to see that beautiful, that exquisite light mercilessly quenched. What you have had to go through in it all, dear Mrs du Maurier, and what you all, and what her young children, have, affects me more than I can say. She leaves us with an image of extraordinary loveliness, nobleness

---

39   Description of Henry James by his friend, the writer, Edmund Gosse.

and charm – ever unforgettable and touching. What a tragedy all this latter history of hers! …

Please believe, dearest Mrs du Maurier, in all the old-time intimacy of your faithfullest Henry James.

He had hit the mark, for Emma had been completely felled by the experience of watching her daughter die. At the back of her mind she knew that she, as head of the family, had to make a decision about the boys, but she couldn't even decide for sure that she would be going to the funeral. Two days later, she wrote to May:

> The arrangements are that we all go up tomorrow (all but Michael & Nicholas) by the one o'clock train reaching London 5.40 … I shall sleep at Campden Hill Square … The funeral is on Tuesday at twelve. I think I shall go … I can't quite make up my mind about anything. Your loving Mother.

In the event, Jack, George and Peter travelled with Barrie in a van, along with Sylvia's coffin, and at every stop along the way Barrie stood sentry outside it. Jack was glad when the funeral at Hampstead Parish Church was over. From there he went to stay with Sylvia's elder brother, Guy, a career soldier, at Longmoor Military Camp in Hampshire, before returning to naval college in Dartmouth, where he found a letter from Michael, the only one to think to write.

Meanwhile Michael and Nico had been invited to stay at the rectory at Oare, where R. D. Blackmore's grandfather had been rector and *Lorna Doone* had actually been written. They moved there with Nanny Hodgson after everyone left the farm to go to the funeral.

It was to the rectory that Crompton arrived on 1 September, with Barrie, George and Peter. He wrote that day to Emma:

We arrived all well and found Michael & Nicholas with Mary [Hodgson] established here. They have been fishing & the time seems passing happily for them. I have written to Hugh Macnaghten [George's housemaster] and Mr Wilkinson [Michael's headmaster] – Michael has written to Jack & we all send you our dear love.

Crompton Llewelyn Davies.

On Wednesday morning, the day after the funeral, Barrie had taken George and Peter to Little's, a shop in the Haymarket off Piccadilly in London, and bought eight-foot fly-rods, and fine casts and flies. This was a considerable step up for any fisherman. There would be no more catching trout with worm hooks. Real fishermen use flies.

The boys were ecstatic. 'We were selfish little creatures,' admitted Nico in hindsight, like Peter, a bit embarrassed that they had accepted the transition to orphan so readily.

Fly-fishing henceforth became the focus of every holiday and a significant part of Michael's life, an activity that made a good fit with his nature, giving him more opportunities to withdraw into another world, a beautiful world, a world of silence and solitude in which he could still his feeling of loss.

The man who owned all the fishing in the area was one Nicholas Snowe, and Nicholas Davies (six) was persuaded by Michael to 'intercede with him for fishing facilities on the grounds that they were of the same name – successfully too', Barrie reported. 'Michael was ten then and I remember we had a grand scheme of reaching Dulverton and fishing some water there.' The Rivers Exe, Haddeo and Barle coalesce near Dulverton and it remains one of the great areas for salmon and trout fishing today.

As their holiday drew to a close Lady Lewis offered Barrie and the boys refuge at the Lewis's palatial abode in Portland Place, but Barrie declared that home was still 23 Campden Hill Square, where they were reunited with Nanny, who now took the role of mother. 'She was the person in our lives,' said Nico later. 'She was the mother.'

But she wasn't to be the only mother, for increasingly Barrie took on that role, which made for continuing unrest with Nanny. The critic Desmond McCarthy, who knew Barrie, made an astute definition of him as 'part mother, part hero-worshipping maiden, part grandfather, and part pixie with no man in him at all', each facet of the description – Barrie's maternal love for the boys, his need to be dominated by Michael at least, his assumption of the mantle of grandfather du Maurier, and the fantasy games of his pixie-self – follow from it.

However, except for staff, No. 23 was now an all-male dominion and the atmosphere seems to have been like that of a public school common room: periods of study alternating with raucous game playing, including cricket in the corridor, but with a certain control exercised by George, the eldest, the leader – a form of society George knew well and which was good practice for Peter, who would be joining him at Eton in the new term.

As a Scot with a tendency to a very British sort of snobbery – ever at its worst when adopted by an outsider – Barrie was exultant at the very notion of the English public school, Eton in particular: 'I am like a dog looking up to its owner, wondering what that noble face means,' he once wrote of the public schoolboy, actually lifting a wonder-love line from du Maurier's *Trilby*, though no one would notice the deep-set irony in so much of what he said and wrote. He would soon have four such noble faces, which could own him, but for the time being two, Michael and Nico, were not at boarding school and would return to the house each afternoon from Wilkinson's and Norland Place respectively.

A new notebook, dated 22 October 1910, registers Barrie's address for the first time as 23 Campden Hill Square. Mackail writes that Campden Hill Square was 'his home far more than the flat, at present'. And Nico: 'As often as not he was there.'

Thus, casually and with minimum fuss, did he get what he wanted. It was not what Sylvia had wanted or what she had specified in a handwritten document headed 'Sylvia's Will'. But immediately after the funeral Barrie had button-holed the du Mauriers and staked his claim. Emma hadn't been happy, but what alternative could she propose? Nobody in the family could cater for the material needs of five boys as well as he, four of whom would go through Eton and university. And clearly the boys wanted him.

What Sylvia wrote that she wanted was that Nanny Hodgson and her sister Jenny would together look after the boys, with Emma, Barrie and her elder brother Guy as trustees and guardians, and with back-up from May du Maurier and Margaret Llewelyn Davies. But Sylvia's will didn't come to light for three months after her death.

The odd thing was that when it did, Barrie sent a hand-written copy of it to Emma, altering 'Jenny' to 'Jimmy', the name by which he was often known, giving the false impression that Sylvia had wanted Nanny Hodgson and Barrie to be hands-on in charge of the boys.

Much has been written about why Barrie did what he did. The die-hards say he must have mistaken the word. This is unlikely because 'Jenny' is so clearly written and Barrie was a stickler for accuracy and precision. The more sceptical argue that he was ever the twister and since the boys were not adopted in law, he needed to show the family that he was abiding by Sylvia's wishes, hence the deliberate fabrication.

No one was chasing him however and it is doubtful that the law would have been impressed by Sylvia's makeshift will, as it gave custody to parties who had not been consulted and who were not prepared to take on the responsibility. Also, 'possession is nine points of the law' particularly to a Scot (it was originally a Scottish expression) and in those days a fifty-year-old bachelor millionaire was seen as more of a scoop than a threat to five orphan boys, whatever might go on behind closed doors.

Barrie didn't need to alter the document. He already had what he wanted. The die-hards call on this in support of their case – it would have been pointless to falsify the will: what had Barrie to gain?

But there *was* a point, a motive which would not normally be considered in such a case, the motive Barrie had for almost everything he did, namely to manipulate and write from life so to make his fictional creation lively and life-like. Falsifying the will was an opportunity to study the family's response, and if it was a worthwhile one, to use it in his work.

Since he modelled Grizel on Sylvia twelve years earlier, her family had been Barrie's paint box. He owed the boys more than anyone in this regard.

The play of Peter is streaky with you … I always knew that I made Peter by rubbing the five of you violently together, as savages with two sticks produce a flame … Any one of you five brothers has a better claim to the authorship than most, and I would not fight you for it, but you should have launched your case long ago in the days when you most admired me, which were in the first year of the play, owing to a rumour reaching you that my spoils were one-and-sixpence a night … You watched for my next play with peeled eyes, not for entertainment but lest it contained some chance witticism of yours that could be challenged as collaboration; indeed I believe there still exists a legal document, full of the Aforesaid and Henceforward to be called

> Part-Author, in which for some such snatching I was tied down to pay
> No. 2 one halfpenny daily throughout the run of the piece.

This is perfectly true, Barrie drew up an Agreement dated 6 December 1903 with Jack on account of something he said that appeared in his play *Little Mary*. That Jack originally insisted on it, that he tied Barrie down to it, is wonderfully in the nature of their precarious relationship.

Barrie's life every single day was a mystery in the making and he wrote about himself as often as he wrote about the people in his web. He was quite ruthless in turning his life to advantage in his work, and crucially, while he 'took an impish delight in decorating or even fantasticating his own portrait, *he never falsified it*', as the critic W. A. Darlington was the first to point out.[40] That was his genius: constantly he challenges us to decide whether it is irony or plain truth that he is delivering. Even as he says goodbye to Arthur and Sylvia, and the faint possibility that he might have had something to do with their deaths passes over our minds, he is writing of their alter egos, Mr and Mrs Darling in the novel *Peter & Wendy* (1911): 'There never was a simpler, happier family until the coming of Peter Pan,' and giving Peter the heartless line, 'I forget people after I kill them.'

Hugh Walpole, who knew Barrie when he was an aspiring journalist, before he was writing books, had no hesitation in concluding that it was the plain truth Barrie was delivering: 'Barrie tricked nine-tenths of us, and knew well that he was tricking us. He was his own murderer, murdered and detective in his own mystery story.'

In 1911, life with the Darlings was moving on and the focus

---

40 W. A. Darlington, *J. M. Barrie* (1938).

was no longer on Sylvia but on Michael alone. The first stage of his scheme – 'to burrow under [Sylvia's] influence with the boy, expose her to him in all her vagaries, take him utterly from her and make him mine' – had been 'relentlessly pursued' and successfully achieved, as Barrie predicted it would be in *The Little White Bird*. Sylvia had throughout been 'culpably obtuse to my sinister design, having instructed Nanny – ever a threatening shadow in the background – that I was to be allowed to share him with her'.

Now, noted Denis Mackail, Barrie had what he had wanted all along:

> Michael was ten last summer. Still looks like his mother, and hasn't escaped her charm. An orphan at ten. Not wax for Barrie – not by any means – but you can steer or lead little boys of ten in a way that you can't do afterwards. The spell is still irresistible when it chooses, and here is the boy – quick, sensitive, attractive, and gifted – who is to be everything else that the magician most admires. There is no cloud between them. From Barrie, as yet, Michael has no secrets. You can call him the favourite, if you like – indeed there are plenty of moments when it is impossible to call him anything else – but his brothers are the last to resent this. He and Barrie draw closer and closer, and perhaps it isn't always Barrie who leads or steers. He has given his heart to Michael – or must one again say one of his hearts? – and has transferred an enormous part of his ambition. Is this dangerous? No answer. One mustn't say so. It may be; but there can be nothing wrong with such kindness and such love.[41]

---

41   Denis Mackail, *The Story of J. M. Barrie* (1941).

Chapter Eighteen

1910–11: Scourie: Learning to Fly

MACKAIL WAS THERE; he knew them all; and although he was writing his biography guardedly (because that was the limitation of the arrangement he had with Barrie's executor, Lady Cynthia Asquith) the tenor rings unusually clear as regards Michael, and clearest about Michael taking the lead. That was the ironic position Barrie liked to adopt with him and initially it increased Michael's self-esteem considerably, as well indeed as giving Michael an influence on his work.

For example, on Michael's say-so the first notes appear in 1911 in Barrie's notebook for a murder mystery, later to be called *Shall We Join the Ladies?* The scene is a (so far) week-long country house party – thirteen are present, twelve guests plus the host Sam Smith, a little old bachelor who sits there beaming on those present at dinner like an elderly cupid. So they think him, but they are to be undeceived, for each has been invited on account of their involvement with the host's brother, who has been murdered.

Barrie never finished the play, some say because he couldn't work his complicated twists and turns into a solution, though it was rumoured that Sam Smith (basically Barrie himself) was the murderer, and Barrie was unsure whether the admission was an ironic step too far in a play that would be watched by thousands. As with Socrates, someone might reach for the hemlock. The first act was produced on its own in a wider programme in 1921, and was (as ever) a hit.

There was the odd titled lady in the cast list and Lady Tree was among the top-line actresses who played them. Titled ladies were a Barrie speciality. It had not always been the case. Once, in the early 1890s, when things were a little rocky for him and Mary Ansell (Barrie had suffered three mental breakdowns during the period he was playing around with hypnotism and shadowing du Maurier), one of them offered them sanctuary in her home. 'She flattered, she spoke honeyed words,' according to Mackail, and Barrie got it into his head that she fancied him. He made love to her in the only way he knew – with laboured, sentimental verbal blandishments – and she had recoiled. It was not at all what she'd intended to encourage, and Barrie was left with egg on his face. A polite retreat was not going to be enough. He had to *get out*. Such humiliation the little man could barely countenance; he had caught sight of himself through her eyes and hadn't liked what he saw, and was deeply scarred.

The result was Lady Pippinworth in *Tommy and Grizel* and Lady

Sybil Tenterden in the play *What Every Woman Knows* – self-seeking, bumptious parasites on society.

But since he had become a success, titled ladies were more respectful to him, and when one in particular, Millicent, Duchess of Sutherland, asked him for ideas for a costume that would make her shine in a high society ball at the Albert Hall in aid of the National Theatre in 1911, he not only came up with some ideas, but engaged a designer to make it for her.

Now, on 20 April of the same year, it was payback time. He wrote to ask her

> Whether you would in the goodness of your heart set some factor in Sutherland searching for a house for me up there for August and September. I bring four boys with me [Jack, of course, was unavailable]; what they yearn for is to be remote from Man and plenty of burn trout fishing, of which they never tire from the rising to the setting of the sun. The rate would not so much matter but there should be space for about ten of us including maids.

The Duchess was a good person to advise on this. In 1872, when the government ordered only the second audit of land since the Domesday Book, the ten leading Dukes in the Kingdom owned over 100,000 acres each, while the Duke of Sutherland, whose money came largely from coal, had 1,350,000 acres. By 1911, some of it had passed into the hands of the Duke of Westminster, but not enough to bother five young boys.

This holiday was meant to be special, the first in Scotland since Barrie had secured his own family. 'I have in a sense a larger family than you now,' he boasted to Charles Turley Smith, the writer of books about schoolboys and member of the Allahakbarries. 'Five boys whose father died four years ago and now their mother last summer, and I look after them, and it is my main reason for going on. The Llewelyn Davies boys.'

By July the holiday was fixed and on the 10th Barrie wrote to his friend again:

> We are going for seven weeks or so beginning of August to Scourie in the west of Sutherland. 630 miles rail, then a drive 44 miles. The nearest small town is farther than from here to Paris in time. Nothing to do but fish, which however is what they want. Now that Miss Corelli and Ranger Gull [science fiction writer under the pseudonym Guy Thorne] have appeared among you I shall expect to see an improvement in your style. You don't say whether you are working much but I hope all is well with you, body and soul. I have nearly finished my P. Pan book. We might play draughts by correspondence so as not to get rusty at it...
>
> I have been teaching Michael to bicycle, running up and down the quieter thoroughfares of Campden Hill and feeling what it must be like at the end of a Marathon race. Have also taken him to a garden in St John's Wood where an expert teaches him fly fishing on a lawn...

Scourie is an unspoilt dream of a village on the far north-west coast of Scotland, a region of white sandy beaches, great boulder mountains, rushing rivers and literally hundreds of fishable lochs and lochans – formed, one cannot but think, from the myriad splashings of some giant who in myth leapt out of the sea at Laxford Bridge.

There are more than 300 of them, including the famous fishing grounds of the Laxford, Lochs Stack and More, and the Lower Duart, noted for its migratory run of fish from the frozen Atlantic.

You can't get much further away from the world of telegrams and anger than this. Barrie wrote of it to Nurse Loosemore (surprising that he was still in touch with her so long after Sylvia's demise):

> It is a remote place, nearly 50 miles from a railway, and when you want food you have to kill a sheep. It is very beautiful with sea & lochs, all as blue as the Mediterranean, and in the course of their wanderings the boys see eagles, otters, whales, seals, &c. The wanderings are all in search of fish, and it is a great place for fishing.

The 630 miles by rail, which will still take you more than twenty hours from London today, brought Barrie and the boys to Lairg, the railhead for the north-west on a similar latitude to Ullapool. Here the early twentieth-century traveller would linger for an hour or two before being bundled into the mail bus, in Barrie's time a horse-drawn waggon of some sort – not until the '20s did it become a red motorised van – a long and rather uncomfortable ride many miles up the single track mountain road to Scourie.

Once in the ultima Thule, one found the gable-stepped houses of the old village by means of a narrow country lane, which spilled out at its north end into the sheltered waters of the old harbour of Scourie, and the Duke of Sutherland's hotel and hunting lodge.

The Lodge, where the boys stayed with Barrie, is tucked behind the harbour in its own landscaped gardens. For fifty-odd years before Barrie took it, it had been home to Evander Maciver, the Duke's factor for the whole of Sutherland, unpopular to this day for his key role in the infamous Highland clearances, which robbed crofters of a living and led to misery in enforced exile abroad for untold numbers.

The hunting lodge and Scourie Hotel, known in Michael's day as the Stafford Arms, combined with a house known as Roseville to offer some sixty-three rooms. Scourie was not a stag-hunting centre.

People came for the fishing, particularly for the fly-fishing – dry, wet, and dapping with a large fly mimicking the action of flying insects such as daddy long-legs or, if there's a hatch in the area, mayflies.

Every day, ghillies would gather outside the hotel to attract the custom of the guests in return for a few shillings. Ghillies knew, then as today, where the fish lie in any of the 300-odd local lochs, which are split into forty-six beats. These men – all self-employed local fishermen – will also tell you which fly to use, and the best of them offer a lot more besides.

It is possible that Barrie found his ghillie on the way from Lairg, as the man's brother was for some time the mail bus driver.

Johnny Mackay turned out to be a lucky strike. He got to know all the boys and Barrie well, but hit it off especially with Michael, ending up his personal ghillie, firm friend and mentor, and reappearing later in his story.

A few months before he died in 1977, Mackay recounted how Barrie, while fishing with the humbler worm, 'looked so scruffy that when the Duchess of Westminster saw him she thought he was a poacher and ordered him off her land; and he was too shy to say who he was, so he went'.

Barrie, no fly fisher himself, wrote that Mackay taught Michael 'everything that is worth knowing'. Used to casting on a lawn in St John's Wood in London, the boy soon found that it was a different matter on water.

Mackay took him back to basics, explaining the stance that would best facilitate the smooth action required in a cast – now like a cricketer at the crease getting stance, grip and body action just right, now like an archer transferring the energy from bow to arrow, as his line snaked over his shoulder and he brought it up abruptly to fall at (hopefully) just the right spot. Michael, a good enough cricketer to make the first XI at Wilkinson's, and with a wrist action soon to be celebrated in a natural aptitude for Eton Fives, picked up on it fast.

Mackay's niece, the sculptor Dorothy Dick, lives in Scourie today and remembers Johnny well:

> He was a good ghillie and a delightful person. As a child I loved his company. He would take me to nearby lochs, but I never really mastered the casting. He could cast the trout line and put it *exactly* where he wanted it.

Mackay was a magician with his casts and Michael began to appreciate the sheer beauty of the shape of them – the wand, as the fly rod is often known, snaking back and forth, back and forth, until whoosh, the line glides in a straight line down upon the water like a wingless bird.

For days Michael experimented with Johnny's techniques, finding those that suited him best, and the ghillie began talking to him about what was involved besides the cast – like how to read the water, how to recognise the different parts of a loch or river and how to unravel its meaning in the same way a trout has to do in order to survive. He also taught him how to recognise where currents have formed, how to cast across currents of different speeds, how to control how the fly line is affected by them, and particularly how to 'mend' when the line gets caught up in them and begins to drag.

MacKay distinguished between those of his clients who wanted to know how to cast and those who wanted to be taught how to *fish*, and once it was clear that Michael was of the latter sort, their conversation turned to flies. As Dorothy recalls, 'Johnny tied his own flies in a shed beside the house. I loved going into that shed.'

There was Claret Grouse and Teal & Yellow, but the fly I remember best was a Jungle Cock. It was beautiful. The feathers looked almost as if they were burnished. They must have come from a tropical bird, I guess: yellow, black and grey … He took one feather at a time and delicately put the thread around to tie it on the hook, so that it looked like the wings of an insect that the fish would like. And then the body of the fly would be silver, like tinsel.

But besides being good at finding the best place to catch a fish he was very popular because he was good at telling stories. Of course people were in those days. There was no other entertainment up here. Johnny was probably very good with Michael. He was very good with me.

A year had passed since Sylvia had died. In all that time Michael, described by Barrie at this age as 'the mysterious boy of the so open countenance … with the carelessness of genius', had found no activity that took his mind off his mother's death, until now. Within a few days of Mackay starting with Michael and Nico, Barrie was taking Nico out on his own to fish. Michael was no longer available.

On 18 August, Barrie wrote to Lady Lewis: 'The fishing is extraordinary good, and Michael does fare better than almost any of the bags we see recorded in the papers…'

Fifteen days earlier, on 3 August, Michael had caught his first sea trout – 2½ pounds. He had waded downstream in the Laxford and cast to the tail of a pool. The fish had taken. He had given the line a short sharp pull backward and up to set the hook, and all his equipment had come alive, throbbing, surging with life. The fish had jumped out of the water and Michael had lowered his rod, giving it slack and then reeling it in, keeping the pressure on, waiting for the fish to tire. It was a battle he had no desire to win and yet knew he could not duck out now.

Afterwards Johnny told him he was a real fisherman now. But, for the first time that day, Michael felt alone. That night he took the sea-trout to bed with him, placing it on a chair by his side. Next day Barrie sent it to England to have it stuffed. But it arrived on a Bank Holiday. The shop was closed and it was taken to the gardener's cottage of one of the firm. The gardener's wife thought it was a gift from some anonymous friend and ate it. Barrie didn't dare tell Michael until he got his first salmon.

Scourie was a most memorable holiday, one of the best, for it started Michael, this young city boy of eleven years of age, on a relationship with nature and replaced something that had been missing since his mother had gone.

When he arrived home in Kensington, he was full of Scourie, but momentum was gathering beneath the wheels of discontent from various relatives, particularly Margaret Llewelyn Davies, as Dolly Ponsonby's diary record for the very day that Michael's sea-trout had arrived in England attests:

Monday Aug 7th, Bank Holiday [1911] M[argaret] & I talked all morning of Sylvia & Arthur's boys – & Jimmy Barrie. M is very desperate at moments about them & I too have felt the pity of their easy luxurious lives. In fact it has been on my tongue to say to J. M. B. does he want George to be a fashionable gentleman? Of course in principle he doesn't. In principle he is all for the ragged raggamuffins & says he wants the boys to be for them too. But in his desire to make up to the boys for all they have lost, he gives them every material pleasure. Nothing is denied them in the way of amusement, clothes, toys, etc. It is very, very disheartening, & when one thinks of Arthur their father – almost unbearable ... J. M. B. takes the boys to very grand restaurants in their best evening clothes & they go on to stalls or box at the theatre. They buy socks costing 12/6 a pair & Michael, aged 11, is given very expensive lessons in fly fishing.

Michael, however, was enjoying life more than he had for a very long time and beginning to fit in more at school, as Barrie recorded in a piece about him, as usual selecting, rejecting and inventing what material he needed to make the story more completely reflect his feelings for the boy. 'Here is interesting autobiographical matter,' Barrie wrote.

I culled [it] years later from the fly-leaf of his *Caesar*: 'Aetas 12, height 4 ft. 11, biceps 8 1/4, kicks the beam at 6-2.' The reference is to a great occasion when Michael stripped at his preparatory (clandestinely) for a Belt with the word 'Bruiser' on it. I am reluctant to boast about him (this is untrue), yet must mention that he won the belt, with which (such are the ups and downs of life) he was that same evening gently belted by his preceptor.

It is but fair to [Michael] to add that he cut a glittering figure in those circles: captain of the footer, and twenty-six against Juddy's. 'And even then,' his telegram to me said, 'I was only bowled off my pads.'

A rural cricket match in buttercup time with boys at play, seen and heard through the trees; it is surely the loveliest scene in England and the most disarming sound. From the ranks of the unseen dead, for ever passing along our country lanes on their eternal journey, the Englishman falls out for a moment to look over the gate of the cricket field and smile.

Let Michael's twenty-six against Juddy's, the first and perhaps the only time he is to meet the stars on equal terms, be our last sight of him as a child. He is walking back, bat in hand, to the pavilion, an old railway carriage. An unearthly glory has swept over the cricket ground. He tries to look unaware of it; you know the expression and the bursting heart. Our smiling Englishman who cannot open the gate waits to make sure that this boy raises his cap in the one right way (without quite touching it, you remember), and then rejoins his comrades. Michael gathers up the glory and tacks it over his bed. 'The End,' as he used to say in his letters. I never know him quite so well again. He seems henceforth to be running to me on a road that is moving still more rapidly in the opposite direction.

This is Barrie bathing in the love he feels for the boy, positioning him for a glorious future from the spring of 1913, when he was due to shine at Eton. But still he manages to slip in that bit about 'the unseen dead, for ever passing along our country lanes on their eternal journey'. And with good reason. He had not given up on the idea for a play drawing on the legend of Kilmeny. Despite the fact that he clearly had misgivings – in March 1911 he'd written to Quiller-Couch that 'No one should come back, however much he was loved' – with the death of Sylvia, the legend had taken on tangible realism. For hadn't he written in *The Little White Bird*, 'There is no other inducement great enough to bring the departed back' than dead young mothers returning as ghosts to see how their children fare?

They glide into the acquainted room when day and night, their jailers are in the grip, and whisper, 'How is it with you, my child?' but always, lest a strange face should frighten him, they whisper it so low that he may not hear. They bend over him to see that he sleeps peacefully, and replace his sweet arm beneath the coverlet, and they open the drawers to count how many little vests he has. They love to do these things. What is saddest about ghosts is that they may not

know their child. They expect him to be just as he was when they left
him, and they are easily bewildered, and search for him from room
to room, and hate the unknown boy he has become. Poor, passionate souls, they may even do him an injury. These are the ghosts that
go wailing about old houses…

Now he had a situation with the orphaned Michael which, if handled
carefully might draw back the veil on 'the ranks of the unseen dead',
if not literally at least metaphorically. Central to the project was the
boy's relationship with his dead mother, which Barrie had already
decided to keep alive by writing her a letter every year, 'telling
her how things now were with her children', though according to
Andrew Birkin he later destroyed these letters.

Sylvia's warning not to press Michael sounds somewhere off stage
– 'He is at present not very strong but very keen and intelligent:
great care must be taken not to overwork him. Mary [Hodgson]
understands & of course JMB knows and will be careful & watch.'

But, like it or not, Barrie's affair with Michael was the driver and
Barrie was ever-driven by the need to write from life, even if he was
also aware of the need to proceed softly. For being *in loco parentis* he
had every opportunity now to witness Michael in the grip of nightmare as it occurred:

I have known the small white figure defend the stair-head thus for an
hour, blazing rather than afraid, concentrated on some dreadful matter in which, tragically, none could aid him. I stood or sat by him,
like a man in an adjoining world, waiting till he returned to me, for I
had been advised, warned, that I must not wake him abruptly. Gradually I soothed him back to bed, and though my presence there in
the morning told him, in the light language we then adopted, that he

had been 'at it again' he could remember nothing of who the name-less enemy was. Once I slipped from the room, thinking it best that he should wake to normal surroundings, but that was a mistake. He was violently agitated by my absence. In some vague way he seemed on the stairs to have known that I was with him and to have got com-fort from it; he said he had gone back to bed only because he knew I should be there when he woke up. I found that he liked, 'after he had been an ass', to wake up seeing me 'sitting there doing something frightfully ordinary, like reading the newspaper,' and you may be sure that thereafter that was what I was doing.[42]

---

42   J. M. Barrie, *Neil and Tintinnabulum* (1925).

Chapter Nineteen

1912: The Outer Hebrides: Catching Mary Rose

THE FOLLOWING SUMMER a boyhood friend of Barrie's from Kirriemuir, Peter Lindsay, put him on to Amhuinnsuidhe (pronounced 'aven-suey'), a castellated mansion situated on North Harris in the Outer Hebrides.

North Harris could just as well be taken for South Lewis, as the isles of Lewis (north) and Harris (south) are geologically one. But the natural boundary line between them – the narrow slip of land at Tarbert – is not the one chosen by their people. So that, while Amhuinnsuidhe has a Harris address, it actually lies within the Lewis land mass.

There are various routes to this remote location, including a two-and-a-quarter-hour ferry ride into the Atlantic, west from mainland Ullapool to Stornoway on Lewis's north-east coast, which takes some beating on a sunny day with dolphins playing all around, but in high winds can be dramatic, even treacherous. Alternatively, one can cross further south and take in Skye en route to Tarbert.

In Barrie's day supplies for the fishing and shooting seasons would be brought to the castle in May on the *Dunara Castle*, the boat coming up almost to the castle door. And guests would be ferried to and from Tarbert on two launches, called *Rover* and *Mabel*.

It was while on their way to Tarbert in 1912 that Barrie revealed to Nanny, Michael and Nico – George and Peter were to follow after school camp; Jack as usual was ruled out – just what it meant to travel with a man with one foot in a magic wood.

'My grandest triumph is that long after No. 4 [Michael] had ceased to believe [in fairies], I brought him back to the faith for at least two minutes,' wrote Barrie.

> We were on our way in a boat to fish the Outer Hebrides (where we caught Mary Rose), and though it was a journey of days he wore his fishing basket on his back all the time, so as to be able to begin at once. His one pain was the absence of Johnny Mackay, for Johnny was the loved ghillie of the previous summer … but could not be with us this time as he would have had to cross and re-cross Scotland to reach us.
>
> As the boat drew near the Kyle of Lochalsh pier [off the south-east of Skye] I told Nos. 4 and 5 it was such a famous wishing pier that they had now but to wish and they should have. No. 5 believed at once and expressed a wish to meet himself (I afterwards found him on the pier searching faces confidently), but No. 4 thought it more of my untimely nonsense and doggedly declined to humour me.
>
> 'Whom do you want to see most, No. 4?'

'Of course I would like most to see Johnny Mackay.'

'Well, then, wish for him.'

'Oh, rot.'

'It can't do any harm to wish.'

Contemptuously he wished, and as the ropes were thrown on the pier he saw Johnny waiting for him, loaded with angling paraphernalia. I know no one less like a fairy than Johnny Mackay, but for two minutes No. 4 was quivering in another world than ours. When he came to he gave me a smile which meant that we understood each other, and thereafter neglected me for a month, being always with Johnny.

'Amhuinsuidhe' is the Gaelic for 'sitting by the river' and indeed one of the salmon and sea trout systems careers across the rocks to the sea right beside the castle. In the vicinity are ten distinct fresh-water loch and river systems, all in remote and beautiful surroundings, variously accessible by vehicle or on foot.

Charles Murray, Seventh Earl of Dunmore, built the castle in 1867, but when he went bankrupt the estate was taken over by his bankers, headed by Sir Edward Scott. Barrie first rented it from Sir Edward's son, Sir Samuel Scott, from July to September 1912. 'This place is very remote,' he wrote to the actress Mrs Patrick Campbell – 'nothing alive but salmon, deer, and whales.'

Wild country, certainly – the birds are especially impressive – huge, white-tailed eagles with eight-foot wing spans, the largest in Britain. But there was also a place to play cricket and a tennis court, which today completely surprises one in the midst of wilderness some miles before you come upon the castle.

In Sir Edward's day, non-paying guests were invited for the hunting and fishing and attended by a staff of forty. But it seems that Barrie took the place over in its entirety, drafting in his own staff

– Nanny and the below stairs staff, Minnie, Lilian and Bessie from 23 Campden Hill Square, and Harry Brown, his manservant/butler from Adelphi Terrace.

Nurse Loosemore, who nursed Sylvia but had had no duties in the household since her death, was also invited and stayed 'for an indefinite period', as Nanny observed. Writing to her sister, Nancy, on 1 September, Nanny said:

> The weather has been very good for Scotland, & the fishing splendid. They (the boys) generally go on ponies & are getting quite expert at riding. Jack is not with us – his holidays do not come convenient. J. M. B. is well, & much better than I have seen him for some years.

Among Barrie's friends to be invited to join the party were: Turley Smith; the E. V. Lucases with daughter Audrey (who stayed for a month); Mason (who stayed for ten days) and Anthony Hope, the celebrated author of *The Prisoner of Zenda* (1894) who had known Sylvia since before she was married; and Hope's wife and daughter, Betty; plus Betty's governess (they stayed for well over a month).

Wrote Nanny: 'We have had (to use slang) the pick of the literary genius's [sic] of England, but alas – either my liver is out of order, or my ideals too high, for at close quarters they are but mortal – & very ordinary at that.'

Auberon Herbert, 9th Baron Lucas, also put in an appearance with his sister, Nan. 'Bron' Lucas was shortly to become President of the Board of Agriculture in the Asquith government, and was an athlete in spite of a wooden substitute for a leg lost as *Times* correspondent in the Boer War.

Typically, Nico, who at eight had two prominent front teeth and a lively, arrogant charm that made him a popular boy at Wilkinson's and somehow excused his impossibly forthright approach and insensitive manner towards adults, had straight away gone up to Lucas and asked him whether he could see his artificial leg. Lucas had taken Nico up to his room immediately, removed his leg and shown it to him.

Betty Hope provided a great deal of the gossip among the boys and seems to have had little time left to study with her governess. According to Nico, she was bedded by No. 1 son George (nineteen) – 'Yes indeed! I'm sure she also took Jack (eighteen) to bed with her, though not at Amhuinnsuidhe as he wasn't there.'

Having just finished his last term at Eton and preparing to follow in his father's footsteps to Cambridge, George had arrived at Amhuinnsuidhe pumped up after a sensational performance at the annual Eton–Harrow cricket match at Lords. He had scored the second highest among Eton's batsmen, bowled out the leading Harrow batsman, and made a spectacular catch at full stretch.

From Betty he found adulation fit for his heroics. Peter (fifteen) described her as 'an attractive *femme du monde* – very easy on the eye, and American', but doubted loyally 'whether [she] ever had a more attractive adolescent to play around with' than George.

So interested was Peter about what was going on between the young couple, particularly in the ancient fishing-huts by the side of these remote romantic lochs, that George had to take him aside and teach him some tact, 'i.e. the necessity of making myself scarce', as Peter put it. Henceforth, Peter 'envied from afar'.

The fishing here was the best to be had anywhere, and Michael (twelve), advised and counselled by Johnny Mackay, was once again exclusively in his element.

The Amhuinnsuidhe experience is of real, uncreated, natural beauty, and of course the fly fisherman enjoys this as a participant.

Sitting in a boat on a loch with the mist closing in around him, it becomes a gateway to his Neverland.

Amhuinnsuidhe isn't of course alone in this. The fly fisher's 'other' world breaks in upon him just as well in the South of England, soothed by the lush water meadows and slow reedy streams of deepest Berkshire when the mayflies are dancing. It has something to do with the peacefulness and curiosity of the occupation, in which he is at once relaxed, detached and enlivened with high levels of attention and observation.

Every sight and sound from the hills, the water and the air in the long periods of solitude which Michael spent in these sublime surroundings sent impulses to his heart, acting upon him inwardly, delivering a sense of the fullness of life and also a humility and surprise understanding that there was something other than himself out there – something unseen within the beauty, which at any moment he might encounter.

In Scourie, in the wilds of Sutherland, Michael realised instinctively that the world of the fly fisherman was one that he definitely wanted to cross over into again. As soon as he was on the water with Johnny, he slipped right back into the spirit of it.

In the isolated beauty of the hills and lochs around the castle he no longer felt lonely or lost, or abandoned by his mother, but found in his solitary occupation what the Romantic poets he was already reading referred to as an immanence within Nature's structure – immutable, everlasting, free of decay.

He was no longer looking at the landscape, but was living it, a shift of consciousness into the hills themselves. He and the landscape were one; part of the one consciousness.

Who he was and where he was going no longer mattered, not even how successful he was going to be that day at fishing. Here, in the silence and stillness of the moment, time disappeared, the world of eternity came near, and what mattered was simply being.

This is what Peter meant when he said of Michael that he had 'the true stuff of the poet in him from birth', because even as a child his appreciation of beauty and enchantment was his first and principal quality. Perhaps it was only a matter of time before he awakened and found a use for the sixth sense which requires no eyes or ears, and which survives into a world beyond space and time so familiar to the du Maurier line. For that is how Mary Seraskier describes living in the afterlife when she dies and returns to visit Peter Ibbetson as he is about to drown himself in the Mare d'Auteil.

It must have been easy to believe that this 'sense' was a quality built up over generations – genetically, hormonally – George du Maurier's 'little spark', Daphne's 'faculty amongst the myriad threads of our inheritance'. D. H. Lawrence recognised it as a more widespread phenomenon – intuitive, instinctual faculties too often dulled by our obsession with ego – and called it 'knowledge in the blood'.

What is certain is that when Michael was orphaned and flung upon the special beauty of the Highlands in the care of Johnny Mackay, wild Nature grew uniquely dear to this reserved but impressionable city boy.

A special sense did prevail, a natural appreciation of the spirit of place led to a sense of a supra-natural spirit within. And now, while George and Betty cavorted, Peter made himself scarce and envied the lovers from afar, and Nico played the clown with Lord Lucas's artificial leg, Michael fished and developed a poetic eye for the stories that appertained to the hills and lochs around them.

With Johnny he explored many of the lochs in the vicinity of the castle, from the adjacent sea run of Castle River, Douglas Pool and Ladies Loch to the remote Brunaval, a walk of six challenging miles even after any recognised track disappears.

But his focus was Voshimid, one of the most productive salmon and sea trout lochs in Europe, located at the end of the Meavaig track, which takes off to the east a few miles south of the castle on the road between Amhuinnsuidhe and Tarbert.

Nanny wrote to her sister of Michael's success here:

> I trust you received the salmon & served it up with mayonnaise sauce. It was one of Michael's catches ... Minnie also sent fish to her home, also Lilian, also Bessie, also Mr Brown (J. M. B.'s butler), also Michael's ghillie – the man who accompanies him in his travels & whom I implore not to bring him back in pieces.

Shrouded in mist after a day of torrential rain, the track to Voshimid is hard going and very wet. The storm-laden river alongside can carry a man to his death faster than he might canter on horseback. After a good half-hour walking against the weather, the small, so-called 'Weedy Loch' emerges through the pall, and then Voshimid herself. The 200-year-old fishing huts where George and his girlfriend romanced are there still, as is the islet in the south-west corner, where, with Michael's help, 'we caught Mary Rose', as Barrie put it.

Was it a case of beauty boiling over and the spirit of Michael's beloved mother pouring through the mist towards him – of love bidding the son 'to find the maid wherever she be hidden,'[43] as the poet wrote?

However it happened, here Michael 'caught' the Ghost Mother,

---

43 William Johnson Corey in 'Amaturus' – Michael knew Corey's work so well that he gave a talk on him a few years later at school.

the first hint of which was noted back in 1894, and who now picked up a more modern echo in the tragic passing of his mother, Sylvia, to become the basis of Barrie's play, *Mary Rose*.

A young married couple, Mary Rose and Simon, go on vacation to the Outer Hebrides, leaving their little son, Harry, behind with a nurse. They visit a small island, which has a bad name among the locals. People, including a young boy, have gone missing there. No one can hear the call of the island except for those for whom it is meant, but once it is heard it cannot be ignored. Mary Rose, who like Michael (and Kilmeny), has an elusiveness of which she is unaware, hears the call and disappears.

We learn that this is a repeat disappearance, the first occasion being in the same place when Mary Rose was Michael's age, on a fishing trip with her father. Twenty days later she returned, unaware that she had been away, and her family never discussed the episode with her.

Now, after her second disappearance, twenty-five years pass before she returns, again unaware that she has been away. She looks for her son, but cannot find him. As a lad Harry ran away to sea. She dies, but her ghost continues to haunt the house, still seeking her son. Three years on, Harry returns and confronts his mother's ghost...

On 'several occasions' at Amhuinnsuidhe, according to Nico, when Michael disappeared off on his own, Barrie ran after him manically calling his name. 'We'd hear this haunting, banshee wail, "Mi-i-ichael-l-l!"' he wrote. 'It was an extraordinary sound as it echoed through the hills. And of course Michael was always perfectly all right, and wondered what all the fuss was about.'[44]

Nico, at age eight, was unaware of what was really going on. He

---

44   Andrew Birkin, *J. M. Barrie and the Lost Boys* (1979).

knew nothing of Kilmeny, the girl of poetic nature, the lover of solitude who wanders off alone at twilight and disappears into the wild among the hills, her friends looking in vain for her, their cries echoing around the glen.

He could so easily have suggested that Barrie had been playing around, but he did not. Even Nico, who understood little of the fantasy life that Barrie was leading, realised that this was serious, that it had something to do with the strangely deep relations between Barrie and his brother, in which he didn't share. Nico's description of Barrie's call as a 'haunting, banshee wail' is utterly appropriate, however, for a banshee is a mythic spirit, a messenger from the underworld, an omen of death.

The basic premise of a mother returning from the dead to commune with her son cannot have been easy for Michael to assimilate in 1912. And yet, the impression we have is that he was an active participant in the passage of the narrative from Hogg's 'Kilmeny' through du Maurier's *Peter Ibbetson* to Barrie's *Mary Rose*.

Here was Barrie, one of our great theatrical geniuses, setting up a scene on a remote loch in the Outer Hebrides for a story worthy of consideration alongside the great myths, because like them the plaster out of which Barrie's play is moulded was *real*, and the forces that charge it played on Michael for the rest of his short life. For Michael did go missing in the hills, and Nico remembers not one but *several* occasions when Barrie chased after him as if the boy was about to make his final communion with Nature, and like Kilmeny and Mary Rose, disappear into her folds.

At this stage Barrie had the Kilmeny legend, Sylvia's death and her son Michael's undying love for her, all providing the plot for his play, but no title, nor yet a name for the mother who would disappear and return from the dead to visit her son.

What the name and title would be – 'Mary Rose' – was cleverly appropriate, because 'Rose' was both a verb suggestive of resurrection and the name of Michael's favourite flower (as revealed in another of Barrie's Querist Interrogations), while 'Mary' was the name of the woman (Mary 'Mimsey' Seraskier) who returns from the dead in the du Maurier family myth.

Once again the playwright was confirming that his work is inspired by the supernatural currents in which he grew up and by his connection to the du Mauriers.

However, Mary Rose brings nothing back from 'the other side', no knowledge of 'what only the dead should know', nor even the poetic promise of Hogg's 'Kilmeny', where 'the glories that lay in the land unseen' achieve expression in the immortal beauty of the girl, which, on her return, suffuses the glen:

> Such beauty bard may never declare,
> For there was no pride nor passion there…
> But wherever her peaceful form appeared,
> The wild beasts of the hills were cheered;
> The wolf played blythely round the field;
> The lordly byson lowed and kneeled;
> The dun deer wooed with manner bland,
> And cowered aneath her lily hand.
> And when at even the woodlands rung,
> When hymns of other worlds she sung
> In ecstasy of sweet devotion,
> O, then the glen was all in motion!

After Kilmeny 'left this world of sorrow and pain' for the second time, 'and returned to the land of thought again', we are left in no doubt of the glories in store for her on the other side. But the absence of a message of hope in *Mary Rose* led Mackail to point to a hollowness at the heart of the play: 'Audiences wept, sniffed, swallowed and choked, without ever being able to explain what had reduced them to this state … nobody knew [the play's] meaning.'

The meaning, and Barrie's purpose in writing it, was plain to the playwright, however. Like all his works written after reading *Peter Ibbetson*, *Mary Rose* was an important episode in Barrie's search for the Neverland, a world beyond the physical realities, but it would be a peculiarly dark reading of that 'other' world, a vision completely at odds with twelve-year-old Michael's joyful response to it in the Scottish landscape.

Years later Nico wrote that Barrie had confirmed that it was here, at Loch Voshimid, that the real seed of *Mary Rose* was sown, but for Michael there were seeds sown in Amhuinnsuidhe for a lot more besides.

'We leave here about the 17th, if all goes well' wrote Nanny, before signing off her letter to Nancy. 'Then Peter goes to Eton alone & George to Cambridge. Michael is now top of his school, & Nico is top but one of his class. I trust mother is keeping well, my love to you all, Dadge.'

Chapter Twenty

1913–14: Broken to Eton

AT THE END of the Easter holidays, 1913, Barrie's friend and colleague, the impresario Charles Frohman, who was a guest at No. 23, spotted Michael lost in a copy of *Child of Storm*, the newly published novel in Rider Haggard's *Allan Quatermain* series. He asked him whether he could borrow it for a moment, and on the fly-leaf, with the blue pencil that he always used, scribbled 'a perpetual pass' for two seats for the Duke of York's theatre. One of the advantages of having Barrie for an adopted father certainly, but also a kindness delivered by Frohman with a few bright evenings in mind for Michael in advance of his first term at Eton, which loomed the following month

Eton College, located in Eton, Berkshire, near Windsor, was founded in 1440 as a charity school for seventy boys from

impoverished families who were given so thorough a classical education that at the end of their time they would be fit to go as scholars
to King's College, Cambridge, founded the following year.

Since then the school has expanded considerably and kept its
charitable status, but not its exclusive remit to educate poor boys.

Exclusivity remains very much part of its character, however.
One of a handful of English independent schools that educates only
boy boarders, Eton's scholars are known as Collegers because of this
connection to King's, Cambridge and because in the old days they
were the only boys to live on site. Non-scholars, known as Oppi-
dans, were boarded out at homes run either by worthy townsfolk or
Eton teachers, 'oppidanus' being the Latin for 'townsman' and Eton
offering a thoroughgoing Classical education.

But this was clearly no longer the case by the time Michael joined.
He entered as an Oppidan a term early and lived on site first as an
Oppidan and then, after taking the Eton scholarship, as an Oppidan Scholar in the house of Hugh Macnagthen, his father's friend,
a house known today as Jourdelay's.

Of the school's many hallowed traditions, some seem geared
to sustaining exclusivity for the sake of it, particularly the tradition of playing sports of their own invention, which could not,
at least originally, be played in a league with other major public schools. The Eton Field Game, Eton Wall Game and Eton
Fives all have their own rules and special courts or pitches, and
characterise an introspective school culture. Today, Eton Fives is
the most widely played off-site, and recently an Eton Fives court
opened to the general public in London. But it took more than
600 years.

Again, there is an Eton terminology running into hundreds of
expressions meaningful only within the school; even school terms

are given their own name – three a year, as elsewhere, but inexplicably called halves.

Eton's shout is that it has educated nineteen British prime ministers and multiple generations of British aristocracy. It was the very fount of privilege in British imperial society. Criticisms of solipsism, snobbism and nepotism do not necessarily attach to individual pupils but have been encouraged by the workings of Pop in particular, that bastion of tradition, the Eton Society.

The development of Pop is perhaps most difficult to square with the school's original socialist blueprint. Members of Eton's most exclusive club – all boys, swells of one sort or another – rule the roost. Its president once had the power to cane (or 'tan' as it was called) in the presence of, and at one time with the assistance of, other Pop members, the miserable miscreant to be clad in a pair of old trousers kept for purpose, so likely was it that it'd be cut to shreds.

To be fair, this abuse was not practised exclusively by Eton; rather a model copied in boys' boarding schools (prep-schools as well as public schools) up and down Britain right into the 1950s.

At Eton, however, the will to power and privilege was more obvious owing to the trappings – three-piece Eton tail suits, stiff collars and sleek black top hats were uniform; there was even a designated movement of hand to check the rim of the hat when passing a master. For members of Pop, classier shirts and striped 'spongebag' trousers were *de rigueur*, along with coloured waistcoats instead of the usual black.

In 1920, Barrie described being taken to the annual cricket match at Lords between Eton and Harrow, another of Britain's leading all-boy public schools:

15,000 tall hats – one cad hat (mine); 15,000 stiff collars, canes, shiny faces – one soft collar, cudgel, dreary face (mine). The ladies comparatively drab fearing rain but the gents superb, colossal, sleek, lovely. All with such a pleased smile. Why? Because they know they had the Eton something or the Harrow something. They bestowed the something on each other, exchanged with each other as the likes of me exchange the time of day. I felt I was nearer to grasping what the something is than ever before. It is a sleek happiness that comes of a shininess which only Eton (or Harrow) can impart. This makes you 'play the game' as the damned can't do it; it gives you manners because you know in your heart that nothing really matters so long as you shine with that sleek happiness. The nearest thing to it must be boot polish.

Besides taking advantage of the fagging system, members of Pop enjoyed all sorts of other privileges, meaningless except as an illustration of the position of power they held over their fellows – such as being entitled to furl their umbrellas, or sitting on the wall of Long Walk in front of the main building.

Wrote Barrie:

Endless tales have been written of the bullying of fags – one of the oldest traditions of Eton is that no senior must let himself get tired or, in the *vox populum*, fagged; he therefore hires a scug to get tired for him. At Eton the bully is an institution, it is his duty to kick the little ones. This makes them hardy.

By far the most unappealing aspect of Pop, however, was that membership was controlled by Pop members themselves and with homosexuality rife in the school, favours could be emotionally quite expensive.

Nico, for whom membership of Pop would be a significant aim from the first half, recalled how he was 'suddenly "taken up" by one or two "Knuts" in Pop who take me for walks'. No junior dared to refuse 'walks'. Elder brother George had managed to get out of just such an invitation from a homosexual swell by convincing him that he'd been invited to walk with some other (presumably less danger-ous) boy, which was then arranged.

Nico, more compliant, was amazed to discover that he was 'put up for Pop at a very young age and only got one blackball too many'. Then one day a Pop friend asked Nico for an introduction to one of his friends, a very pretty boy who was also quite good at games, called Fitz-Wright. Suddenly Nico saw what a fool he'd been, let fly at the Pop 'friend' and the next time he was put up for member-ship of Pop he got the maximum amount of black balls. He was also discriminated against when his name came up in other contexts, such as sports colours.

This sort of environment was hardly tailormade for a sensitive boy like Michael – 'very reserved – not a seeker after popularity', as Clive Burt, a boy in the same year as he, recalled.

Macnaghten, Michael's housemaster and tutor, wrote that in May 1913 Michael came to Eton 'very full of anxieties, a boy of a tender heart and delightful feelings, full of promise'. This was euphemism. Whereas Nico, when he arrived three years later, was in Michael's words 'the heart and soul of the house', and 'happy after the first five minutes', Michael became dreadfully depressed and in Nico's remembrance 'more or less cried for the first two years'.

On 10 May, Barrie wrote to Turley Smith:

Many thanks for the bluebells and a squeeze of the hand for everyone you plucked [this seems to have been an annual present from Turley

Smith, who lived in Cornwall]. Still more for the affection that made you know how sad I would be about Michael gone to school. He is very lonely there at present, and I am foolishly taken up about it. It rather broke me up seeing him crying and trying to whistle at the same time.

Typical Barrie tosh, but Michael's going off to boarding school cannot have been easy for either of them. Things became so bad for the boy in his first year that his nightmares returned. Barrie described an occasion when Michael's 'Dame' – the term used to describe a woman who assists an Eton housemaster in looking after the boys' health and domestic arrangements –

remained with him all night, as he had been slightly unwell, and she was amused, but nothing more, to see him, without observing her, rise and search the room in a fury of words for something that was not there. The only word she caught was 'seven'. He asked them not to tell me of this incident, as he knew it would trouble me. I was told, and, indeed, almost expected the news, for I had sprung out of bed that night thinking I heard [Michael] once again defending the stair … There are times when a boy can be as lonely as God. What is the danger? What is it that he knows in the times during which he is shut away and that he cannot remember to tell to himself or to me when he wakes? I am often disturbed when thinking of him (which is the real business of my life), regretting that, in spite of advice and warnings, I did not long ago risk waking him abruptly, when, before it could hide, he might have clapped seeing eyes upon it, and thus been able to warn me. Then, knowing the danger, I would for ever after be on the watch myself, so that when the moment came, I could envelop him as with wings. These are, of course, only foolish fears of the dark, and with morning they all fly away … I have a new thought that, when he is inside me, he may leave them there deliberately to play upon my weakness for him and so increase his sock allowance. Is the baffling creature capable of this enormity? With bowed head I must admit he is. I make a note, to be more severe with him this half.

Barrie decided to write to Michael every day and more or less did so for the five years he attended Eton and then when he went to Oxford. Some 2,000 letters were eventually destroyed by Peter, who found them 'too much'.

In loco parentis Barrie's interest was no longer in the acquisition of power over the family. He had that. His aim now was to be loved by Michael, 'to know each other without asking questions', to dwell in Michael, so that Michael would dwell in him and together they could take a step into eternity. It was, as Michael's contemporary at Eton, Robert 'Bob' Boothby, told Andrew Birkin, to be 'a great love ... something beyond ordinary affection'.

Michael's misery was in that sense an opportunity, for as Barrie's old friend, the poet and novelist George Meredith, for whom education and the emancipation of women were special subjects, wrote: 'At this period, when the young savage grows into higher influences, the faculty of worship is foremost in him.'

If Barrie played his cards right, Michael would 'turn to his father affectionately reverent' and to that end he first made a firm friend of Michael's tutor and housemaster, Macnaghten, and consulted Meredith for inspiration.

During the early 1900s, education was a question of the greatest importance. Meredith espoused Rousseau's ideal for minimum intervention in the life of a child initially. He even advised the parents of a lad who later became a friend of Michael not to disturb his freedom by teaching him to read before seven years of age. The philosopher

Rousseau's great contribution was to give expression to the freedom, innocence and contentment of childhood as the period of life when man most closely approximated to the 'state of Nature' in which he might live a free and untroubled Garden of Eden existence.

Barrie had written about the consequences of society reverting to such a state as early as 1902 in his brilliant play *The Admirable Crichton*. The play told of the family of 'a haughty, aristocratic English house, with everyone kept in his place' being shipwrecked and beached up on a desert island, whereupon the lowliest, the butler of the house, the admirable Crichton, takes charge. In the end, when they are rescued and returned to London, the old order is restored. Lady Mary does not forget who proved himself the best man on the island, but Crichton will hear nothing of it. 'On an island, my lady, perhaps; but in England, no.' She replies, 'Then there is something wrong with England.' Crichton has the last word, proving his supremacy: 'My lady, not even from you can I listen to a word against England.'

Barrie wanted both a State of Nature and Eton – Crichton and a stable, class-conscious England. Meredith had no time for any system that would encroach on the freedom of the individual, and was much more modern than his younger fan and friend. But in his novel *The Ordeal of Richard Feveril*, to which Barrie (and quite possibly Michael under Barrie's direction) now deferred, Meredith is realistic:

> At this period, when the young savage grows into higher influences
> … Jesuits will stamp the future of their changing flocks; and all who
> bring up youth by a System, and watch it, know that it is the mallea-
> ble moment. Boys possessing any mental or moral force to give them
> a tendency then predestinate their careers; or, if under supervision,
> take the impress that is given them: not often to cast it off, and sel-
> dom to cast it off altogether.

Meredith's stylistic obscurity is the reason his prose isn't read today, though his position in the literary firmament of his day was secure. He was counselling that a boy is bound to fall under the influence of one system or another, that thirteen is a moment in time when he is at his most impressionable, and that whatever is impressed upon him will likely determine his future.

Like Sir Austin Feveril, Richard's father in Meredith's novel, during Michael's difficult time at Eton, Barrie 'took care that good seed should be planted in [him], and that the most fruitful seed for a youth, namely Example, should be a kind to germinate in him the love of every form of nobleness'.

Specifically how Barrie guided his young charge was shown when Michael had to write an essay at Eton on 'What makes a Gentleman'. Having read it his tutor commented that 'he seemed to me to show a kinship in spirit to his guardian'.

'I believe', Michael wrote,

> I am right in saying that John Ball made use of the following couplet in his discourses:
>
> 'When Adam delved and Eve span,
> Who was then a gentleman?'
>
> Doubtless Ball used the word gentleman in the more degrading sense, denoting one of the upper classes – I think he was wrong. Adam was no gentleman, not because he was not Lord Adam, but because he gave away his wife in the matter of the apple … Laurence Oates, a very gallant gentleman, went out into the blizzard because he knew he could not live and wished to give his friends a better chance. He was a gentleman because when he knew he was being brave he did not say 'I'm a hero and I'm going to die for you', but merely remarked he was going out for a bit, and left the rest to their imagination.

This was the heroic code of the day, Barrie's morality to the letter. Oates met his death in Scott's disastrous 1911 expedition to the Antarctic. He was both a hero *and* an Old Etonian. The connection between Barrie and Scott and Michael made him an especially relevant model for Michael's education.

Barrie told the story of Michael's transition at Eton in a short story 'Neil and Tintinnabulum'. The boy leaves his prep school, captain of the football team and a cricketing legend, and arrives at Eton where his fag-master is 'a human reminder of the brevity of human greatness'. Equating the adjustment Michael must undertake to survive at Eton with the breaking in of a wild horse, Barrie leans over a bridge on the Eton campus, 'enviously watching the gaiety of two attractive boys, now broken to the ways of the school', wishing that Michael was one of them, 'till I heard the language…'

The image of breaking a wild horse suggests that the boy would have to lose his natural freedoms and the inner joy he discovered in the wild hills and lochs of highland Scotland and replace them with the dissatisfaction and perpetual agitation of being an Eton swell, a creature irrationally driven by self-esteem, even vanity, and as Rousseau put it, condemned 'to the legally sanctioned servitude necessary to preserve his god, the Institution of Private Property'.

We watch as, in Michael's unhappiness, he turns to his guardian, and Barrie enjoys 'being the one needed', just as Meredith predicted. And we pity Michael as Barrie creeps around the playing fields of Eton, 'so that he may at least see me nigh though we cannot touch'.

But this isn't the whole story, for Michael was a very bright boy. Macnaghten described him in a book he wrote about his fifty years at the school as the brightest boy he had ever taught. When Michael took the Eton scholarship he came fourth of all entrants, three places higher than Peter, and much was expected of him.

According to Nico, Michael was the most 'intellectual' of all the brothers, but also the best all round at sport, though he added, 'Heaven knows how different we all would have been if our parents had lived and the little wizard of Thrums had ganged awa'!'

Through this period of despair Michael, on the threshold of puberty, turned to Barrie, and Barrie was a welcome influence at this point. But also Michael showed a natural directing force of his own – a force approaching spirituality – which proved itself capable of making the adjustment to the System, *but on his own terms.*

Macnaghten's outcome report reads as follows: 'In 1914 Michael resolved to face every event with absolute self-possession, however much it cost him.' At Christmas 1914, his Division Master wrote of him, 'He may go very far if he finds an ideal … could be formidable in opposition with a will like adamant, but does not set himself in opposition.'

As usual at public school, the sports field was deemed the most telling of character. 'At any crisis he was glorious, self-controlled, and almost always controlling the result,' wrote Macnaghten.

> In a Junior v. P. V. Broke's he came in last with a bandaged hand, which he could only trust for a single stroke: we had lost on the first innings and needed four runs to win, with only five more balls to make them. He smothered the first two balls, chose the third and drove it hard and low through the hedge into the Datchet Road for six, splitting his hand again; but he had done what he had determined to do, and he alone showed no trace of emotion. Not without reason a good judge of character wrote six months later: 'Very anxious not to give himself away or show any excitement about a game'.

The deep cause 'for this self-imposed law of self-restraint',

Macnaghten believed, was that 'Michael judged it to be necessary for the training of his soul'.

The key phrase in all this is that Michael 'could be formidable in opposition with a will like adamant, but does not set himself in opposition'. He had come out of himself with an adamantine will – 'adamant', the legendary, impenetrable stone, unyielding, inflexible, unbreakable. But he was not employing it, as many did at Eton, to his own aggrandisement or to someone's detriment. He was, as his contemporary Sebastian Earl put it, still 'wholly un-Etonian'.

His was the optimum combination of what he had been with what they wanted to make him. He may never extend Eton's list of prime ministers, a spiritual appreciation of beauty sadly not being the *sine qua non* of political advantage, but there was a new edge to the 'more than earthly aura' that surrounded him: 'Michael was a cat that walked alone,' according to Clive Burt.

Macnaghten wrote further of the boy that 'his judgement is unerring … a boy of terrific power, though still "very anxious," he was marked out as inevitably Captain of the House: "there are no limits," said his predecessor, "to what he might do for good."'

One boy, a year older than Michael, took special notice. Roger Senhouse, a romantic creature, sensitive to beauty in nature and literature – Shakespeare, Wordsworth, Keats above all – was described by a boyfriend some years later as having 'a melting smile and dark grey eyes'.[45]

In his twenties Senhouse would become perhaps the very last recruit to the Bloomsbury set, and an editor and translator of exceptional quality. His skill in translation from the French was to be largely responsible for a revival of British interest in Andre Gide and

---

45   Lytton Strachey.

Colette. In 1936 he would co-found the famous publishing house of Secker & Warburg and bring the Italian existentialist writer and sexual libertarian Alberto Moravia to the English-speaking world for the first time. He was also himself a poet, but like Michael wrote in secret, too modest to allow it to appear before the public gaze.

Senhouse thought Michael a genius, but he was first bowled over by the eldest Davies boy, George. He'd caught sight of him standing naked in the shower opposite his room after an Old Etonian football match – 'I shall never forget that Blake-like effulgence. I wanted to extend the Davies family in my mind and these early memories have held an important position in my life.'

But then 'the ineffable subliminity' of Michael took over, he 'who in a sense assumed a kind of father figure for me and in some strange way replaced that of your brother George', he wrote in 1960 to Nico.

> I have never again since Michael's death felt that those astonishing years have been equalled in intensity – the élan vitae in all its phases … I was then in touch with life forces that have since eluded me and this is not to be accounted for by the age of puberty and the threshold of life.

Michael and Senhouse appeared inseparable and were fleetingly lovers, according to Bob Boothby. Although forbidden by English law there was nothing unusual in sex between boys at Eton. There was virtually no opportunity to have sex with girls. So unusual were heterosexual relations that one Harold Barker became famous around the school for indulging. Barker broke out of Eton one night, fell in love with a girl at a ball and gave her his School Shield, which you'd get if you won a cricket net. The girl told her father and Barker was expelled.

Even Nico confessed to an affair with a boy at Eton. It happened with Fitz-Wright, following the debacle of his attempt to be admitted to Pop. Indeed, it was Macnaghten's habit to appraise new boys on their arrival of the likelihood of it happening – 'that some boys kissed other boys etc', as Nico, who refused to believe it when his housemaster came out with it, recorded.

Senhouse wrote that one of his earliest recollections of his affair with Michael 'was being helped down the stairs by the toe of [his brother Peter's] boot and being called a dirty little boy ... It is the sight of [Peter's] gown descending that most often stays in my memory,' he mused fifty years later.

But, unlike Nico with Fitz-Wright, it was always more than sex between the two boys. Michael was 'the one profound influence in my life', he wrote in his diary. 'I became so wrapped up in him that I faltered, soon I began to fail in concentration on my work.' Macnaghten observed what was going on and told Barrie 'how obsessed I was with him'. But it seems to have been taken as a force for good. His obsession led Senhouse to taking

> Extra Works [extra-mural studies] in Trials [internal exams] in a futile
> attempt to keep some sort of pace with Michael ... Macnaghten was
> slightly jealous of our friendship, almost worshipping Michael him-
> self & always encouraging me to prevail upon him when depressed
> 'because I know how very close you are to him'.

Michael, it seems, was flooring them all and it was now increasingly obvious – if not to his Division Master – that he already had an ideal: the aesthetic he'd brought with him, the ideal of beauty, something he had naturally from a child and reinforced in the Highlands and Islands of Scotland at the end of an eight-foot wand and a hooping, snaking yardage of fly fishing line – an ideal that could be applied everywhere and in everything, even at Eton.

Not appreciating the potential of such an ideal in the big wide world, Barrie's friend E. V. Lucas, while noting a growing 'thoughtfulness for others' in Michael, referred to him as 'an elvish spectator rather than a participant', something of an analyst of the pitiful world, not unlike Barrie.

But no one spoke of him as cynical, as they did of his guardian; nor was he thought of as narcissistic, although Narcissus is one of the mythical figures often linked to a Peter Pan (and it is easy to see why).

Certainly the boy yearned for love, but not at that time of himself – he yearned for a love for another that might consume him like his passion for lochs and mountains, a love that would speak to his soul and move it, a love that would eclipse the images of the dead – that old dead foe which disturbed him – a love that would make him feel blessed to be alive, and once found would seem always to have been within him. For, as Sylvia's beloved son knew from his reading of the poets, such a love might set him free. As Meredith might have put it of the new Michael: 'Beauty was his handmaid … and sweet Romance his bride.'

It is perhaps no coincidence that Macnaghten took to encouraging his pupils to learn by heart Meredith's twenty-verse poem 'Love in the Valley'. If they succeeded, he let them off the 'saying lesson' for the rest of the term.

Owing to Barrie's commitments in London, the Scottish holiday in the summer of 1913 had been brief. He had rented his friend the spiritualist Marie Corelli's home in Killiekrankie – a spacious stone house built in an 'L' high up above the famous Pass, a magnificent wooded gorge with the River Garry flowing through it.

There were games of cricket in the garden (with many a ball disappearing into the gorge beneath), great fishing, and rousing stories of the first Jacobite Rising, a short-lived victory for the Jacobites on 27 July 1689, fought nearby.

Then in January 1914 he took them, with Brown the butler, to Murren in Switzerland. Wrote Mackail:

> George twenty-and-a-half. Little Nicholas over ten. But Michael still and always the special companion, in Switzerland or anywhere else. Unspoilt by it – but a bunch of brothers can help here. Malleable, but already less malleable than you might suppose. Character here; so much that even Barrie couldn't always bend it.

Thence to Paris in April, which proved to be a last hurrah for George, Peter, and indeed for the Belle Époque itself, as, in the months following, the Balkan conflict led to the violence that erupted into the First World War.

The boys went everywhere from their base at the fashionable Hotel Meurice in the Rue de Rivoli, and did everything: the Louvre; the Left Bank; the bookstalls by the Seine; the red-light district of rue Pasquier; a game of L'Attaque organised by Michael – a famous game of military tactics, strategic battle and manoeuvre; tea at Rumpelmayer's, the chic place for Paris gourmets owned by a family of Austrian pastry-cooks and situated between the Tuileries and the Louvre; finishing at the Café de Paris, properly attired of course in tail coats and white ties.

It was George's first taste of Paris. He 'took to all this like a duck to water', wrote Peter, 'and it was then that he and I first clearly saw what Jack had missed by being sent into the Navy instead of to Eton'.

Then, at the end of July, Barrie booked Auch Lodge on the

30,000-acre Auch Estate in the Grampian Mountains, close to the Bridge of Orchy at the bottom of a glen that runs up from Tyndrum towards Rannoch Moor and Glencoe.

The L-shaped stone house with six bedrooms, four bathrooms and annexe stands surrounded by trees beneath three 3,000-foot hills – Beinn Dorain, Beinn Chastiel (pronounced hastle) and Beinn Odhar, overlooking the confluence of the Allt Kinglass (a significant tributory of the Orchy) and Allt Coire Chailein rivers.

Salmon and trout from the Orchy; trout from the Kinglass. As ever, Johnny Mackay was there to act as Michael's ghillie and although he was supposed to be there for Nico too, the ten-year-old generally opted for something else to do, as Barrie wrote to Lord Lucas on 31 July:

> Nicholas is riding about on an absurdly fat pony which necessitates his legs being at right-angles to his body. The others are fishing. The waters are a-crawl with salmon, but they will look at nothing till the rain comes. The really big event is that Johnny Mackay (Michael's ghillie) has a new set of artificial teeth. He wears them and joins in the talk with a simple dignity, not boastful, but aware that he is the owner of a good thing – rather like the lady who passes round her necklace.

But the diplomatic manoeuvring between Austria-Hungary, Germany, Russia, France and Britain following the assassination of Austrian Archduke Franz Ferdinand in Sarajevo at the end of June left everyone with a sense of foreboding, of unease of what was to come, and indeed of uncertainty as morning papers only occasionally arrived on the date of issue at Auch.

Barrie wrote in his notebook: 'The Last Cricket Match. One or two days before war declared – my anxiety and premonition – boys gaily playing cricket at Auch, seen from my window – I know they're to suffer – I see them dropping out one by one, fewer and fewer.'

Even on 4 August, the day Britain declared war on Germany, which Barrie noted was 'vilely wet & windy' in Auch, he was writing anxiously to Nan Herbert, ignorant of when war would come:

> We are so isolated from news here, that when I wrote last I was quite ignorant that Europe was in a blaze. We occasionally get the morning paper in the evening, and there may be big news today. I don't see myself how we can keep out of it long in any case, and if so, probably the sooner the better. You will be terribly far from the centre if you go to Servia, and I should think you ought to wait, but you know best. It seems awful to be up here at such a time catching fish, or not catching them, for it has rained four days and nights and is still at it, and all the world is spate and bog.

The news reached Auch the following day. Wrote Mackail: 'We know now that it was the end of a world which can never return again.'

Barrie, George and Peter left at once for London, both boys joining up with the Special Reserve at Sheerness, beside the mouth of the Medway in Kent. Jack of course was already in the navy, somewhere unknown. Michael, Nicholas and Nanny Hodgson alone remained at the Lodge, where at least the fishing was good.

Towards the end of the month George and Peter returned for a few days' fishing until 9 September, when George wrote in his diary: 'In the morning I threw a farewell Jock Scott, Blue Doctor, & Silver Doctor over the Orchy. Not a rise. The fish were very lively, evidently owing to the rain that came after lunch. Fini'

Chapter Twenty-One

1914–15: Loving, J. M. B.

THE FIRST WORLD War marked a terrible frontier between innocence and adult worldliness. For Peter, first-hand experience of the horrors would consign blissful childhood visions to doubtful memory and shatter his nerves so that he would never truly recover.

Damage went deep into the very culture of Britain. The war broke the continuity of life and of ancient custom. 'Not all the good will in the world could construct the fabric of the old ways; in the years immediately after the war, they vanished like snows touched by the sun, like a dream "remembered on waking",' as the historian A. L. Rowse put it in his memoir, *A Cornish Childhood*.

Poets, such as Edmund Blunden, would return from the horrors and explore country life again looking for confirmation of their

early childhood experiences, which had formed them and seemed
to have disappeared into thin air. Nothing would be quite the same
again. The war drew a line between the Old World and the New.

In January 1915, professional soldier Guy du Maurier, who had
gone out to France to fight with 900 men and had only 200 left,
wrote to his wife:

> The trenches are full of dead Frenchmen. When one is killed they
> let him lie in the squelching mud and water at the bottom; and when
> you try and drain or dig you unearth them in an advanced state of
> decomposition ... There are many dead Highlanders just in front –
> killed in December I think – and they aren't pleasant. One gets used
> to smells ... Two hundred of my men went to hospital today – mostly
> frost-bitten feet; bad cases are called gangrene and very bad cases the
> toes drop off ... When we've done our four days I'll try and go over to
> see George who I think is only two miles off. I haven't seen anyone I
> know lately. I fancy most of the Army I know are killed or wounded.

George's letters to Barrie, two miles up the Line from Guy, show
less of the ghastly realities of trench warfare in a brave and touching attempt not to worry his guardian. On 27 January he wrote to
Barrie to reassure him that

> There's nothing for you to be anxious about. Of course, there's always
> the chance of stopping an unaimed bullet, but you can see it's a very
> small one. And I am far too timorous a man (I am a man now, I think)
> to run any more risk than I must.

George's first calamity was to be wounded in the leg two weeks later,
but he made no mention of it to Barrie.

On 3 March, Michael, who was laid up in bed at Eton 'with a belly-ache' wrote a nine-page letter to his eldest brother, telling him in minute detail what was going on at home, having been on leave from school the previous weekend. Barrie had been rehearsing plays with a bad cold and took Michael and Nico to some sort of musical evening at the Coliseum in London, typical of the sort of undemanding fare he selected for the boys' attention, with, as ever, no expense spared.

> We had the Royal Box, which I had not been in before. There was a man attired so as to represent Nero (the Roman card) with huge legs and arms attached, and Nico has been copying him ever since … Also there was a very good singer, Jack Norworth [a famous American singer songwriter and vaudeville performer]. He sings 'Sister Susie's saving shirts for soldiers', and also a new song which begins 'Mother's making mittens for the Navy, Bertha's bathing baby Belgian refugees'. He is in Uncle Jim's new burlesque. On Saturday Peter had large dinner at the Savoy with old Etonians, i.e. Pemberton & co. On Monday besides going to Uncle Jim's rehearsals we (Sir J and I) lunched at the Automobile Club with Lieut Gen Sir David Henderson, the head of the flying corps, and his wife. He was very nice. I had no idea he was so important until Nico told me that crossed swords and a star means Lieutenant General. The Automobile Club is an enormous place. I went and saw the baths and gymnasia (I feel that Aunt Margo would approve of 'gymnasia'). The evening passed in the usual way:
>
> Tea: then wait, wait, wait, wait, with futile attempts to play Rat-tat etc: books for Mary to pack: taxi comes early: wait: bag in taxi: hurried farewells, and station: crowds of boys: greetings which freeze on sight of Sir James: shouts of Good Lord here's Davies! on finding a carriage:

walk up to tutor's on arriving, to feel you haven't been to leave at all, except for the atmosphere of purses replenished and change suits: supper & prayers after which tutor comes in & asks all about George & Peter & leave in general, while doing his best to obliterate the foot of the bed. Then lights suddenly go out at ten when a new book by Wells [H G] or Bierce [Ambrose] becomes very interesting. Wake in the morning to the refrain of 'Nearly a quarter to seven, Mr Davies. Are you awake, sir?' To which the only possible reply is a grunt. A superhuman effort drags you to the shower-bath etc.

Yesterday I managed to aid my partner in vanquishing the first-round opponents in school-fives and as the second round people have scratched we are in the Final which is not bad. I am in the Final of Junior Fives too. As for house-fives (school) I forget if I told you this, but as Cheney & Neville stayed out O'Peake and myself had to represent the first pair as well as the second. Playing for the first pair v. Brintons IV (first courts Tuesday) we won. For the 2nd pair v. R. S. de Hs II (2nd courts ditto) we lost. It was a very strenuous day. I hope to win my tutor's junior house fives as I have not a bad partner and as good as anybody else's. I think I would have won last year's, only I got mumps in the final. Tom and Jack Bevan were down yesterday. I believe Tom was a pal of yours. I had a letter from Jack this morning in which he says he has done over 3,000 miles in the last twelve days which seems rather a lot. There is only a month till the end of the half [term] now, which seems an awful little when you say four weeks or four x seven days.

The other day, I among others was made a temporary platoon commander in G Coy [Company], & I was even more astounded than anyone else at my voice. It is awful in G Coy now because Chaffey, of all people, has been taking us lately. 'Sap it up, you chaps!' 'Dash it all you boys!' "Pon my word, you know, you are a bad Disgusting little bounder!' And the Adjutant McNeil is not much better. You should hear the songs they sing about him, such as 'What she we do with the acting Adjer' etc etc –

My dame has just come in and at my suggestion asks me to give you her best regards & as he is very interested to hear about you. Coupled with this is the touching information to go up to the night [meeting] only when I feel inclined thereto! And no lunch.

Again enters Mrs d'a with castor oil in Brandy, which now reposes in my belly. She has gone for a punch. The doctor (Ansler) used to live near grandfather du Maurier in Hampstead – enter my dame with Punch – and was interested in my pictures, besides pummelling my bolster and laughing at the fact that I had crumpets and fried eggs for tea yesterday.

My source of information is now beginning to dry up and I feel that you will have to be satisfied with nine pages or thereabouts. I think it is about time you got leave home. It seems ages since you were home. You will be an awful dog when you get back, and must certainly come down to play against the school, and in your uniform. You could play in pop shorts & khaki stockings. I cudgel my brain, but I can find nothing more to say. So I fear I must finish. 'J'ai fini!' Now for a letter to Jack, and then the night only.

Michael

George will have loved to hear from his younger brother about home and Eton, where he'd been both successful and happy. 'J'ai fini!' was the phrase the boys used as very small children to let Nanny know they had finished on the potty.

On 11 March, Barrie had to inform George of the death in action of Guy du Maurier, and in his own strange way wrote of his deep concern for him:

Of course I don't need this to bring home to me the danger you are always in more or less, but I do seem to be sadder today than ever, and more and more wishing you were a girl of 21 instead of a boy, so that I could say the things to you that are now always in my heart. For four years I have been waiting for you to become 21 & a little more, so that we could get closer and closer to each other, without any words needed. I don't have any little iota of desire for you to get military glory. I do not care a farthing for anything of the kind, but I have one passionate desire that we may all be together again once at least. You would not mean a featherweight more to me tho' you come back a General. I just want yourself. There may be some moments when a knowledge of all you are to me will make you a little more careful, and so I can't help going on saying these things.

It was terrible that man being killed next to you, but don't be afraid to tell me such things. You see it at night I fear with painful vividness. I have lost all sense I ever had of war being glorious, it is just unspeakably monstrous to me now. Loving,
J. M. B.

If this was the tenor of his letters to George, we can begin to see why Peter destroyed the 2,000 he wrote to Michael because they were 'too much'.

In the same month the Ninth Infantry Brigade, Third Division, to which George belonged, prepared for an attack at St Eloi (today known as St-Elooi), south of Ypres in Flanders. Having just received Barrie's letter about the death of Guy, George was sitting on a bank along with the rest of his Company, being addressed by his Colonel before the attack, when he was shot through the head and died almost immediately.

That same night, Nico and Nanny were awakened by a loud knocking on the door of 23 Campden Hill Square. (Michael was away at Eton.) The knocking was Barrie. Nico sat up in bed listening as a 'banshee wailing' filled the house. He then heard Barrie mount the stairs and come into his room. He then sat on Nico's bed in silence.

He sent a telegram to Peter at Sheerness to come at once. Peter recorded that the effect on Barrie of the death of George, whom 'he had loved with such a deep, strange, complicated, increasing love', was 'dire'. Among George's effects was a copy of *The Little White Bird*, which he had taken with him to war, and a letter to Barrie written only hours before he was shot, exhorting him once again to 'Keep your heart up, Uncle Jim … carry on with your job of keeping up your courage. I will write every time I come out of action.'

With George's death Barrie lost any idea of war being heroic. No longer was he with Wendy in *Peter Pan*, when Hook brings her to see the lost boys walk the plank and she awes the pirates by saying: 'We hope our sons will die like English gentlemen.'

It fell to Barrie to write to Josephine Mitchell-Innes, Norma's sister. George and Jack had met them at a dance in Cheyne Walk thrown by Sylvia's sister, May, some three years earlier. George had stayed at the family's homes in Scotland and Hertfordshire. He and Josephine had become close.

Barrie wrote:

> My dear Josephine I send you on those other letters in a box. It was very nice seeing you, and still nicer liking you as much as I wanted to do. But I was not afraid. I knew there was one matter on which George could make no mistake. I hope we shall always

be friends, though it has begun in a way so much more sad than it was planned.

Yours affectionately,
J. M. Barrie

The Mitchell-Innes connection is interesting historically for Norma's insight into George's opinion of Barrie. She commented that while many people found Barrie 'rather shivery', George 'was deeply fond of him, and understood him so well – saw through him a little, I think'.[46]

The same might have been said of Peter, Michael and Nico, whose friends likewise found him a bit weird. Michael's friend Sebastian Earl recorded:[47] 'I was terrified [of Barrie] … He never said a word, just sat like a tombstone.' While Nico's school friend, Cecil Day Lewis, to become Poet Laureate in 1968, wrote of a similar experience:

> On one occasion [Nico] took me back to his guardian's house in Camp-den Hill Square, and introduced me to him. I remember a large dark room and a small dark man sitting in it: he was not smoking a pipe, nor did he receive us little boys with any perceptible enthusiasm – indeed I don't think he uttered a single word – which was a bit out of character on his part, since the small dark man, Nico's guardian, was the author of *Peter Pan*. After this negative encounter, we went up to an attic and fired with an air-gun at pedestrians in the Square.[48]

---

46   Interview with Andrew Birkin, 1978.

47   Andrew Birkin, J. M. *Barrie and the Lost Boys* (1979).

48   C. Day Lewis, *The Buried Day* (1960).

It was not at all out of character. He had the same effect on many outside the *Peter Pan* inner sanctum, particularly now that he had the boys to himself, which was ultimately the most important thing to him and nullified the need ever to look over his shoulder again at anybody or anything, other than time. For time would eventually take them away from him and this war had dealt him the first irreversible, heartfelt blow.

There was genuine affection from three of the four boys who remained, who had learned to live with Uncle Jim's strangeness, respecting his space and giving any put-downs (which never applied when Michael was near) ample opportunity to disperse, not because, or solely because, he was their meal ticket, but no doubt too because, like George, they thought they saw through him a bit.

The war did undoubtedly bring them closer. 1914 was the first year in which Barrie signed himself off in letters to the boys with the word 'Loving' instead of 'Your affectionate'. Peter was the first to adopt the same sign-off when he replied from the Front.

For it was Peter's turn now to feel his guardian cared. On 7 August he wrote to Barrie from Sheerness that he was 'simply burning to go [to war]', although in the same letter that it was 'just the time of year when I begin to feel the desire for Scotland in my veins, and I wish I was with you'.

Chapter Twenty-Two

1915: The Blue Bird of Happiness

IN 1915, IT was the Tomdoun in Glen Garry. Barrie, Michael and Nico, the sole travellers that year, set off on the Scots Express from King's Cross at 7.20 p.m., taking a sleeping berth to Spean Bridge, just short of Fort William, where they picked up the West Highland Railway going north through unforgettable scenery to Invergarry. Thence, they drove the single-track road ten miles west along the north side of Loch Garry, probably in a vehicle belonging to Peter Grant, the landlord of the remote Tomdoun, whose family built the hotel in 1893 and had it right into the 1960s.

The hotel is situated beside the single-track road on the side of a hill, its verandah overlooking a paddock and wide section of the

Garry waters. In 1746 the Young Pretender, Charles Edward Stuart crossed the river by means of a ford, which disappeared when the river was dynamited into a deeper channel. On a summer's evening there can be few more beautiful views from any hotel in the Highlands.

Scattered homesteads, a Kirk (still there) and a turning once led along the main road from the south to Kintail and onward for the Skye and Hebrides ferries, the Kyle of Lochalsh, the Sound of Sleat and the Sandaig archipelago, location of one of Scotland's greatest literary love affairs, between Gavin Maxwell, an otter named Mij and the great Romantic poet Kathleen Raine.

It is stunning country and has always been one of those secret havens for fly fishers and naturalists, the deer browsing in the sands on the banks of the Loyne and the golden eagle flying from its eyries in the Quoich Forest. It also had something of a reputation as a resort for partially dispossessed boys of Empire to be hardy and learn to fish, boys deposited in English boarding schools by parents abroad in the Foreign Office or in the armed forces.

The fly fisher Geoffrey Braithwaite, whose *Fine Feathers and Fish* remains a collector's classic and who was a regular at the Tomdoun in the first decade of the twentieth century, knew everybody in the Glen and recalled the simple fare at the hotel at the time Barrie and the boys were there:

> Mutton broth, trout and then mutton, which one could seldom masticate with any ease. So far as bath was concerned, and you were fortunate enough to get there first, you might manage to find a trickle of tepid water and God help those who followed. The bedrooms were always spotlessly clean but had the oldest iron bedsteads and the mattresses so hard that only through real tiredness after a hard day's fishing that sleep came one's way.

The hotel wasn't open all year round, only for the fishing season
and the stag hunting. It was, in fact, as local inhabitant Ken Brown
records,

> both a family home and provided accommodation for the staff that
> worked on the farm the Grants owned. It also housed the telegraph
> office. There were four or five 'suites' to let, guests had a bedroom and
> adjoining sitting room and shared a bathroom/WC. Meals were provided,
> either in the private rooms or in the dining room. You took what was
> offered. There was no bar, but drinks could be taken in the drawing room.

It became a Mecca for real fly fishermen. You could get finer accom-
modation in nearby Glenquoich Lodge, with 'Bear' Ellice as host,
partying with the great and the good of society. You could rent the
more modest Kinlochquoich Lodge. But at the Tomdoun you were
part of a legend.

Salmon fishing was the draw in those days before the dams went up,
and once again Michael was in his element, fishing the Horseshoe,
the pool on the stretch of river in front of the hotel, as well as Kingie
Pool and the Tailings, which could be leased for a weeks at a time.

The hotel was manned by a team of expert ghillies, whose names
recalled many of the Scottish clans: Hector MacDonald, Willie Ross,
John and Neil Stewart, Ronald Gillies and Ian MacLennan were
the regular ones, although when Barrie, Michael and Nico stayed
there in 1915, every one of them was off doing something for the
war effort, and their duties fell to Barrie who followed his charges
with their coats and ginger beer.

As a branch line from Spean Bridge station offered service north
up the Great Glen to Fort Augustus, terminating at a pier on Loch
Ness, the trip also supplied an opportunity to revisit Dhivach Lodge

and reminisce about the last proper holiday with Sylvia after Arthur died, still only eight years ago.

On 15 August, Nico (now almost twelve) wrote to Nanny Hodgson, telling her of the nostalgic expedition:

> We saw the fall in the burn and the place where Uncle Jim and George and Jack played cricket ... In the arbour we found the initials of all our names still there ... Was the flicker-show any good? Did you like Charlie Chaplin? I had a long letter from Jack. He went ashore on Gallipoli with a letter to the French Headquarters ... I miss you here very much. I have caught five trout here and Michael 15. But then Michael – !!
>
> Well love from
> NICHOLAS LLEWELYN DAVIES

Tomdoun was clearly a hit, as Barrie returned with the boys in 1918. But Peter and Jack and the threat of war were never far from their minds. Deeply affected by a sense of doom for a whole generation of boys and concerned to do something, Barrie had financed a hospital at Bron Herbert's Bedfordshire house, Wrest Park, for casualties of the war. He had also given E. V. Lucas's wife, Elizabeth, £2,000 to set up a refuge and temporary hospital for women and children variously stricken and orphaned by the war in a large chateau at Bettancourt, in north-eastern France.

Now, from Tomdoun, he wrote to Bron's sister, Nan, of a recce he had personally undertaken on French soil:

> I went to see that little hospital I told you of. It is in a desolate chateau consisting largely of underground passages where French officers

wander and is on the Marne. The guns are to be heard in the distance all day, and I was usually wakened in the morning by aeroplanes. In the stillness they fill the world with sound. The patients are children and women, either extremely wounded or destitute and ill. One little boy had his leg blown off by a shell at Rheims, and so on. The villages in that part are in a dreadful condition, some of them have about one house standing in fifty. They were destroyed by the Germans in their rush for Paris. There are thousands of Germans buried thereabout, and a grim notice has been issued on the Marne ordering all people to chain up their dogs at night. The dogs have taken to wandering and digging. The Germans stayed in the chateau but didn't damage it.

The Highlands are very lonely this year. Almost every able bodied man seems to have gone, and we are alone in a big hotel. I was loath to come but it seemed best for M. and N. I am wondering whether Bron has gone yet. Give him my love, and do let me hear from you and how things are going at Wrest. I wish I could be walking up the steps at this moment and seeing you come down the stairs in your nurse's garments. This is a big job you have taken on and trying to keep at it so long, but at any rate there is no doubt that it was worth doing…

Barrie also wrote to Elizabeth Lucas at the Chateau in Marne along the same lines – how all the Highlands were 'denuded of their young men [and] there are scarcely any tourists' and that he 'had to knit my teeth to come away at all', adding 'Michael would like me to take him to the chateau but I suppose better not … Now I'm off to read *War and Peace*.'

Towards the end of August the party struck out 100 miles south to Kimelford, a village beyond Oban and opposite Mull, in the area of Gleann Mor (Glenmore), close to another archipelago of islands and sea lochs.

Where the dam is today ran the famous Pass of Melfort, a mountain trail cut into the rock along which an open coach drawn by five horses would transport some twenty or more passengers from M'Gregor's offices near the Station Hotel at Oban, southwards to Glenmore.

The journey to the Cuilfel Hotel in Kimelford – the seventeenth-century drover's inn which was the Barrie party's destination – was reckoned in those days to be fifteen miles from Oban but took two hours to reach. So narrow was the pass and high the walls and deeply laid the adjacent rushing river that it is not at all clear from surviving photographs how any vehicle coming in the opposite direction could do anything but turn back.

The Cuilfel offered deep-sea fishing off the coast as well as sea-fishing in the tidal Loch Melfort, and fresh water fishing up in the hills above the village, where a multitude of lochs were stocked by the Cuilfel with the much-prized Loch Leven and Fontinalle, or Great American Brook Trout.

John McFadyan was the keeper of the inn. Tennis and hot and cold baths were supplied 'and all conveniences connected with hotels', which may seem a little vague. Normally, local ghillies were supplied to take people across the road from the inn and up into the hills for the day, but once again Barrie appears to have been happy enough to take on that role.

On a warm, windy day in summer the hills above the Cuilfel are a heady potion of clover, ling, alpine meadow flowers, white and purple thistles, bog-loving bulrushes and grasses, the odd crimson foxglove, underscored by the pungent nutty scent of bracken – warm, wet; the scent of fertility. It is a gem of a place, sheep grazing on the sides of gentle, round-topped hills, with serene freshwater lochs, like Lapis Lazuli dropped in their midst. You never know when you will find another such jewel over the rise.

Perhaps the pastoral beauty reminded Barrie of a visit he'd made with Peter on short leave in June to Montgomeryshire in rural Wales, for it was now that Michael began pestering him to take him to meet a family which had for some time been referred to as the 'Welsh Lewises', so to distinguish them from the solicitor Lewises of Portland Place.

On 1 September, he wrote from the Cuilfel to Eveline, the mother of the Lewis household at Glan Hafren, the large, detached, listed property at Penstrowed, just outside Newtown, where the family lived:

Dear Mrs Lewis,

I wish there were a few more like you, but it is perhaps better that you should remain unique … It has been rather grim in Scotland this year. The Highlands in many glens are as bare of population owing to the war as if this were the month before Creation. I have just Michael and Nicholas with me and they feel it too, but they climb about, fishing mostly, and if you were to search the bogs you would find me in one of them loaded with waterproofs and ginger beer … I wish we could hurl ourselves straight upon Glan Hafren, but we shall be here till the 8th and that only gives us an exact week before Michael returns to school, and we need that time in London. It shows how much we must have talked of you that he (the dark and dour and impenetrable) has announced to me that he wants to go to see you. I was never so staggered.

He was 'never so staggered' because as Medina, one of the daughters of the Welsh Lewises later wrote, 'Up to then, Michael's one idea of a holiday seems to have been fishing in Scotland.' A date

was fixed for Barrie, Michael and Nico to visit Glan Hafren the following Easter.

The Welsh Lewises were very Welsh and very Lewis, so that,
for example, Eveline's husband, Hugh Lewis (1860–1921) was the
son of Lewis Lewis (the younger) and grandson of Lewis Lewis (the
elder), who took over a tannery in Newtown, which became the
family business.

Hugh had studied at Cambridge University before returning to
help run the tannery, and married Eveline Griffiths, Headmistress
of Newtown County Intermediate School for Girls, where Hugh
was Chairman of the Governors.

Hugh and Eveline had three daughters and two sons, one of whom,
Hugh Griffith Lewis Lewis, died just before his eleventh birthday.
In descending order, the other children were: Katherine Medina
(Medina), Janet Ellen (known as Eiluned, which became her pen
name), Eveline Mary (May), and Hugh Peter Meredith (Peter).

Hugh and Eveline played a large part in the life of Montgomeryshire, now a part of Powys. He was High Sheriff in 1902–03,
Chairman of the County Council from 1910 to 1918. Both were
JPs and Eveline was a County Councillor. Both were very involved
in the Montgomeryshire Liberal Party.

They came into Barrie's circle after Hugh became embroiled in
a tussle as Chairman of the Education Committee, which had dis-
owned responsibility for the management of the elementary schools
of the county. In the course of the disagreement, George Meredith wrote in Hugh's support, they became friends, after a difficult
moment when Meredith appeared to think that they had abused
his friendship (he was not an easy man), and eventually Meredith
accepted Hugh and Eveline's invitation to become godfather to
their youngest child, Peter.

Siegfried Sassoon, who wrote a book about George Meredith, was deeply envious of the intimacy they enjoyed with his subject, writing to Mrs Lewis:

> It must have been a wonderful experience to hear G. M. talk. For 18 months I literally lived with him in my thoughts, until I almost felt that I had known him. And the more I studied him & his works the more I admired his character. I suppose he had rather a sharp tongue; but his actions seemed to show how generous and immensely courageous he was. Anyhow, you will find it all in my book!

Very likely it was Meredith who gave Peter a copy of his friend Barrie's book, *The Little White Bird*. He may not have read it because Peter was the one who, on Meredith's advice, was not to be burdened with the toil of learning to read until he turned seven. If so, Eveline read it to him and Peter liked it so much he made a drawing, which Eveline sent to Barrie towards the end of 1912 with only 'Glan Hafren' for a return address, not wanting to seem like an autograph hunter.

Wrote Peter later, 'As a small boy I drew a picture which I called "The Long Walk taking the Broad Walk for an outing (in a pram)". Eveline was amused and decided she would send it anonymously to Barrie. Somehow he managed to trace the sender and correspondence followed.'

Something about the letter persuaded Barrie to respond, which he did with a copy of *Peter Pan in Kensington Gardens*. Correspondence with Mrs Lewis led to Barrie taking Peter Davies to visit the family in September 1914, when Peter was on short leave from Sheerness and after Michael had returned to Eton.

The two eldest girls, Medina and Eiluned, were also away at

boarding school in Wimbledon at the time, but Barrie and Peter met Hugh and Eveline and the other two children, May and Peter, and thoroughly enjoyed the warm Welsh family atmosphere, likening it to the idyllic rural life of Dr Primrose, his wife Deborah and their six children in Goldsmith's minor classic, *The Vicar of Wakefield*.

Meredith had died in 1909, so he couldn't have had a hand in progressing the relationship between the two families, although it is of course possible that he had earlier confided in Barrie that he was Peter Lewis's godfather. But there was a clear rationale for the meeting to happen on another level.

Wrote Medina: 'I think that these holiday visits, which meant such an enormous amount to us, were also welcome to the boys, for as Eiluned has said they provided a background of family life, complete with sisters of their own age, which the boys had not known before...'

What's more, Wales was the Llewelyn Davies's native land. Barrie was in a very real sense bringing them home – home into a world that hadn't changed in centuries and was not noticeably changed by the advent of war.

Unlike in other parts of the country, life at Glan Hafren continued more or less unimpaired.

> Our coachman and gardeners were old, so not called up, and there were no munition works at hand to absorb our few maids. We had kept our horses and carriages, and were still able to get about, while so many other households – with only cars – were immobile. We did not farm but kept cows, chickens and pigs for our own use, so food was never short.

All this combined with the clear benefit of a traditional family environment, which Barrie will have sensed Michael would enjoy, that led him to take the step (most unusual for him) of pursuing contact with the Lewises.

It should also be said that Eveline shared Barrie's interest in the paranormal, which was then being re-examined in the new terminology of modern psychology.

There are letters from Eveline to, among others, the philosopher H. H. Price, Wykeham Professor of Logic at New College, Oxford, and to Whateley Carrington, who was a parapsychologist with a particular interest in telepathy.

According to the family, Eveline herself was telepathic. Her letter discussed ideas put forward by Maurice Maeterlink in *The Unknown Guest* (1914). Carrington was riveted by her theory that linked 'the telepathic, etc, phenomena with the concept of Deity, via what I should call the Common Subconscious or Mind or Spirit of Man', as he wrote.

He corresponded with the Society for Psychical Research on her behalf: 'She adopts the hypothesis of what we should now call a Common Subconscious … of virtually unlimited knowledge and powers, with which the individual "finite" mind may somehow or other "make contact".'

Her idea seems to have been that the 'Common Subconscious' (what Eveline actually referred to as the 'Infinite Unconscious') can be a means of communication beyond the space-time continuum – in telepathy (in the present with another living person), in séance (with the past), in precognition with the future.

Dealing with phantasms and the like, Mrs Lewis writes: 'We may take as an example of the point of contact some such simple idea as the perception of a room or place in which the individual is at the time. Immediately the contact is made his idea of the room becomes enlarged by some addition from the Infinite Consciousness. This addition may be borrowed from the past or the future ... Thus the individual may become suddenly conscious of some scene formerly enacted in that spot, or he may have a prophetic vision of events that are to come.'

How this connects with the concept of deity is that we live a kind of epiphytic existence on the Infinite Unconscious, which is more or less a projection of what people understand by the Deity. The psychiatrist Carl Jung later came up with a not dissimilar idea when 'translating' the work of German theologian Meister Eckhart into modern psychoanalytical terms.

There is no evidence that Eveline had read du Maurier, but the latter's notion of a 'sixth sense', which survives after death, with its infinite knowledge and powers, is accommodated within her ideas, and Peter Ibbetson and Mimsey Seraskier's plumbing of the mysteries of the Infinite Unconscious in their communication with past, present and future, which is at one point joyously telepathic, is precisely Eveline's preoccupation.

So, Eveline understood the du Maurier family myth, which was one very good reason why their meeting was such a success.

It wasn't long before the members of the Lewis family absent from their first meeting in 1915 were invited to Adelphi Terrace. On 20 June, Peter Davies wrote to Peter Lewis a playful letter after their visit, which also contained the information that 'your mother and father and two sisters are coming to tea this afternoon', Medina and Eiluned on leave from their Wimbledon boarding school.

So, Barrie had met the entire Lewis family by Easter 1916 when Michael and Nico were introduced to them for the first time. Yet, according to Medina, it had been obvious that Barrie was anxious that the holiday might yet be a failure. Probably he was worried about how Michael would react, for in company that bored him he could be as moody as Barrie himself.

He needn't have worried. All the children got on brilliantly. 'Glan Hafren had never seen such days,' wrote Peter Lewis.

> As well as riding and occasional fishing, there were competitions in croquet and tennis (carefully drawn so that if possible each one of the Lewises would win in turn). There were also fancy dress teas. I can remember [my father] Hugh dressed in a genuine Chinese costume and Sir James appearing in a dressing gown and large cosy from the spare room with Dwr Poeth (warm water) embroidered in silk. Sir James became devoted to Eveline until he died.

Michael and Nico were at Glan Hafren again in September, without Barrie this time, and Michael wrote thanking Eveline on the 17th, as soon as they were home.

> Dear Mrs Lewis,
>
> We reached Paddington in safety, & y'day evening Sir Jas went off to Wrest [Nan Herbert's hospital]. He is returning today. Thank you so much for the lovely time you gave us – I feel I ought to write to every one of you, but will you thank everyone for me. Nico is going to make an attempt to write.
>
> … I am sending Medina a little letter for the Levanian [the magazine of Levana School, Wimbledon]. I hope she accepts it, as it is not so very often that I get my little things accepted. It'll probably be the old old story. 'Dear Sir, I fear the Levanian has no great use

for yr style of work, spicy and vivacious tho' it be. Yrs very sincerely, K Medina Lewis, Editor Levanian.'

Please give my love to Mr Lewis and Medina, and Jane, and May, and Peter, and Sir John, and Peregrine,

Yrs Michael Llewelyn Davies

Michael got on with everyone, but especially Eiluned, whom he now addressed in his letters as Jane rather than Janet or any one of the variety of nicknames (besides Eiluned), from which he could have chosen – Luned, Bittie or Bits among them. She had been christened Janet Ellen but didn't like either, and Michael wanted his own name for her. She was just five months younger than he.

In the 1970s, in response to a question about whether Michael ever had a girlfriend, Nico recommended Andrew Birkin, who was researching his film *J. M. Barrie and the Lost Boys* to get in touch with Eiluned: 'I've no idea whether she and Michael even held hands, but she might well have a clue as to his feelings towards girls.'

Eiluned was the one who perceived the true spirit of Glan Hafren and in her thirties captured it in a bestselling novel, *Dew on the Grass* (1934), still in print today. She was a poet as well as a novelist, and a journalist who rose to become assistant editor of the *Sunday Times*.

Dew on the Grass is the story of a rural childhood based on her own at Glan Hafren. It is an evocation of a lost world – not only of childhood, but of a whole way of living in rural Wales as she was growing up, when the year revolved around the seasons, the village, the church and the festivals. It was, as A. E. Housman put it in *A Shropshire Lad*, a 'land of lost content', a land in which time stood still, life was one endless summer day and Eiluned was borne along by its very current.

There is little of Housman's melancholia here, only Eiluned's strikingly clear, joyous remembrance of what it was like to be Lucy, an imaginative little girl of nine years of age growing up in rural Montgomeryshire in the first decade of the twentieth century: a wholly natural, idyllic environment of which she and her three siblings – Delia (eleven), Maurice (six) and Miriam (three) – were intensely aware, but never consciously so.

For Lucy there was 'real' and 'pretend' and the latter 'was often the most important of the two'.

Like when she drew imaginary pictures on the ceiling with one finger – pictures of knights on horseback, and ladies with flying hair, running, running as fast as they could through haunted woods … 'They said that she looked like a half-wit, lying in bed, waggling her finger at the ceiling; but the moment they were out of the room she began again…'

Like playing games of hide and seek with her sisters and friends from the village in the endless garden and outbuildings – hiding in the coach-house terrified that 'a groping hand might suddenly touch you, dreading the flight and pursuit: feet running behind, drawing nearer every minute…' Knowing that it was 'something infinitely disastrous that would catch you in the end', but then becoming so lost in thought in the dark that time did stand still, and when they found her it was by the light of lanterns and the game was long over and the visiting children had gone home.

Like knotting a skipping rope around your waist so that it resembled a cartridge belt, drawing the elastic of your hat on to your chin, and choosing a pea-stick to become Hawk-Eye, Leather Jacket and La Longue Carabine in James Fenimore Cooper's *The Last of the Mohicans*, which in those days of great adventure (before television) all children were reading, even girls.

Like playing with a pretend friend, Joseph, who when you went for walks and people said, 'What a beautiful view,' preferred 'the muddy lanes that go twisting in and out, and the little trees blown crooked in the wind, and water where it lies on top of a weir and curves over the edge, gently, gently, before it goes crashing down below'.

Like writing plays for your brother and sisters to act out and poems to recite – 'conscientious rather than inspired' – always laughing and dancing, sometimes spontaneously for joy, and sometimes for the travelling harpist John Roberts, who, when he was through, turned his harp 'a little towards the south-west, so that we heard a faint sighing in the strings as the breeze swept through them and passed on its way'.

Among her many poems, Eiluned wrote 'The Birthright', which puts what she laid before Michael at Glan Hafren perfectly:

We who were born
In country places,
Far from cities
And shifting faces,
We have a birthright
No man can sell,
And a secret joy
No man can tell.

For we are kindred
To lordly things,
The wild duck's flight
And the white owl's wings;
To pike and salmon,
To bull and horse,

The curlew's cry
And the smell of gorse.

Pride of trees,
Swiftness of streams,
Magic of frost
Have shaped our dreams:
No baser vision
Their spirit fills
Who walk by right
On the naked hills.

Eiluned's older sister Medina wrote modestly that the contact with JMB and the boys meant an enormous amount to them 'in our quiet country life, broken only by boarding school. Of course to them, with their far wider circle, it meant much, much less.'

This was not the case for either Michael or Nico.

Nico was the life and soul of the games and wrote nostalgically to Eveline more than thirty years later, 'Bless you for those many happy memories you were largely responsible for giving me...'

When Michael first arrived at Glan Hafren he was fifteen. Had he found Eiluned as a younger child, they would have been dubbed the heavenly twins. Now that he could reflect on his early youth, he believed, as he had just written in the *Eton Chronicle*, that the only true pleasure is happiness coming unconsciously from within. He loved Eiluned's still-unconscious empathy with all that was beautiful about Glan Hafren. Children were children for longer in remote rural parts and Eiluned had lost nothing of her innocent charm. Though she and Medina were in their young teens, their mother told Medina years later that 'watching us on the lawn one day JMB had remarked, "It is so innocent, it almost hurts.'"

Michael's short piece in the *Chronicle* in February had been about 'pleasure – *voluptus*'. He'd quoted Keats, from 'Ode on a Grecian Urn', in support of the idea that pleasure pursued for its own sake must always 'leave a heart high, sorrowful and cloyed', and cited Maurice Maeterlink's 1908 play about the Blue Bird (the ancient mythical harbinger of happiness) in support of the idea that true happiness is unconscious, and can only be found at home.

Now here was Eiluned at home, the epitome of all that he had written about happiness unconsciously pursued. When writing his 'pleasure' piece he'd had in mind the happiness he felt in the Scottish Highlands fly fishing. Now, at Glan Hafren, Michael had found a similar happiness, for the first time since his mother's death, in female form.

He was over the original pain of his mother's death. 'It is a common phrase, "to indulge in the luxury of tears",' the fifteen-year-old wrote, 'but until that luxury has been indulged in, it is not possible to realise how expensive this form of pleasure may become.'

He was done with crying, but not with love and wonder, and making the wild his home. He was reading Shelley and Keats, and Meredith's 'Love in the Valley' –

> *Shy as the squirrel and wayward as the swallow,*
> *Swift as the swallow along the river's light*
> *Circleting the surface to meet his mirrored winglets,*
> *Fleeter she seems in her stay than in her flight.*
> *Shy as the squirrel that leaps among the pine-tops,*
> *Wayward as the swallow overhead at set of sun,*
> *She whom I love is hard to catch and conquer,*
> *Hard, but O the glory of the winning were she won!*

He would soon be giving a public recitation of William Johnson Corey's 'Amaturus' at Eton –

> *Somewhere beneath the sun,*
> *These quivering heart-strings prove it,*
> *Somewhere there must be one*
> *Made for this soul, to move it;*
> *Some one that hides her sweetness*
> *From neighbours whom she slights,*
> *Nor can attain completeness,*
> *Nor give her heart its rights;*
> *Some one whom I could court*
> *With no great change of manner,*
> *Still holding reason's fort,*
> *Though waving fancy's banner;*
> *A lady, not so queenly*
> *As to disdain my hand…*

Michael was yearning for love but the solitude of spirit that drove his soul to create its own world meant that he found it at least as difficult to be gay – the word widely used in those days for its original sense of carefree and merry – as any teenager who had no experience of girls.

Typically, his letters made the switch from his earnest side by dropping into an Etonian vein, as this public-school-boyish letter to Eiluned on 17 January 1917, when both were sixteen, shows. But that he wrote such letters to a girl and was making what for him was an almighty effort to engage Eiluned, is itself a mark of his feelings, as he didn't write them to anyone else. Naturally, he used his pet name for her.

Dear Jane,

I choose the prettiest in your bright constellation of names.

I hear Levana has again taken you to its ample bosom but without the Editress, or rather the Ex; Ed; Lev. I don't know if May will be there with you, but from my more world-wide experience, if she is, I think you will then look back with great regret to the days when you were the sole representative of Glenhafren and Levana. Have you stepped into your sister's illustrious shoes on the Editorial staff? … Salute them all six (or is it we are seven?) from me, but two to Margo, the dear girl! Tell me not that Gertrude has left! If so – I must know at once where I may seek her. You can picture the scene thus: – as the last note died away, the audience burst into a storm of clapping, & Gertrude was preparing to take her encore, when there was a sudden commotion in the crowd – a tall commanding young man thrust passionately through, & bending, whispered into the girl's shell-like ear 'Come,' he said simply & they rose together & went out … Wish me luck! Heaven help me if she hath been faithleth!

Sir James, Davies minor, and yr humble servant have just returned from Brighton, with its poisonous people piers postcards picture palaces & penny in the slots. Have you been there? I trou not, else you would not be the pure & innocent maiden that you appear. We have luckily got a week more before Eton, in which I shall trot around London with a pail of red paint.

I hope Monsieur & Madame, your parents, are in excellent health, not to forget M. Peter, Mdlle May, & Mdlle K. Medina, to whom I must write. Peter D is now at Sheerness, preparatory to France again, & Jack D in the North Sea. Nico D is entirely the 'young Eton' that you w'd expect. He grows in all directions. Believe me, madam, I am hoping this finds you as it leaves me.

Yr obed serv

Michael Ll. Davies

P.S. Any message to Colonel David Davies if I meet him in the House?

P.P.S. Offly jolly that in your paper about the Names on the Wall.
What? I sh'd like to know that girl!

P.P.P.S. If there's any literature you want, Lindsay Gordon or anything, command me, I beg.

P.P.P.P.S. Do you want a Rolls Royce?

In 1979, not long before Eiluned died, when the only surviving
Barrie-boy, Nico, approached her directly and touched on the subject
of Michael's girlfriends, she moved the focus effortlessly but almost
too swiftly onto Audrey Lucas – 'Oh, of course Audrey Lucas was
the one, wasn't she? Is she alive?'

Nico knew, as did everybody (including Eiluned), 'that there
wasn't a whiff of an affair' with Audrey, though she and Michael
had been friends for many years.

In one or two letters presently in the possession of Eiluned's daughter,
Katrina Burnett, there is a hint of Barrie trying to get Eiluned and
Michael together more. 'He was far too canny to push it,' Katrina
writes. But not so canny as to see how infuriating Michael must have
found it when Barrie subsequently adopted Michael's pet name for
Eiluned in correspondence with her.

Nico was of the opinion that if Michael hadn't had an affair with
Eiluned then he never had an affair with any girl in his life, and that
this might be 'a tinge of a clue', as he put it, to Michael's sexuality.

Chapter Twenty-Three

1916–17:
Home Fires Burning

MICHAEL'S FRIENDSHIP WITH Roger Senhouse, which had been intimate and remained close, and the new experience of friendship with Eiluned meant that this was an especially intense time for Michael. Macnaghten observed that 'for the next year he was strangely difficult. He never means to be rude, but he is too clever not to see the weak points in his Tutor and others.'

From 1916 until 1920, Michael saw Eiluned a great deal. At first Scotland diminished in importance because of the war, but also she and the rest of Glan Hafren contributed so much to his emotional and spiritual life. Although it would be the males in Michael's life who would steer him, Eiluned made him happy in a way no female had since he was ten; quite possibly he enjoyed his greatest happiness with her, though not when they went swimming in the nearby River Severn. 'My mother always said Michael was frightened of water and never enjoyed bathing in the Severn with the others,' remembers Katrina Burnett today. In Welsh the River Severn is 'Afon Hafren' – Hafren being the name of a legendary British princess who was drowned here.

Happiness spread through all the participants. Wrote Peter, Eiluned's young brother:

> I shall never forget being there [at Barrie's Adelphi Terrace apartment], seeing the wide view of five bridges over the river, the woven mesh matting and the great fireplace with school caps for Eton worn by the boys, pale blue for the first eleven at cricket, scarlet one for the Field (Eton football), all the boys were brilliant at games … I can remember a most memorable half term when Sir James entertained the whole family to a box at the Coliseum for a performance in aid of War Charities, of *The Admirable Crichton* with Ellen Terry in the lead role.

Hugh Lewis brought his own special character to the friendship. Barrie wrote of him after his early death:

> He was one of the most lovable most honourable men I have encountered in my wanderings through the years; every one who met him whether intimately or casually must have been the better of it. He not only gave much happiness but received it. I think I can really call him about the happiest man I have ever known.

Medina said that her 'boyish' father brought 'all sorts of jokes and nonsense with the boys, which JMB with all his wit could never do', but that was because she never knew the Barrie of the Kensington Garden days. *That* Barrie was a good deal less visible now.

She recalled one incident which puts the fun the two families had together perfectly in focus. The Lewises had gone down to Eton with Barrie and Nico to watch Michael play cricket.

> Coming back, and walking up the Paddington exit, my mother and JMB were in front, his perpetual cough was worse than usual, and she was very concerned. We young ones were loitering behind at the end of a long hot day, and my father and Nico, one each side of the street, were making faces at each other like a couple of school boys. A taxi came along, JMB hailed it and got in, followed by Nico. My father, as a parting shot, made a 'long nose' at Nico, who responded by acting 'the death of the Fat Boy' over the back of the open taxi, JMB still coughing and ignorant of the antics going on beside him. 'The Death of the Fat Boy' was a wonderful invention of Nico's, in which with puffed out cheeks and rolling, squinting eyes he gave a life-like representation of an apoplectic fit. The road was practically empty at the time, but I can still see the puzzled, disapproving expression of one lady passing by.

Nico's corpulence was a running joke and he never begrudged any of those who gathered around the Welsh Lewises a joke at his expense. There is a relic of the period, purportedly written by Michael, which shows just how far the joke was taken and the kind of innocent fun everyone at Glan Halfen enjoyed, adults and children together.

Glan Hafren

Newtown,

Wales

Mon, 18 April, 1920.

SOCIETY for REDUCTION of NICO.
REPORT for 1920–21.

Jan 3. The Society met to discuss what policy it should adopt for this year, being unanimously agreed that the methods employed during the previous year achieved dangerously little.

The Hon. Pres. (Miss May Lewis) in throwing the debate open to the House, expressed a hope that any if not all, of the distinguished visitors present would give the House their views on this tremendous subject.

Mr Lewis (Dick) Davies at once sprang up.

– He had been riding (he said) along the Dolfor road on Christmas eve with the debated subject, and had observed that the back of the subject's mount had sagged in an alarming manner. Was this sort of thing going to –

– One moment, Dick, said the president, rising from her seat with a swish, of frou-frou, – what the BLAZES d'you mean by not addressing the House in time-honoured fashion?

The Hon. member sat down discomfited.

The member fra' Forfar took his pipe out o'his mouth. – Miss P, and G, (he said) The Insurance laddies has refused tae insure ma unco flat because of this wee nannie (laughter) Syne he waur tae gang bump, d'ye see…? (he waved his hand in an expressive manner) Thon's al a'hae tae whustle.

He curled his legs under him and sat.

At this period there was a struggle in the back of the House, and simultaneously with the appearance of a smallish sandy-haired gentleman who spluttered something about being squashed, a lady with red-rhododendronian hair dragged him down, folded her arms, and exclaimed in the tongue of CYMRI:

– Fwls, he is but a feeder – I have dandled him lightly [*sic*].

(Instantaneous uproar, shouts of Oh No, Impossible, Withdraw. The reactionary female is ejected, also the sandy-haired lad, who has been discovered to be an emissary of the REDS.)

When the tumult had subsided a stranger of very striking mien rose to his feet and delivered the following in a voice vibrating with emotion:

– There are three reasons (he said) why this house MUST, I say, go through with its work. ONE, because now it is not possible [for] the subject and the billiard-table to be in the room together at the same time, TWO because he has to go up in the lift, which will carry 5 persons [only]. THREE because he has rolled on me twice. You will understand me if I say that I AM HIS BROTHER.

The HOUSE rose to its feet & sang MEIN Fader its ash Appenzeller.

After this there were a few hesitating speeches, among others from Mr Hugh Lewis, who mentioned a broken back-axle, and Mrs Hugh Lewis, who told of ominous cracks in her dining-room ceiling.

The Hon. Pres, then rose and proposed: THAT WE DO FORBID NICO TO VISIT GLAN HALFREN BECAUSE HE HAS TOO MUCH THAT IS GOOD TO EAT THERE.

Mrs Lewis opposed pro forma. Susie seconded. Carried.

The House then adjourned.

Present: The Hon. Pres., Mr & Mrs Lewis, Preece, Dick Davies, Kinsey, Sir Jazz Band Barrie, Susie, Emily, Ray Lankester, Fatty Arbuckle.

There were guests of that house: Cargantus, Caruso, John Watts, the BIG FOUR, and the Neapolitan Giant.

London was all this time in the grip of war, with Zeppelin raids and food shortages. On 24 September 1916, Barrie wrote to Nico in his first term at Eton:

> We had zeppelin excitement last night as you will have heard, and two down is a good bag. When I was at the kitchen window the first one fell and so I missed it. I would have seen it if I had been at my corner window, which I had just left. I watched them shelling one, which looked to be just over the Cecil Hotel. I hope you have had a first good Sunday…

As with the others, it was signed, 'Loving, J. M. B.'

There were also food shortages, and Glan Hafren stepped into the breach, Barrie writing to Eveline in May 1917:

> How truly splendid and magnanimous of you to send the potatoes. When they were revealed to my astonished eyes my hand (I am sure) went instinctively to my head to take off my hat. Brown looked as if he ought to be singing the national anthem. Cheers for Glan Hafren! How sorry we were to go.
>
> You will be interested to hear that Nico finished *Ivanhoe* several minutes before returning to school and came out head of his division in the exam. Michael is now captain of his house XI 'with power to tan'. Nothing so triumphant to record about myself. My love to all and looking forward to seeing you before long in London.

Glan Hafren was the opposite to war. Peter Davies wrote from the

Front on 16 August 1916, that he'd received 'a cake and some peppermints inside it' from Eveline. Immediately his thoughts had turned to Glan Hafren, to bathing 'in the cool stream of the Severn or the Pool', and walking the slopes of Plynlimmon, a massif that dominates the countryside of northern Ceredigion, memories of a landscape beauty so at odds with the ghastly reality of the front line.

Peter (nineteen) was fighting in the Battle of the Somme when he wrote this. Between 1 July and 18 November 1916 more than one million men would be wounded or killed.

A month earlier, at his first sight of 'the Line', he had been awed by the apocalyptic beauty of star-shells bursting above him in the air, casting an extraordinary light all around. But within a few days of continuous rain and cold, despite being in the middle of summer, he had his first night in the trenches in 'a foot and a half of mud and water, with no shelter to speak of'. At no point were the trenches deeper than six feet, so Peter had to walk with a stoop, aware that one false move would provide a target for a sniper like the one that shot his brother. As a signalman the shelling was especially ominous, for while you crouched down in your trench like the rest of the men, listening to the shells whispering overhead and waiting to be hit, you also knew that after it was over you would have to mend the communication lines, which meant prowling around No Man's Land on your stomach at night even 'to within about 50 yards' of the German line, mending the wires. The Line was now 'the most desolate, ravaged place imaginable … damnable beyond all powers of description'.

On 25 July he wrote that a certain Captain Wilson of Edwardes Square, close to Campden Hill, had joined the battalion. Peter had discovered that Wilson was a scholar at Winchester, and both turned their classical education to advantage, forging a special bond of homespun intimacy by 'quoting the ancients' to the 'amazement of our comrades'.

Two days later he wrote excitedly about Michael making 'Sixpenny', the under-sixteen cricket team at Eton, and captaining the winning junior cricket team. On 30 August a strong breeze across the battleground reminded him of Voshimid at Amhuinnsuidhe – a breeze 'such as delights the heart of him who lures salmon from the loch'.

Michael received Peter's letters knowing that it would be his turn in 1918. Each successive year of war since 1914 brought rumour of its ending and then certainty that it would continue into the next. Everyone was scared of dying. Everyone wondered when it would end. Physically, Michael would cope, but emotionally? War was the desecration of his ideal, which was neither the heroic idea of Barrie's Castaway games, nor the Victorian values that had led to this war.

On 21 August, Peter wrote to say that Wilson had been mortally wounded. He had come upon him shortly after he was hit and recognised at once 'that horrible colour of dirty chalk...'

Then, three weeks later, he wrote to say that he was lying 'between clean sheets, after a long hot bath, in a hospital at Etaples'. He'd been invalided out with impetigo, which covered him in a rash, the result of the filth and the mental and physical strain. Once home he was admitted to Wandsworth military hospital, thin and haunted, his nerves shot.

But, by 14 July 1917, he was passed fit to go back again and by 12 December he felt 'called upon to write in a "pacifist" strain...' Drawing support from his Aunt Margaret's views, 'firmly convinced of the hopeless and grotesque folly of the war', he wrote that his 'dislike of it all is infinitely greater than it was before, and I often feel as though I should wake up a raving lunatic at the end'.

As for Jack, no one ever seemed to know where he was, only that he was still serving in the Royal Navy on a destroyer, with yet another gold band on his arm.

In January 1917, shortly after writing to Eiluned about his visit to Brighton, Michael went down with chicken pox and for some unaccountable reason suddenly began to draw like his grandfather du Maurier.

People were already expecting Michael to do great things. '[He] was going to be something pretty remarkable sooner or later,' wrote Mackail. 'There was never a moment's doubt about that.' Naturally, a tutor in art was found to bring the new talent along.

> And still – getting on for seventeen now – he was the closest com-
> panion [to Barrie] of all. No secrets. No shadows. Character and
> cleverness, fully authenticated by his housemaster as well. Yet always
> one dread. What if the war weren't over in time, and Michael's turn
> must come too? An icy terror that gripped at the heart, and then must
> be hidden; for if this had to be, there must be no weakness at which
> even Michael could guess.

Michael's record in the spring half of 1917 included a poem in the *Eton Chronicle* and first prize for throwing the cricket ball in the sports. It was in this year too that Barrie gave him a copy of a play he'd written and asked his opinion of it.

Barrie had worked his way into the boy, given him his own ambition, and now loved to be dominated by him. He liked to say that even as a schoolboy, Michael was 'the sternest of my literary critics'. And this was perfectly true.

Wrote Barrie: 'Anything Michael shook his head over I abandoned, and conceivably the world has thus been deprived of a masterpiece ... Sometimes, however, No. 4 liked my efforts, and I walked in the azure that day when he returned *Dear Brutus* to me with the comment "Not so bad."'

Chapter Twenty-Four

1917–18:
Michael Turns Away

*D*EAR BRUTUS OPENED at Wyndham's Theatre in the West End on 17 October 1917. It ran for 365 performances, almost to the end of the war. Five years later, it ran again at the same theatre for 258 performances.

Its theme was one that Barrie had already raised in *The Little White Bird* and was ubiquitous in his notebook thereafter. The context in the 1902 novel is Peter Pan being locked out of his mother's love, calling,

'Mother! Mother!' but she heard him not; in vain he beat his little limbs against the iron bars ... What a glorious boy he had meant to

be to her! Ah Peter! We who have made the great mistake, how differently we would all act at the second chance. Solomon was right
– there is no second chance, not for most of us. When we reach the
window it is Lock-out Time. The iron bars are up for life.

His mother has been crying, 'and he knew what was the great thing
she cried for, and that a hug from her splendid Peter would quickly
make her to smile. Oh! He felt sure of it...' But the 'great thing
she cried for' was 'the great mistake', which Peter had made and
we are never told about, so big a mistake that a hug is not going to
be enough.

What locked Barrie out of his mother's love, as he describes in his
biography of her, is the death at thirteen of her favourite son David
in a skating accident, after another boy bumped into him and he fell
and hit his head on the ice. Her exclusion of David's six-year-old
brother Jamie was catastrophic, it probably crippled him emotionally for life. It is possible that little Jamie Barrie was involved in his
brother's accident, which is why his mother was so hard on him –
'Ah, Peter! we who have made the great mistake, how differently
we should all act at the second chance.' But, whatever is the truth,
it is enough to know that while we all believe there are no second
chances in this world, no way back from our great regrets, Barrie
thought that he had found a way by opting for a life of fantasy and
illusion, and that is the burden of *Dear Brutus*.

Dear Brutus dramatises what happens when a cast of characters,
all of whom long for a second chance in life, enter an enchanted
wood on Midsummer Eve and go back in time to re-shape their lives.
Barrie's technical mastery is superb – how he convinces the audience
that there can be such a thing as a magic wood into which we, the
audience, might find our way. As is the stagecraft, in convincing us

that the wood has crept right up to the house in the eerie moonlight and is suddenly visible through the windows of the drawing room – all this is pure genius and completely convinced audiences in 1917.

It is the plot, however, that is so troubling, now that we know so much more about Barrie than the 1917 audience did. One character, Will Dearth (played by Sylvia's brother, Gerald) finds himself in the magic wood with a fantasy daughter (clearly based on Gerald's favourite daughter Daphne du Maurier). The scene imitates and embellishes Gerald's special love for Daphne with titillating, even erotic and incestuous undertones, all delivered so smoothly in Barrie's trademark style that it is easy to allow it as simply the whimsy we expect from him (indeed the play is actually billed as a comedy).

But it isn't quite like that. Will Dearth possesses his daughter utterly. Absent is any notion of the disinterested love a father usually feels for his daughter. In particular the girl's approaching independence of her father is anathema to him, and appears to him to cheat him of what is, by rights, his.

The best time in a father's life is the year before his daughter 'puts her hair up', when a girl turns eighteen. The girl counters that there is one time better, 'The year she does put up her hair.' She then puts her hair up and asks him, 'What do you think? Will I do?' Dearth's eyes fall on 'the young woman that is to be', with 'the change in his voice falling clammy on her', as Barrie's stage direction reads.

Smitten, Dearth speaks 'with an odd tremor' in his voice, and his daughter manhandles him, 'bumping into him and round him and over him', saying he will be sick of her with her hair up before he has done with her. Then she teases and tantalises him with the thought of one day being in love with a boy.

Their dialogue has a quasi-erotic ring. Daddy is controlling; he has taught her all she knows, like a master teaches his dog how to catch a biscuit in its mouth. He even takes credit for her beauty: 'I wore out the point of my little finger over that dimple.' Daphne's dimple on her chin was a feature as a child. His rights over his daughter are repressive. There is nothing about the girl that Daddy does not regard as his, and he holds ultimate power over her.

Afterwards, as the child recedes from his imagination, he, despite all that she does to dissuade him, leaves her in the wood on her own, and she cries: 'Daddy, come back; I don't want to be a might-have-been.'

With her dismissal as a might-have-been, the playwright gives the girl no more reality than the fading colours on the artist's easel, because of course she is just a figment of Dearth's imagination, alive only in the magic wood.

The effect on ten-year-old Daphne du Maurier, who was no stranger to her father's first nights, was devastating. She fled from the theatre in floods of tears because she recognised herself and her relationship with Gerald immediately.

Years later, John Gielgud revived the play and admitted,

> I kept remembering how marvellous [Gerald] du Maurier had been as the painter Dearth. I could not touch him in the part. – …when he came on in the last Act, his face when they told him that the child was only a dream was so extraordinary I remember thinking what a pity it was that he never played in Chekov or Ibsen.

Again, as Noël Coward put it, in *Dear Brutus*, 'Gerald tore your heart out.'

Perhaps no playwright other than Barrie *could* have had Gerald play it as he did. Gerald was already having a relationship with his favourite daughter very like the one between Will Dearth and his dream-child daughter. As Daphne admitted, she became engaged in 'a sort of incest' with her father, her feelings 'tragic' because they never would be fulfilled. It was as if Gerald had brought Dearth home into their relationship. There was even an estrangement between Daphne and her mother (as was also predicated in the play).

Dear Brutus and all that followed gave Daphne what she called a 'Daddy complex', which muddled her sexuality, and in time developed into a serious inner conflict which infected her work and finally brought her to breakdown.

In the play the theme is put to positive use – after Dearth's experience in the magic wood he and his wife Alice emerge as the two characters in the play capable of learning from their adventures, and as the critic W. A. Darlington wrote, 'There is a hint that they will come together, and that the dream-daughter will no longer be a might-have-been.'

But in reality the intensity of the relationships between Gerald and Daphne and of course in parallel between Barrie and Michael was less easy to square. Where did it leave the dream-child who was being used and might be disposed of at will? There was this pornographic notion of disposability, which disturbed Daphne so deeply at ten years of age that she ran from her seat in tears, and showed that Barrie simply didn't understand what parental love is.

As Nico, who'd always been immune to resurgent Pan, saw it, Barrie had been 'in love with' George originally and was now in love with Michael, 'as he was in love with my mother [Sylvia]', while Barrie's feelings for Nico himself, Peter and Jack 'came nearer to normal deep affection'.

The difficulty of Barrie's love for Michael, loaded as it was with his own needs, was already causing some concern, both from Nanny Hodgson and, in the autumn of 1916, from Jack's fiancée, Geraldine

'Gerrie' Gibb, who provided a new, sensitive and objective view of the relationship.

Nico was right. Barrie was in love with Michael in the only way he could be. When Michael was younger that probably meant he had to suppress feelings towards him of a sort which, in 1917, he couldn't help but expose in the whimsically erotic parent–child relationship of *Dear Brutus*.

To Andrew Birkin, Gerrie described Barrie's love for Michael as

> very intense … I think it was bad for Michael to be so much the centre of Barrie's world. And Barrie made demands on him, writing to him every day and all this kind of thing … You must let your children go free. But Barrie certainly clung to Michael.

But to be fair, Barrie did give the boys real affection, which was clearly reciprocated – George and Peter's letters from the front exemplify this. And there was another amazing dimension to his love for them. Barrie paid for, educated and entertained Michael and his brothers like no other could have done.

Nevertheless, Barrie was becoming aware that Michael was 'building seven walls around him'. In 'Tintinnabulum' he described him as receding 'farther from my ken down the road which hurries him from me … he no longer needs me as [he] did, and he will go on needing me less... On the last night of the holidays he was specially gruff, but he slipped beneath my door a paper containing the words "I hereby solemnly promise never to give you cause for moral anxiety."'

Senhouse, still the closest of Michael's friends, will have been of particular concern to Barrie and was possibly the reason Michael put that paper under Barrie's door. Senhouse described how, on a weekend spent at Barrie's London flat in 1918, Barrie had not addressed one word to him from first to last. But he was the same with other of Michael's friends. It was the behaviour of a man who wanted Michael to himself.

Barrie decided to reignite the spirit of his relationship with Michael with a holiday in Scotland, not visited since 1915. He, Michael and Nico went first to Edinburgh, where they were due to meet Jack and his fiancée Gerrie. All five met on a platform at Edinburgh station and then went off for dinner, an event Barrie later wrote up as a spoof in a letter to Lady Juliet Duff, the humour harbouring truths about each character just below the surface, and Barrie pretending that the whole thing went off at the Trossachs Hotel in Loch Katrine, where in fact they gravitated to later on.

As he wrote it to Lady Juliet on 14 August:

We were all outwardly calm, but internally white to the gills; Nicholas kept wetting his lips, Michael was a granite column, inscrutable, terrible; I kept bursting into inane laughter, and changing my waistcoats. So the time of waiting passed, the sun sank in the west and the stars came out with less assurance than usual. What is that? It is the rumble of wheels. Nico slips his hand into mine. I notice that it is damp. Michael's pose becomes more Napoleonic, but he is breathing hard. The chaise comes into view. I have a happy thought. They are probably more nervous than we are....

M. What do you think?

N. I like her awfully.

M. Don't be an ass. You don't know her at all yet. What do you think, Uncle Jim?

J. (with a great sigh of relief). The first impression is very favourable.

N. Rather! What is favourable exactly?

M. Do shut up, Nico.

J. I should call her tall, dark and pretty.

M. (who knows more about it). She is pretty. The question is, is she very pretty?

N. I think—

M. It doesn't matter what you think.

J. I should say she is very pretty.

M. She is. It's not a common type of prettiness.

N. No, it isn't. What is type exactly?

J. She's elusive, that's what she is.

M. (guardedly). It may be that.

N. Yes, it's that. What is elusive?

In the meantime another conversation is going on in another part of the edifice, which is probably to this effect.

Jack. Buck up, Gerrie, that's the worst over.

Gerrie. Oh dear, I was so nervous and they were all so calm.

J. It was a biggish ordeal to you, but of course it was nothing to them. Besides, they are three to two.

G. How do you think I did, Jack?

J. Splendidly. I never admired you so much.

G. I took to Nicholas at once. I feel I can get round him.

J. Rather. What about Michael?

G. He alarms me. Did anybody ever get round Michael?

J. I can't say I ever did. After all the third chappie is the important one.

G. (gasping). I know. Oh, Jack!

J. Yes, he's a bit like that. His heart's all right.

G. Is it? His face is so expressionless.

J. It's an uncomfortable face of course.

G. He never smiled once.

J. I bet you he thought he was smiling all the time. That's the way he smiles.

G. Good gracious!

J. He's really rather soft. We can all twist him round our fingers.

G. (looking at her fingers). I wonder.

J. You see he is essentially a man's man. He doesn't know what to say to women. They don't interest him. I think he's a woman-hater.

G. Don't!

J. What are you to wear for dinner?

G. Does it matter? He won't notice.

J. No, but Michael will. He takes Michael's opinion on everything. All depends on Michael. If Michael says 'Let them marry next week—'

G. Oh oh oh!

J. If Michael says that, Uncle Jim will fix it up. If on the other hand Michael says 'Delay for three years,' it will be fixed that way.

G. Oh, if he should say that!

J. He won't.

G. How can you be sure?

J. I should kick him.

Transferring to Loch Katrine, the boys had two weeks' fishing and on 17 August, Barrie wrote to Nan Herbert:

I don't know if you were ever here. It is pre-eminently the spot where you are supposed to stand on a rock and recite Sir Walter Scott from the guidebook. A very wet rock too at present. May is the best month for fishing if you come in August, and August is the best month if you come in May. You can, however, fall in all the year round.

Thereafter, Barrie, Michael and Nico transferred to a shooting lodge

near Fort Augustus in Inverness-shire, lent to them by Lord and Lady
Astor. And a week later, having picked up a new croquet set on the
way, they wound up at Edgerston, a 3,700-acre estate six miles south
of Jedburgh, a charming, historic border town.

Edgerston House was originally built in the seventeenth century, with two Regency wings added to the older part of the house
a century later. Today fully restored to its original splendour, with
formal gardens, burn, natural pool, acres of woodland climbing the
surrounding rounded hills, and a library of Walter Scott first editions, it is easy to see why Barrie warmed to the place immediately.

The Rutherford history of Edgerston brought Walter Scott into
the picture – Scott's mother, Anne, was a Rutherford, hence the
first editions. The story goes that as a young girl she became very
ill and was declared dead by her father who was a doctor in Edinburgh. She was buried and, that night, grave robbers dug her up
to get the jewellery that she was wearing. It was a custom in those
days to bury one's jewellery with the person. When they couldn't
get her ring off, they started to cut her finger off and she arose and
screamed. Persons living nearby heard it and came to her rescue.

Barrie arrived at Edgerston as the guest of Frederick S. Oliver and
his wife, who had bought the estate from William Edward Oliver-
Rutherford (1863–1931) in 1915. Frederick Oliver was an outspoken
British political writer and businessman. Though this was Barrie's
first visit, he had stayed before at the Olivers' house in Berkshire,
but it was clear that Frederick Oliver had already found his way into
the spirit of the place to an almost magical degree.

Later Barrie wrote to Mrs Oliver:

> I wish I was still among your rounded hills. You have a prospect as fair
> I think as any in Scotland, and though you all love it, it means most

to Fred. One day as I watched him from a window stalking in the garden with the round hills for company I made a discovery about him
that I have probably been on the verge of discovering for years and
then missing – that he is really a figure in some unwritten tale by Walter Scott. The scene of it is certainly Edgerston and the whole thing
would begin to move if something very small could happen, such as
the opening of a gate down by the burn. I could go on in this way for
a long time, and for the moment at any rate it is my chief memory
of that happy visit. I seem to know a little more of Scotland than I
ever knew before … I felt very much at home at Edgerston. I give you
many thanks for that. You were the chief conspirator.

This was pure Barrie sorcery, but he warmed also to the nearby market town of Jedburgh, where he found history everywhere he looked,
his imagination turning with delight to the Young Pretender, who
stayed in Castlegate in the town in 1745, also to Robert Burns,
who lodged in Canongate in 1787, and to Mary Queen of Scots,
who stayed in Queen Street in 1566 at what is still known as the
Queen's House, and was visited by her lover, David Rizzio, in nearby
Hermitage Castle.

The town is redolent of the history of conflict between Scotland and England, and Barrie liked to think of Edgerston as the last
house in his native land. So attached did he become to it that he
was still coming in 1932 to celebrate the centenary of Sir Walter
Scott's death.

For Michael there was fishing in the burn and the Tweed, but
Barrie was in fantasy mood with them. On 30 August 1917, he
wrote to Turley Smith:

I am up here with Michael and Nico – the last house next to the

English border. Three German escaped prisoners are lurking about and Nico is looking forward to being compelled to exchange clothes with them some day when they catch him fishing. He is then to Sherlock them.

My love to you.

Jedburgh conferred the Freedom of the town on Barrie, and he became so embedded in the culture of the place that he was asked to present the prizes at the estate school. As a result we have a little snapshot of him from a schoolgirl who won a prize that day.

Elizabeth Dodd, who lived on an isolated farmstead three miles away and walked to school and back each day, remembered Barrie as 'a very odd little man in crumpled clothes and with a faraway look in his eyes. I would sooner have met Mr Anon whose works I knew better. The nearest theatre was over fifty miles away, so what chance had I of seeing *Peter Pan*.'

Dodd grew up to be a famous, bestselling author and broadcaster and was honoured with the MBE – her pen name, Lavinia Derwent. She said she would have been bursting with pride if only her prize was being awarded for something to do with brains. 'The truth was, it was for the best-dyed egg.' Worse, Jessie had made it, she hadn't done it herself at all, as she wrote in *A Breath of Border Air*.

I stood trembling in front of the famous man, hanging my head in shame and wondering how I would confess my sins. Sir James was very complimentary. He had never seen such a beautiful egg. If only hens could lay them like that every day ... What a clever little girl I was, and what pleasure he had in presenting me with the first prize which I richly deserved.

Every word he said cut me to the quick and made my sins seem more scarlet. More so when I saw the prize. It was a book of bible stories with a picture of the Good Samaritan on the cover. I clutched it under my arm and was sure that I would be struck dead.

Chapter Twenty-Five

1918: The Real Peter Pan

PERHAPS SENSING THAT Gerrie was an ally, which indeed she turned out to be, when Michael returned home he reached out to her in a letter, showing her the kind of life he led with Barrie, telling her that he was taking him and Nico to four theatres before their return to school:

> A musical thing called 'Chap' being the only one as yet – but we are going to a play called 'Trelawney of the Wells' tomorrow and my Uncle Gerald's play – 'A Pair of Spectacles' [by Sydney Grundy] on Saturday. So we shall soon be painting London red in earnest.
>
> We go in daily fear of air-raids just now – at least we are supposed to. I believe the thing to do is to lie between two mattresses on the ground floor out of range of glass – with a Book of Common Prayer

in one hand and a loaf of bread in the other – in case of interment while alive! I think of going to the Red Lion myself. Don't you think it w'd look well on the placards.

ANOTHER BLOW FOR THE PUBLIC SCHOOL SYSTEM

A young Etonian has just entered the Red Lion in Notting Hill Gate where he was a regular visitor when a bomb entered through the ceiling striking the unfortunate young debaucher on the right hand, as he was raising a glass to his lips, caused immediate death by laryngal congestion.

The Pink 'un w'd put me down as 'Died as he lived.'

Nico returns to Eton on the 19th and I on the 21st – and hope you'll pay us a visit on our Lordly Stairway.

I hope you're tying Jack down with the dear old blue ribbon.

Don't bother to answer.

If the last line sounded abrupt, perhaps Michael hoped that Gerrie would be in touch but was afraid to burden her with his case, not surprising as Barrie's involvement with Michael now was increasingly and depressingly marked with a preoccupation with death.

On 20 February 1918, Barrie wrote a letter from Adelphi Terrace to Elizabeth Lucas:

I emerge out of my big chimney to write to you. I was sitting there with a Charlotte Bronte in my hands (when I read her I think mostly of Emily) and there was a gale on the roof; it is probably not windy at all down below but with the slightest provocation the chimneys overhead in their whirring cowls go as devilish as the witches in Macbeth, whom they also rather resemble in appearance. I hope, however, it is a sufficiently dirty night as the sailors say to keep the air-raiders at bay…

I had an odd thought today about the war that might come to some-thing, but it seems to call for a poet. That in the dead quietness that comes after the carnage, the one thing those lying on the ground must be wondering is whether they are alive or dead. Out there the veil that separates the survivors and the killed must be getting very thin, and those on the one side of it very much jumbled up with those on the other. One can see them asking each other which side of the veil they are on, not afraid that they may be dead so much as curious. And then the veil thickening a little, and the two lots going their different ways. You could even see some going with the wrong lot, a dead man with a living, a living man with a dead. Perhaps it is of this stuff that ghosts are made. These be rather headachy thoughts. I expect the lot on the other side of the veil have as many Germans as British, and that they all went off together quite unconscious that they had ever been enemies. To avenge the fallen! That is the stupidest cry of the war. What must the fallen think of us if they hear it. Audrey would be amused with the subject Michael had to write a poem about in the *Eton Chronicle* – not had to but greedily pounced on it…

This may have been written some time after Barrie's dream. Indeed, he may not have had the dream at all. For the play he had been work-ing on in his mind for some time (A *Well-Remembered Voice*) was based, of course, on George, and he will have been concerned that people might find that insensitive, so he was testing it on Elizabeth.

He may already have tested it on Michael, as he did all his works in progress. If so we, don't have Michael's opinion of it. Neverthe-less, significantly, Michael chose this moment to make a speech at Eton, which suggests that his mind was far from ruminating with Barrie on 'the mighty dead'.

The subject was Frederic W. H. Myers's essay on the novelist and dramatist Victor Hugo (1802–85), who was the literary force behind the Romantic movement in France. Myers was a poet and one of the founders of the Society for Psychical Research. He was sufficiently to the fore in the thinking of the times to be said to have influenced the philosopher William James and the psychiatrist Carl Jung.

Hugo's spiritual views changed radically over the course of his life. In his youth he was a Christian, then he became a Spiritualist, believing, as Barrie said he did, in the existence of immortal spirits with beneficent or maleficent influences on the physical world, and participating in séances conducted by the French author, Madame Delphine de Girardin.

Eventually spiritualism was discarded and he developed an acute appreciation of Nature, which led him to an acceptance of a spiritual dimension not dissimilar to Michael's. A reviewer in the *Eton Chronicle* praised Michael's speech not simply as well researched, but recognising it as a personal credo: 'He spoke clearly and with an understanding quite unusual.'

The holiday at Edgerston in the summer of 1917 had been a return to the Scotland that had reformed Michael after his mother's death. But that wasn't all that the Highlands had meant to him at that stressful time. It offered him relaxation and release certainly, but not merely escapism in the manner of Barrie's 'lost boy', who runs farther and farther into the wood, singing joyfully to himself and hoping that no adult will turn up and compel him to face life's harsh realities.

Since Scourie and Amhuinnsuidhe Michael had come to understand that the source of his new-found calm was both within and around him in the highland landscape, and that the degree of peace it afforded him was in direct proportion to that more mysterious awareness.

Michael had spoken well of Victor Hugo because his transition had been similar to his – both away from Barrie's morbid spiritualist preoccupation with the dead and towards the apprehension of a spiritual dimension within and around him in the natural world.

The hours Michael spent fly-fishing – still and poised to perform some deft movement – induced in him a sort of mystical transcendence. He was a bright boy, but intellectual capacity had nothing to do with it. The natural environment, the stillness and peace, the requirement to listen, to concentrate, to *attend* rather than to think, brought him to it. What died to the process were words from Barrie, images of islands and pools, thoughts of any kind, petty concerns, ambitions and *self*-consciousness – all instruments and material effects of the external world.

After a century or more of analytical introversion, it is not easy for us to appreciate that the spiritual effect of purposeful activity in a landscape of great sublimity has the potential to be more productive than psychology.

The joy of liberation from the tawdry and the trivial and the sense of unity with all Nature may indeed be as blissful as du Maurier described in *Peter Ibbetson*. It is the same for Michael as for Peter Ibbetson – the discovery of the real Peter Pan within, an inner sense not directed like our eyes or ears towards the external world. With it, one can see the most heavenly music and hear the sun shining on earth. With it, blindness made no difference to Homer and Milton, nor deafness to Beethoven.

To cousin Daphne it was 'an other-world intimacy', which as we grow up becomes 'etiolated by disuse'. For she too associated it with the real Peter Pan, calling it 'the secret of the elixir of youth'.[49]

---

49   'The Archduchess' from *The Breaking Point* (1959).

The question remained as to whether Michael could carry this inspirational quality into the hurly burly of life. If the real Peter Pan did remain in the ground of his being, it would be the making of him and those around him.

Meanwhile it would have to withstand being beaten down by more and more of Barrie's morbidity, as the plot of his play, *A Well-Remembered Voice*, unfurled:

A group of people are gathered for a séance for a young male victim of the First War, including the boy's mother and sometime sweetheart, Laura (in real life, Josephine Mitchell-Innes).

The boy's father, Mr Don, is sitting 'in the inglenook', paying no attention to the party round the table. So famous was Barrie's seat in the inglenook, the massive fireplace of the main room of the Adelphi Terrace flat, that he was painted in it by Sir John Lavery. We are to see Mr Don as Barrie.

The séance yields one phrase only from the other side, 'Love Bade Me Welcome', which later turns out to be the password that facilitates the son's passage over from 'the other side'.

Eventually father and mother are left alone, and their attention is riven by their son's fishing rods against the wall. The mother says. '[The rods] are sacred things to me.'

At last, the father is left alone. 'He stands fingering the fishing-rods tenderly, then wanders back into the inglenook. Through the greyness we see him very well in the glow of the fire. He sits on the settle [in the inglenook] and tries to read his paper. He is a pitiful lonely man.'

Dick, the son, appears. A well-remembered voice says, 'Father.' Mr Don looks into the greyness and sees his son.

It is a touching reunion. Dick has no taste for sentiment. The disadvantage of the hereafter is that there are no risks to run, and Dick will admit that his gaiety is part put on to help his father, which was *so* George. His voice is 'as boyish as ever', but 'there is a new note in it ... Dick may not have grown much wiser, but whatever he does know now he seems to know for certain.'

They are in the inglenook together now and the boy 'catches his father by the shoulders', the very behaviour that he would remember of Michael so vividly after his death. They discuss their times fishing together. Dick confesses that he put a stone in the mouth of his prize catch to make it a seven-pounder. They laugh. Then they speak eerily of the battlefield, the lightest of veils that separates the living from the dead, and of 'what a little thing' death is.

We are with the living wounded and the dead, feeling the quietness of death, the concatenation of the two worlds, and the passing over. 'When I came to,' says Dick, 'the veil was so thin that I couldn't see it at all; and my first thought was, Which side of it have I come out on?'

It is touching, but irredeemably sad. We may feel sympathy, but the words are those of 'an inspired and desperate alchemist hoping to still these obstinate questionings by forcing some lone ghost to render up the tale of what we are'.[50]

A *Well-Remembered Voice* characterises the context in which Barrie's relationship with Michael moved to its tragic conclusion. Barrie couldn't help himself. As early as July 1909, he had written to Q, 'I fancy I try to create an artificial world to myself because the one I really inhabit, and the only one I could do any good in, becomes too sombre. How doggedly my pen searches for gaiety.'

He even invented an alter ego that he called 'M'Connachie', blaming him for his sombre shivery side.

---

50   P. B. Shelley, 'Alastor' (1816).

M'Connachie, I should explain, as I have undertaken to open the innermost doors, is the name I give to the unruly half of myself: the writing half. We are compliment and supplement. I am the half that is dour and practical and canny, he is the fanciful half; my desire is to be the family solicitor, standing firm on my hearthrug among the harsh realities of the office furniture; while he prefers to fly around on one wing. I should not mind him doing that, but he drags me with him.

So he claimed, a medical condition meant that he had lost the battle to stand firm on his hearthrug and now preoccupied himself wholeheartedly with death. It was the theme not only of *A Well-Remembered Voice*, first produced at Wyndham's theatre on 28 June 1918, but also of Barrie's long awaited realisation of the Amhuinnsuidh play, *Mary Rose*, adjudged by W. A. Darlington the last of his great successes in the theatre. It appeared at the Haymarket on 22 April 1920, just one year before Michael himself died.

The medical condition was cramp in his right hand, his writing hand. He wrote to Charles Whiblet, also a writer:

My dear Charles … It isn't so difficult as you might fancy to write with the left hand but 'tis the dickens to think down the left side. It doesn't even know the names of my works. Also it seems to have a darker and more sinister outlook on life, and is trying at present to egg me on to making a woman knife her son [*Mary Rose*]. Always love, J. M. B.

To the actress Mrs Campbell:

My right hand has gone on strike – writer's cramp – and I have had to learn to indite with the left. We scarcely know the right hand nowadays – we pass the time of day and so on, but nothing more. At first the left was but an amanuensis. I dictated to it, but I had to think down the right arm. But now the left is my staff. Also I find the person who writes with his left is quite another pair of shoes from the one who employs his right; he has other standards, sleeps differently, has novel views on the ontology of being, and is a more sinister character. Anything curious or uncomfortable about the play of *Mary Rose* arises from its having been a product of the left hand.

Later he would backdate the influence of the release of the sinister side of himself upon the world to the writing of *Dear Brutus* (1917), as Darlington noted. 'Nobody seemed to see till later that *Dear Brutus* was, as Barrie himself described it many years later, an uncomfortable play such as he could only have written with his left hand.'

Of course, the left-hand/right-hand business was another piece of Barrie nonsense. But the trouble was that once this fanciful, sinister side started operating in the real world, people could get hurt. It was this tension that he needed in his life in order to create. And Michael was the key.

Nanny became increasingly concerned. But what could she do? Her loyalty to Arthur and Sylvia remained as strong as ever, she could not bring the family into disrepute by taking her fears to someone outside. Anyway, who would listen? But something had to be done.

When Nico went as a boarder to Eton in 1916, she had decided to offer her resignation. Barrie saw immediately that that would not do. He did all in his power to persuade her to stay. She agreed reluctantly.

Then all of a sudden, on 24 June 1917 – Midsummer's Day – he moved from his flat on the third floor of Adelphi Terrace House (fifth if you looked at it from the Embankment side) to a studio apartment on the top floor of the same building, large enough to accommodate Michael and Nico.

No expense was spared in its redesign by Edwin Lutyens. A large study room ran the length of the apartment to huge casement windows looking out over the Thames, making it even more like the Captain's bridge than the flat below.

The walls were mahogany-panelled. Large brown wooden bookshelves were installed. The overall impression was one of brown-ness. Immediately to the right on entry was a large inglenook fireplace, into which Barrie, at just over five feet, could wander without bending and tuck himself away on a hard settle, to read in the light of a log fire. The floor of the room was covered with matting, and later rugs chosen by Michael. In one corner stood a polished iron stove, where Barrie liked to brew tea when his manservant was not in attendance.

'Somehow the apartment seems just like him,' wrote a visitor.[51] Dark, bookish, imposing, hard, it would not be out of place in the opening scene of *Faust* as the 'high-vaulted, narrow Gothic chamber' where we first see the scholar sitting restless at his desk.

Without consulting Nanny, Barrie arranged for Jack and his new wife, who were married in September, to take over the running of Campden Hill Square.

When the young couple arrived, Nanny, unprepared and piqued at the assault on her authority, turned her back on the young couple and refused to speak to Gerrie, who was to take her place. Jack was furious, but Nico and Michael wouldn't have a word said against her.

Nanny refused to talk to Gerrie. Tensions ran wild between the two factions. Matters became fraught.

---

51   Charlie Chaplin, who Barrie fancied to play Peter Pan on film.

Then one night Nanny pushed a note under the door of Jack's bedroom, which read: 'Things have been going on in this room of which your father would not have approved.'

It is not known what Jack made of it, but the response within the family was shameful. Gerrie later recalled that Edward Coles, husband of May du Maurier, and therefore Michael's uncle, read the note and quipped: 'She probably heard the bed squeaking.'

A joke in bad taste, but the likelihood was that sex was the last thing going on in that room. Much more likely, given Nanny's choice of phrase and the plays Barrie and Michael were now engaged in – one about George coming back from the dead, and the other about Sylvia – is that the 'things' going on in the room of which Arthur would not have approved, were séances. Would Nanny have stood by for so long had Barrie and Michael been having sex? I think not!

But why did no one do anything? 'Because they were intimidated,' said Gerrie to Andrew Birkin in 1975. 'All the other relations said they were intimidated.'

Certainly, Barrie could be intimidating if it suited him. We have already met with Dolly Ponsonby's wariness of him, the alarming way he 'sees right through one'. Mackail recalled that he would meet your conversation with an expression 'horribly like a sneer … Oh, yes, we have suffered. No, don't let's remember … the faint, Caledonian grunt with which our desperate observations are received.'

There's a wonderful description by the cricket writer Neville Cardus in his autobiography[52] of a weekend he spent in Barrie's Adelphi apartment a couple of years after Michael's death, interesting because it gives us Barrie as he was at his most intimidating. Nico described it as 'vividly true and to me extremely funny'.

---

52 Neville Cardus, *Autobiography* (1947).

Cardus had written to Barrie about Kathleen Kilfoyle, a young actress he had seen playing Mary Rose. When Barrie replied, he told Cardus he had for years been reading his books and articles on cricket and invited him to Adelphi Terrace. Cardus accepted. By this time, Barrie's butler, Harry Brown, had been replaced by Frank Thurston.

Cardus arrived on a Friday evening and was shown to his bedroom by Thurston.

This Thurston I have subsequently found out was a grand and sterling character, he spoke various languages, and would correct any loose statements about Ovid that he chanced to overhear while he was serving dinner. He had a ghostly face; he was from a Barrie play – so was Barrie, and the flat, and everything in it; the enormous cavern of a fireplace, the wooden settle and old tongs and bellows, and the sense the place gave you that the walls might be walked through if you had been given the secret. Barrie trudged the room smoking a pipe; on the desk lay another pipe already charged, ready for immediate service; he coughed as he trudged and smoked, a cruel cough that provoked a feeling of physical pain in my chest; and his splutterings and gaspings and talk struggled on one from the other.

At last he came to sit facing me in front of the smouldering logs, and for a while the silence was broken by groans only to be heard in our two imaginations – the groans of men separated for ever by a chasm of shyness and uneasiness. Until midnight we lingered on. He offered me no refreshment. Thurston apparently went home to sleep each night. Or perhaps he merely dematerialised. Barrie knew I had dined on the train, but a nightcap would have been fortifying to me, I am sure; for already the spell of the flat high amongst the roofs of Adelphi was gripping me.

Next morning, having been given the information, 'unnecessarily as I still think', that it was Michael's room he'd been sleeping in, Thurston came into his bedroom with tea and showed Cardus the bathroom, 'the most unkept I have ever known'.

> The towels were damp and soiled; and round about the shelves were one or two shaving brushes congealed in ancient soap. A rusty razor blade on a window ledge was historical. Barrie had his private bath-room; the unclean towels puzzled me. Was it the custom to bring your own towels when staying with distinguished people for a week-end? I dried myself as best I could, and now Thurston directed me to the breakfast-room, where he attended to me in complete silence.

On the Sunday, after a dinner party the previous night enlivened occasionally by E. V. Lucas's 'low chuckles', Thurston again served tea in his bedroom and informed him that Barrie had gone away until Monday. Cardus spent the day in the parks, dined in Soho and let himself into the flat just before midnight.

> Not a sound. A cold collation had been laid for me on the table, with a bottle of hock and a silver box of cigarettes. I explored the book-cases, almost on tiptoe; there was a row of volumes of the Scottish philosophers – Hume, Mackintosh, Hamilton. I sat at Barrie's desk but got up immediately for fear I might be caught in the act. The great chimney corner, with no fire in it, glowered at me.

At breakfast, to his surprise, he was met by Barrie's sister Maggie, who invited him in her boudoir on the Tuesday evening to take part in a little musical 'conversazione'.

On the Monday night he was met again with a bottle of hock and light meal, but this time, as he sipped his wine in the cold silence of the flat, he heard the lift arriving outside the flat door and the metal concertina gates opening, 'and presently the door opened and a young man entered, in a dinner jacket'.

Without a sign of curiosity at my presence or at the absence of others, he remarked to me that it had been a lovely day. He sat on a couch, smoked a cigarette, and talked for a few minutes about the cricket at Lord's; he hadn't yet been able to look in at the match himself, but he had enjoyed my account of Saturday's play in the 'M. C.' I was liking him very much when he arose, and with an apology left the room and the flat. To this day I do not know who he was – probably young Simon out of *Mary Rose*.

The following night Barrie was present but excused himself from his sister's musical 'conversazione' as he was tone deaf. However, he took Cardus to Maggie's boudoir, 'remotely Victorian in fragrance and appearance [with] an upright piano with a fluted silk front', before escaping. There followed a rendering of a work of Maggie's own, entitled *1914–1918*, 'with a battle section in the middle and a finale of bells and thanksgiving. She next sang a number of Scotch songs in an expressive if wan voice. When the music was over she asked me about my early life and of my struggles.'

Next morning Maggie was at breakfast waiting for him and admitted to having been 'in communication with my mother "on the other side" and that my mother and she had loved one another at once, and that my mother was proud of me and that they, the two of them, would watch over and take care of me. I was naturally ready to perspire with apprehension.'

Thurston then appeared and brought one scene to an end and the final one into focus. Barrie wished to say goodbye before Cardus left.

He was in bed in a bandbox of a room, bare and uncomfortable – what little I could see of it through thick tobacco smoke, for his pipe was in full furnace as he lay there, frail in pyjamas, like a pygmy with one of those big pantomime heads. He hoped I had enjoyed my stay and would come again; the flat was open to me at any time: I had only to give him short notice. Thurston carried my suitcase down the lift cage. He got me a taxi. In my highly emotional condition – feeling I had emerged from another dimension, and only just emerged – I forgot to tip him.

Chapter Twenty-Six

1918: Within the Gothic Chamber

WHEN NEVILLE CARDUS'S long weekend was over he concluded: 'I prefer my Barrie plays on the stage in front of me, where I can see what they are doing.' But those closer to him were 'on stage' most of the time.

After nothing happened when Nanny passed the note under Jack's bedroom door, she issued an ultimatum to Gerrie to leave Campden Hill Square. She and Jack repaired to a Knightsbridge hotel, where Gerrie suffered a miscarriage. Nanny broke down, resigned and refused compensation of £1,000, made up of £500 left to her in Sylvia's will and £500 put up by Barrie.

On 20 January 1918, from Tillington in Sussex, where Barrie had taken Michael and Nico to stay with E. V. Lucas and Audrey (Lucas had by this time separated from his wife Elizabeth) Michael wrote to Nanny in an effort to conclude the whole dreadful business. He expressed the fear that it was a callous letter, but there is a certain maturity here, which at least wrapped the whole thing up, and before we reach judgement on his style we should remember our innocence of the often-patronising way family–staff relations were dealt with in those days.

Michael is not disloyal to Barrie, although his hand in the whole business lurks beneath the surface of the letter. He doesn't give the impression that it was his adoptive father's deeply laid strategy that brought him to Adelphi Terrace, and yet he attends to Nanny's fears of what will become of him there with telling candour: 'As to whether going and living at [Barrie's] flat will be worse for Nico and me, that rests with our own strength of mind, don't it – and particularly with mine I believe.'

My dear Mary,

Do you mind if I try to reduce the painfulness of things by putting them down here in writing? I believe I can do it.

I am assuming that matters have gone too far to turn back now, though whose fault I will not say, tho' I shrewdly suspect it had a little to do with everybody.

Before going any further, let me assure you with the utmost assurance that it will not be at all possible for Nico and me to continue living at 23 with Jack & his wife – as you suggested. The proof lies in the last three weeks, whatever you say. This may be hard luck on Jack, but the fact remains, & when a man marries, his family is the one he is setting up for himself. You yourself said that Jack is hav-ing too much done for him [by Barrie]. That is so, so why sh'd he be allowed to go on in this easy way, undisturbed and disturbing?

It w'd be hardly possible for us to go on living at 23 even without Jack and Gerrie, unless you came back. As to this last it rests with your 'pride', & with your opinion as to the importance of maintain-ing 23 as a home for Nico. (I hope all this doesn't sound callous. You know me too well to make that mistake.)

The present scheme I believe is to let things remain undecided for a month or two, so as to see which way to turn. As to whether going and living at the flat will be worse for Nico and me, that rests with our own strength of mind, don't it – and particularly with mine I believe.

And of course the chief reason of 23's importance was that you were there – & – do not say I am wrong – I am sure we shall see very nearly if not as much of you as before. Let us weigh the past with the future:

Past. We have seen you only in the holidays, which has not been very much. We have written about once a week or so (when old Nico could be roused).

Future. Of course we shall write as much if not more (when I can rouse old Nico). And in the holidays – mind you! – you're to come with your gingham & take up your quarters in the attic we'll have ready for you – if only to see my mustache grow! And besides that you will overcome yr dislike of travelling, & be dragged off in the summer holidays, or whenever we do disappear in the wilds. And – mind you! – this is absolutely serious – none of your absurd ideas of pride or absurd ideas of Uncle Jim not wanting you! That's what I call false pride, & harmful at that. Think how glad he'll be to get us off his hands for a time!

This frivolousness of pen really hides the most serious inwardness I've ever had. I'm going to draw up a form for you to sign.

The chief sadness this week then is the leaving of 23, & that was bound to come, so don't let us be cowards.

Also – & I know this is not my business at all – do take that paltry thousand to please Nico & me, if only to start a social revolution! We'd have made it a billion only that's not a billionth part enough. I know it's twice as hard for you as it is for us, and that's precious hard. Nico is unaware of the state of affairs, so please Mary don't make it harder by refusing anything.

AU REVOIR.
MICHAEL.

Nine days later, Barrie wrote to Elizabeth Lucas:

Michael's letter to Audrey has told you of our adventures at Tillington where we had a very happy time, and M. discovered an old shop at Petworth and triumphantly bought a soap-dish for his room here. That room is not finished yet, indeed three rooms are still in confusion, which will give you some idea of the difficulties with workmen nowadays. I have got into the study now, however, and at last the chimney behaves and certainly it is a very attractive room, and the little kitchen off it is good too. I had begun to feel in my bones tho' that it was all too fine a flat for me and that for my lonely purposes all I really needed was this room and the bedroom. Brown could have done for me so, and I had quite planned letting the rest with its own door. However the way has been cleared by trouble at Campden Hill. Mary is going sometime in February.

Michael was now co-editing the *Eton Chronicle*. On 29 March, Barrie wrote a little sadly about how he was missing him:

Dearest Michael,

Pretty lonely here for this week-end, 'Bank holidays' are always loneliness personified to me, but I think that you & Nico are almost on
the way [home] and rejoice with great joy. Nico said you might get
off on Monday after all, but I'm not counting on it, too good to be
true. I got your dressing-table out [of No. 23] all right & have been
trying various plans to make the rooms nice. I have brought a few –
very few – things from 23, but of course everything I've done is very
open to re-arrangement – in fact it is wanted. The Red Cross sale cat-
alogue is just out & is a most interesting volume as you will see. The
sale begins on the 8th … We can go to Christie's and see the things
before the 8th. Your account of the boys' musical in the *Chronicle*
makes me want to see the M.S. thereof. Would it be possible for you
to get the loan of it?

Loving,
JMB

By Easter 1918, Michael and Nico were installed at Adelphi Terrace, and Barrie was hard at work on *Mary Rose*.

Barrie's oddly unsettling corruption of Hogg's hauntingly beautiful
'Kilmeny' poem, began during the 1912 holiday at Amhuinnsuidhe
and was now to be filtered into *Mary Rose* by means of Barrie's archaic
idea of the 'little gods … tricky spirits' that looked after him.

They first appear in the play as 'seekers' responsible for making
'the call' to Mary on the island at Voshimid – 'soft whisperings from
holes in the ground – "Mary Rose, Mary Rose".' Then 'in a fury as of
storm and whistling winds that might be an unholy organ [which]
rushes upon the island, raking every bush for her. These sounds

increase rapidly in volume till the mere loudness of them is horrible,' writes Barrie in the stage directions to the play.

They have a counterpart – 'You have forgotten the call,' says Harry to his mother in the end. 'It was as if, in a way, there were two kinds of dogs out hunting you – the good and the bad.'

'Unseen devils' appear and disappear time and again in the play, and they are not confined to Barrie's script. A seeker is 'one that keeps step, as soft as snow' with each of us, and if, like Michael, your 'childhood may have been overfull of gladness; they [the seekers] don't like that', wrote Barrie in 1922.

Before long Michael was himself writing a poem from a Scottish island in which 'the white mists eddied, trailed and spun like seekers', and Daphne, who came under Barrie's influence strongly after Michael's death, would, far in the future, write a poem called 'Another World' in which they are 'the loathly keepers of the netherland' and she hears 'their voices whisper me from sleep'.

Daphne leaves us in no doubt that this is a different Neverland to the one Hogg ascribes to Kilmeny, rather the nightmare one of Barrie's own gloomy imagination, but it is impossible to be sure to what degree he deliberately darkened Michael's mind or believed what he impressed upon him. He was, as Peter wrote, such 'a fantasy-weaver that anyone he made much of ended up by either playing up to him or clearing out'.

The author Jon Savage[53] concluded that the Barrie boys, whose lives had been 'filleted' for Barrie's plays, had been the subject of an 'act of transference, if not possession' by Barrie. If you can make people believe something of your dream, it will cleave to their perception of reality. Every magician, every religious leader, every politician knows

---

53   Jon Savage, *Teenage: The Creation of Youth 1875–1945* (2007).

this to be the case. But Michael had the literary image to hand that explained his situation best. As 'the foster-child of Silence and slow Time' held on the sculpted surface of Keats's beautiful Grecian urn, Michael was trapped within Barrie's morbid works.

In the opening stage direction to *Mary Rose*, Barrie explains that what the resurrected Mary Rose cannot tell us of 'what only the dead should know' is available for us all to see in the 'disturbing smile' of Leonardo da Vinci's 'Mona Lisa'. Two years later he pointed to Michael as the one who 'half knows' this secret – 'something of which [his fellows] know nothing – the secret that is hidden in the face of the Mona Lisa'.[54]

Once, lingering long in the lonesome hills of Amhuinnsuidhe, Michael's smile had been closer to the beauteous visage of the mythical maiden caught by Hogg in 'Kilmeny' than to the Mona Lisa's ironic, or as Barrie would have it 'cynical' smirk, almost a sneer. But because of the gloom inherent in having as one's keeper a man who wandered over his world 'lone as incarnate death', the boy was rapidly fulfilling Barrie's projection of him as 'the dark and dour and impenetrable'.

The nature of the gloom under which he lived is nowhere more obviously found than in the story of Mary Rose, whose ghost prowls about the cold house looking for her son, 'searching, searching, searching', just as Michael once prowled around the house searching in his nightmares for 'the old enemy. It was always the same nameless enemy he was seeking,' Barrie wrote. 'I stood or sat by him, like a man in an adjoining world, waiting till he returned to me...'

Not only had Barrie elected to write a play about summoning up a dead mother to visit her son, a woman whose role he had usurped,

---

54   Barrie's rectorial address at St Andrews University, 23 May 1922.

but he had co-opted the son in the venture and connected his mother's state of mind to his experience of nightmare. There was a storm cloud gathering. Even while he was moving into Adelphi Terrace, life was becoming increasingly dark for Michael.

Meanwhile, the War Office was still asking for more men.

Michael's housemaster Macnagthen recorded that his star pupil was not faring well under the pressure, though Macnaghten didn't know the half of it: 'It was a time of great strain: the war was still raging; his friend Roger Senhouse, who was half a year older, had left, and Michael was uncertain whether to stay on another Half. He was obviously unwell.'

In the middle of May, Macnaghten called Barrie down to talk things over. Michael told them he wanted to leave at the end of the summer term. He was going to enlist in the Scots Guards and at the end of the war, he was going to study art in Paris, as his grandfather du Maurier had done before him.

Barrie had wanted him to try for the Cambridge scholarship, but taken by surprise by his frank and forthright message it was arranged that Michael would leave Eton at the end of the Half.

The regiment was Peter's idea. He had written on more than one occasion that Michael shouldn't underestimate what it was like for an Etonian in the ranks: 'Without accusing myself of snobbishness, I feel in this battalion like a survivor of a dead race, and sometimes wonder if I'm being pedantic when I speak the dialect which is my native tongue.'

Peter's concern reminds us of a significant aspect of life in 1918, the class war. Michael was an *ingenu* when it came to the big wide world. Also, he was increasingly forthright in his approach to people. It was Peter's view that his life would have been made miserable by the more streetwise squaddies.

So, he would join the Scots Guards. But not before one last summer holiday with rod and gun this time (good practice at the expense
of the grouse): Edgerston and Tomdoun again: 'Leading a bucolic
life up here,' reads a letter from Barrie to Gilmour.

> The great event is going out in a dog-cart to bring home the lamb.
> We won the lamb in a raffle, but always when we go for it, it is 'up in
> the hills', so we keep going. Fine hay crop, but no fishing owing to the
> want of rain. Michael shoots grouse. He will be going to Bushey for
> Scots Guards in November ... The war news heartens one up a bit.

Meanwhile, Michael was persuaded to think again about leaving
Eton. 'Subsequently,' wrote Macnaghten,

> he wrote in the quiet of the holidays asking if he might return. He
> was welcomed back, and the record of his last Half is, 'A wonderful
> Captain [he was made Head of House]: he worries, but his judgment
> is unerring, and his actions swift as lightning: the most admirable boy
> who has ever been in the house.'

And then in October the war was obviously ending – Bulgaria,
Turkey, then Austria bailed out, and on 9 November the Kaiser
abdicated. It was over.

Michael had been spared.

Chapter Twenty-Seven

1919: Oxford

ON 22 NOVEMBER, Barrie wrote to Eveline at Glan Hafren:

> So it actually is ended! It was dear of Peter [Lewis] to say that about Michael. You can guess how thankful I am. I don't think he will be wanted for the army now, and I'm going to Eton on Sunday to go into his future. They marched at Eton with their bath-tubs as drums [on Armistice night] and the night ended with Michael getting 500 lines! (For standing on his head on a roof when he should have been in bed, or something of the kind.)

At the Sunday meeting at Eton, Michael, who was so thrilled to be speaking about any kind of future, was persuaded to go to university.

Eiluned saw the folly of his bending to Barrie's will, believing that Barrie should have allowed him to go to Paris. She could see that Michael's artistic talent was something of his own, un-seeded and un-moulded by Barrie, who had no appreciation of art.

Had Michael been firm, a bohemian existence in Paris might have been the making of him, as it had been in the case of his grandfather. But Michael conceded his life to Barrie, in return for which Barrie would buy him a car and, indeed, a cottage, which he would never take up. His adopted father's largesse knew no bounds. Michael would have £5,000 in his bank account in 1921, the equivalent of £170,000 today, and he hadn't worked one day in his life.

However, Michael did not get a scholarship or an exhibition to Cambridge. On 20 December 1918, Barrie wrote to the Dean of Christ Church College, Oxford: '[Michael] went in for the Cambridge Trinity Scholarships this year [and] just failed to get an Exhibitionship. But in any case his wish was to go to Oxford…'

Michael matriculated from Christ Church, as the expression goes, on 23 January 1919. From Hilary term (January–March) 1919 through Trinity term (April–June) 1920 he resided in college at what is known as Peck 1:5, short for Peckwater Quad, Staircase 1, Room 5; a second floor apartment, quiet, wood-panelled, fairly dark. The living room overlooks the quad – the college library to the south.

On 17 January, Barrie wrote to Elizabeth Lucas:

Michael went off today to Oxford and Christchurch [sic] full of suppressed excitement. He has a very nice panelled sitting room, with furniture that would make you shiver. He hopes to be able to put in pieces from Campden Hill in place of it. Freyberg [Bernard Freyberg, VC, DSO, a warrior, a hero, and a close friend who adjusted well to sudden immersion in the gushing waters of Barrie's esteem] has been staying here for the last fortnight also and got on very well with the boys. Nicholas just come in and calling for billiards...

The following month Barrie sent Michael some small dining room chairs and a sideboard and sofa from No. 23, the rest of the furniture being put into storage and the house let to an artist called Speed.

Michael took Mods – the first public examinations in Latin and Greek, in Hilary term 1920. Mods, or Moderations, are the first part of the Classics degree course known as Literae Humaniores or, colloquially, Greats. Honours Mods for Classics students have been called the hardest examinations in the world. They lead to Second Public Examinations – Finals.

Macnaghten, who saw Michael occasionally when he visited Eton, noted in his book that for a year and a half he was still very restless: more than once he made up his mind to leave.

That may have been the case, but he also had some fine times too. Among his friends were a number of Old Etonians, among them Roger Senhouse and Bob Boothby, who was interviewed at length in the 1970s by Andrew Birkin.

Boothby, a Magdalen College man, was the only son of Sir Robert Tuite Boothby, a banker from Edinburgh. The aristocratic, moneyed, Scottish and Etonian background would have pleased Barrie, who did appear initially to have been happy that Michael was invited by Boothby's parents to stay at the family home in Scotland.

Boothby, who was bisexual, described Michael as 'a very desirable undergraduate' and classed him as a brilliant scholar who read widely – 'he'd have got a First in anything'.

Boothby did not have an affair with him. He described Michael as 'introverted and moody', 'very emotional', a young man who concealed his emotions, but if there was one word that described

him best, it was 'Romantic'. Sebastian Earl, another contemporary
Etonian, who rowed for Oxford in the 1920 Boat Race, agreed: 'He
was someone who cared for poetry and I would have thought music,
though music didn't mean *much* to my generation. Nothing like it
does today.'[55]

Michael did have an interest in music. Nico told a defining story
about Michael's taste when a large wind-up gramophone appeared
at the flat in Adelphi Terrace at some point after he and Michael
began living there. Barrie gave them each a ten-shilling note to buy
some records. Nico's choice was *Japanese Sandman* and *Whispering*
by Paul Whiting, which became a number one hit in 1920, while
Michael chose Rimsky Korsakov's *Scheherazade*. He said to Nico,
'You bloody fool. You'll want to throw yours away in half a minute.'
(Nico told Andrew Birkin this in January 1976 – and he still had
his copy of *Whispering*.)

But Michael came out of his shell with Boothby and there was
laughter. There developed a little group of them: four young men
– Boothby, Michael, Senhouse and Clive Burt – 'all tremendous
friends, and frightfully gay'.

Of course, Boothby knew about Michael's affair with Senhouse,
but said that Michael wasn't physically homosexual. 'He had emotional relationships with a great many people.'

There was nothing unusual or particularly homosexual in this.
It was quite normal for two men at Oxford at this time to enjoy a
casual, free-and-easy friendship that was intimate intellectually,
spiritually and emotionally, yet singularly pure by nature.

Nico said of his brother that he had 'a number of friends who were
girls, rather than that he had a number of girlfriends'. He wondered

55   Andrew Birkin, *J. M. Barrie and the Lost Boys* (1979).

whether Michael's inability to get a girl, 'as a presumed more normal friend would have been doing in Oxford days', was the reason for his restlessness.

Boothby thought not. He himself made love to a woman for the first time at twenty-five. In those days at Oxford, it wasn't natural to have a girlfriend. 'Occasionally undergraduates would go up to London, have a woman and come back in "the fornicator", but the idea of having anything to do with any woman in Oxford – it wasn't on.' No change from Eton, then.

In July of 1919, the four young men went to France for a holiday together. They went to Tour Solidor, near St Malo in Brittany, and stayed at a pension. It was then that Boothby realised Michael was afraid of water.

In fact, that summer Michael went home and announced that he was going to learn to swim properly, because they had a punt the following term.

In Brittany Boothby watched Michael gamble for the first time. They played boule, a game similar to roulette. Michael won and 'was terribly excited. We had a marvellous month in France, drinking green chartreuse.'

From there they travelled to Paris for a peace procession, where Michael tried to trade on his relationship with Barrie for a suite for all of them at the Meurice. It didn't work out. Instead, they trawled the bistros, climbed into a tree in the Champs-Elysées and sat in it until the peace procession came by.

After it all broke up Boothby took Michael and Senhouse to stay with him in Scotland, where they drove all over the place in a Ford car.

Boothby had no idea that Michael was dissatisfied with Oxford, only that he felt pressured about what he should do with his life.

He described Michael as 'brilliant with his pen – painting people. What he would have done, God alone knows.'

Barrie was on his case, as usual. When Michael heard that Violet Bonham Carter had heard what a brilliant mind he had and that she wanted him to join the Liberal Party and go into politics at Oxford, he was furious – 'Who is this bloody Mrs Carter who thinks I'm clever and wants me to go into politics?' he bawled. The answer was that she was the daughter of Herbert Henry Asquith, Liberal Prime Minister up until 1916, and Barrie's secretary Lady Cynthia Asquith's sister-in-law.

Politics would never have been for Michael, for whom opposition of any kind was anathema. He also understood that the moment he defined a goal or ambition, he would be trapped in it. He wanted his freedom, not only from Barrie, but partly as a result of the pressure he was under, from the whole world of time and space – freedom simply to *be*.

When Boothby met Barrie, he saw at once, without Michael saying anything, precisely where his problems lay. 'It was an unhealthy relationship. He was an unhealthy little man, Barrie, you know? I mean in a mental sense.'

As Boothby saw it, Barrie pulled Michael down into his own black moods; also that he was the only one who could get Barrie out of them. 'It was morbid,' he said.

Boothby spoke of going to the apartment in Adelphi Terrace one day and being overwhelmed by the atmosphere. When they left, intending to drive to Oxford, Michael had been furious and slammed the door of the car as they got in. Boothby said what a relief it was to get away, and Michael agreed with him. But he never spoke to Boothby about getting away from Barrie. It was a complex relationship indeed: 'Sir Jazz-Band Barrie, he used to call him. He loved him. It was a great love. He was very grateful to Barrie. Barrie did do a tremendous amount for them all.'

Chapter Twenty-Eight

1919: Garsington

LESS SUCCESSFUL THAN his friendships with Boothby and the others was Michael's foray into the so-called Bloomsbury Group, members of which Michael had links with on both sides of his family, one might even say on all three sides.

The group formed around 1905 in conscious revolt against the repressively male ethos of Victorian society and its hypocrisies. It was time now for courage to live one's life in broad daylight with integrity and truth, a time to champion the freedom of the individual and denounce the unquestioned authority of institutions, particularly that of the Church. It was a time for free love, too, which the group exercised with particular commitment and imagination.

Although Barrie was to fall to the new post-war writers, led by D. H. Lawrence, Virginia Woolf, James Joyce, Ezra Pound and

T. S. Eliot, most of whom were part of the Bloomsbury Group, he might claim to have been in some ways quite modern. The war had diluted his child-like adoration of the heroic and shaken his views about pacifism, for example, and he had never been religious in the conventional sense.

But he was in one important way precisely what the group abhorred. He lived a double life, his public life was a model of morality, while, as with the Calvinists back home, it concealed what really consumed him. Barrie did not live his life in broad daylight; he was a master of illusion. As on stage, so in life, it was second nature to him to create an illusion around him, hence the scene in the flat with Neville Cardus. When Cynthia Asquith, daughter-in-law of the Prime Minister who led Britain into the war, became his secretary in 1918, he was, according to Mackail, who was writing his biography of Barrie under Cynthia's direction, 'completely successful for a long time at representing himself in several very false lights'. Then would come 'a burst of frankness and truth, and the observant secretary found another impression to discard'. It was impossible for Barrie to be straight with anyone. Quite a few of the group knew of Michael before he came upon them. First, they knew him as the grandson of du Maurier, a great friend of Leslie Stephen, whose children Vanessa Bell, Virginia Woolf, and Thoby Stephen were all Bloomsbury participants.

Again, Michael's uncles Crompton and Theodore Llewelyn Davies had both been Apostles at Cambridge – members of the secret society that originally spawned some of the most impressive members of Bloomsbury such as the philosopher G. E. Moore, the poet Rupert Brooke, the economist John Maynard Keynes, the political theorist and author Leonard Woolf, and the strange author and ideological anarchist Lytton Strachey.

Lady Ottoline Morrell also had connections with Michael's family. The Morrell house at 44 Bedford Square in Bloomsbury, London, gave the Group their name, but the Morrells' estate at Garsington, seven miles south-east of Oxford, was the base from which she extended her patronage to writers such as Aldous Huxley, Siegfried Sassoon and T. S. Eliot, and artists Dora Carrington and Gilbert Spencer.

Ottoline was the sister-in-law of the daughter of the local grande dame at Kirkby Lonsdale (Lady Bective). Margaret Llewelyn Davies knew her well, as did Crompton, who kept up his friendship with Ottoline to the end of his life. As a result, Michael's brother Peter recalled visiting Ottoline at Bedford Square, and the same connection ensured Michael of a welcome at Garsington Manor.

The third side of the family to have connections with the Bloomsbury Group turns out to have been Michael's adoptive side. For Barrie's ex-wife Mary Ansell had married the writer Gilbert Cannan (the man who cuckolded the author of *Peter Pan*), and he had become something of a catalyst in the development of the Bloomsbury Group.

In 1913, after reading his novel *Round the Corner*, Ottoline Morrell invited both Cannan and Mary to visit her at Bedford Square. 'The poor fellow,' she wrote afterwards, '[he] must have a dim time of it with his wife who's years older than him and very distressing.'

Through this association, Cannan became friendly with Lytton Strachey. Then, in 1914 and quite separately, he met and became closely involved with the writers D. H. Lawrence, Middleton Murry, Murry's wife Katherine Mansfield, and the artist Mark Gertler, who were living within a few miles of Cannan in the countryside around Cholesbury in Buckinghamshire. They took to having dinner together, and Cannan threw a celebrated Christmas party where Gertler and Katherine Mansfield enacted a play in which they were supposed to pretend to be in love and Gertler made it all rather too realistic.

During the war, Cannan was a pacifist and conscientious objector, and was involved in the National Council Against Conscription. He and his new friends shared a deepening hatred for the First World War and began to see it as their responsibility to make it a watershed between the old world and the new.

Lawrence was then writing *Women in Love* (completed in 1916, though no publisher could be found for it until 1920), which denounced the heroic values that he saw at the heart of Victorian imperialism and identified the same values within the collective unconscious of Germany – hence the war.

Cannan introduced Lawrence and Gertler to Ottoline Morrell. Gertler he knew especially well. Cannan's novel *Mendel* was based on his early life (Mendel being his Yiddish given name), and Gertler painted a picture of Cannan, 'Gilbert Cannan and His Mill', with reference to the mill at Cholesbury where he was living. The picture also shows the Cannans' two Newfoundland dogs, Sammy and Luath, the latter the inspiration for Nana of course, the Darling children's nurse in *Peter Pan*.

Mary Ansell, who was still seeing her ex-husband occasionally, brokered a meeting for Barrie with D. H. Lawrence. Barrie claimed not have liked the amount of sex in Lawrence's novels, but regarded *Sons and Lovers* (1913) as 'the best novel that he had read by any of the younger men', while Lawrence said that Barrie's autobiographical novels, *Sentimental Tommy* (1896) and *Tommy and Grizel* (1900), had had a profound effect upon him. There was a correspondence between the two men before the war, but the letters were lost, generally a sign of something of interest in the more secret aspects of Barrie's life.

They finally met in London in 1915 – the year that George Llewelyn Davies was killed and Barrie began to question the heroic values on which he, as boy and adult, had based many a personal friendship, the values which Lawrence, as I have said, was at that moment decrying in *Women in Love*.[56]

If that suggests some common ground, it appears that they did not, after all, get on. Certainly no further meetings took place, even though Lawrence became a friend of his secretary, Cynthia Asquith. In 1921, Lawrence wrote to Cynthia, telling her that he had arranged for her to receive a copy of *Women in Love*, and added in a postscript – 'Tell J. M. [Barrie] what I think of him.'

It is fair to assume that what Lawrence thought of Barrie had been influenced by what Mary Ansell, who 'knew where the bodies were buried', had told him. To meet the character Herr Loerke in *Women in Love* is to see what Lawrence made of Barrie –

> the little man with the boyish figure and the round, full, sensitive-looking head, and the quick full eyes, like a mouse's [who] held himself aloof … His body was slight and unformed, like a boy's, but his voice was mature, sardonic, its movement had the flexibility of essential energy, and of a mocking penetrating understanding.

Gudrun is spellbound by him, just as Sylvia had been, and the psychology of Loerke in the narrative does not disappoint in his kinship to Barrie, any more than the physiology does.

What all these connections meant was that Michael was not only welcome, but that he arrived at Garsington raising no small amount of interest. There is a picture of him, looking rather uneasy, with

56   Harry T. Moore, *The Priest of Love: A Life of D. H. Lawrence* (1980).

Dora Carrington (who lived with the bisexual Lytton Strachey) and
Julian Morrell (Ottoline's politician husband).

Usually Michael took Senhouse to Garsington Manor with him.
Senhouse was for some time after Michael's death Strachey's boyfriend, famously engaging in a sado-masochistic role-play of the
crucifixion of Christ, even to the point of making the cut with the
centurion Longinus's spear. Strachey of course was the one playing
Christ. Blasphemy gave him a rise. Afterwards, he wrote to Senhouse:

> My own dearest creature. Such a very extraordinary night! The physi-
> cal symptoms quite outweighed the mental and spiritual ones – partly
> because they persisted in my consciousness through an unsettled but
> none the less very satisfactory sleep. First there was the clearly defined
> pain of the cut (a ticklish business applying the lanoline – but your
> orders had to be carried out) and then the much vaguer after pangs
> of crucifixion – curious stiffnesses moving about over my arms and
> torso, very odd – and at the same time so warm and comfortable – the
> circulation, I must presume, fairly humming – and vitality bulking
> large … where it usually does – all through the night, so it seemed.
> But now these excitements have calmed down – the cut has quite
> healed up and only hurts when touched, and some faint numbnesses
> occasionally flit through my hands – voilà tout, just bringing to the
> memory some supreme highlights of sensation…

Strachey liked Michael very much, saying of him that he was 'the
only young man at either Oxford or Cambridge with real brains'
– hyperbole in anyone else's mouth, but he had wide experience
of young men at Oxford and Cambridge. Writing to Ottoline after
Michael's death: 'I am sure if he had lived he would have been one
of the remarkable people of his generation.'

Dora Carrington found him 'so lovable and rather a rare character', and Michael was perhaps a prime example of someone who
might make good use of the freedom-loving Bloomsbury group,
in order to break free from Barrie and be his own man. However,
Michael couldn't relax at Garsington. When the parties got going, he
became impassive. Carrington put it down to 'the gloom of finding
Barrie one's keeper for life'. Certainly, he was to a significant degree
what Barrie had made him. Artistic and intellectual by nature, but
so influenced by Barrie that, as his friend Sebastian Earl said of him,
he was 'quite a conservative member of the bourgeoisie – continua-
tion of the Victorian bourgeoisie into Edward VII's time'.

Given that Strachey drove a stake through the heart of Victorian
hypocrisy in his trail-blazing biography *Eminent Victorians* (1918),
and dismissed said Victorians in a letter to Virginia Woolf as 'a set
of mouthing bungling hypocrites', perhaps Michael was after all
better off back at college.

Chapter Twenty-Nine

1920: Romance

FIRST A ROMANTIC, second a Victorian, it wasn't clear that he was going to find his way in the turmoil of a revolution that was gathering not only in Bloomsbury – especially as an artist, which Michael now planned to be.

The Romantics, and beauty per se, were out. In the 1850s, when Michael's grandfather was studying to become an artist in the Swiss painter M. Gléyre's studio in Paris, nothing could have been further from the case, what with the Impressionists and soon the Pre-Raphaelites finding their way. But in 1900, the year Michael was born, Picasso had pitched up in Montmartre and with Georges Braques forged Cubism, their purpose to ditch Impressionism and make an abrupt break with the past: 'We were trying to move in a direction opposite to [it],' Picasso said.

That was the reason we abandoned colour, emotion, sensation, and everything that had been introduced into painting by the Impressionists, to search again for an architectonic basis in the composition, trying to make an order of it ... I hate the aesthetic game of the eye and the mind played by those connoisseurs, those mandarins who 'appreciate' beauty. What is beauty anyway? There's no such thing.[57]

However, one boy who pitched up at Christ Church in October 1919 was deeply sympathetic to Michael's natural Romantic bent.

Rupert Erroll Victor Buxton was born on 10 May 1900, just one month before Michael, the youngest of seven children – one sister and five brothers – of Sir Thomas Fowell Victor Buxton, the 4th Baronet Buxton, who had died in the year Rupert arrived at Oxford.

The family was at that stage wealthy. Rupert's grandfather, 3rd Baronet Sir Thomas Fowell (1837–1915), Governor of South Australia, had bought Warlies, a country house near Waltham Abbey in Essex, and built another house close by at Woodredon.

Before he arrived at Oxford, Rupert was for six months at Cambridge University. No record remains as to why the transfer took place. He had been Head Boy at Harrow School in north-west London, and before that attended Summer Fields prep school in Oxford.

He was an unusual and enlightened boy who had been writing poetry since he was eight. He was also musical. He had belonged to the Choral Society at school and written with verve to his mother about such as Chopin's *Études*, Mendelssohn's 'Messiah' and the German composer of opera, Christoph Willibald Gluck.

He arrived at Oxford with the highest references. His headmaster wrote:

---

57   Françoise Gilot, *Life with Picasso* (1964).

He was one of the best boy-examples and boy-influences I have ever
known at school: the protector of the young, the friend of all, even
those with whose opinions he was least akin. His own opinions were,
and I expect still are unsettled – but they were all built on the foundation of love and service to others.

His housemaster Archer Vassall concurred – Buxton was 'a charming boy of the highest ideals, taking a great interest in philanthropic
and social work, and a "minor poet" of some competence'.

Buxton's consideration for others had extended at school to never
using his privilege as Harrow Head Boy of beating other boys. This
was unheard of in any English public school at the time. His social
conscience also led him to make friends with people outside his own
class, 'strange, out-of-the-way people such as pavement artists and
street hawkers', as one Harrovian put it, and to go into London for
days at a time on philanthropic quests.

Rupert's letters to his family, particularly to his mother Anne,
Lady Buxton (née O'Rorke), whom he addresses at first as 'My
dearest Mother', then 'My own darling mother', are deeply loving.
It is through his letters to Anne that we can draw a detailed portrait of Rupert.

He hadn't liked the idea of going to Harrow and it isn't clear
why it was chosen for him, as at least two of his brothers went
to Eton. One of them, Maurice, a year and a half older, Michael
certainly will have known. After taking the scholarship exam at
fourteen, Rupert wrote to his mother, 'I'm not sure that I'm frightfully impressed with Harrow, although I suppose I shall get to like
it.' However, by December he wrote to his brother Roden, 'I am
enjoying myself like anything at Harrow and am awfully glad I
went there after all.'

Like Michael, he loved Scotland and fishing. On 3 July 1915, he wrote to his mother envious of her going to Scotland to see Roden, who was based there. Mother and son embarked on a fishing expedition together – 'I can imagine how glorious the scenes must have been up there, as I think Scotland is easily the prettiest and most magnificent country I have ever seen.'

Being a boarder at Harrow, any opportunity to see his mother had been a great bonus, but frequently she seems to accept his invitations to attend concerts and the like. He took to sending his poems to his grandmother – Mrs O'Rorke of St Mark's Square, Regent's Park, asking for criticism. But by 14 November 1915 (aged fifteen), he was sending his mother three books of his poetry –

I should like you to keep [these], they were mostly written when I was in bed. I have been reading a good deal of Shelley while in bed ... he has written some marvellous things ... I have been made a member of the Literary Society – whatever that is! I believe you write a paper on a given subject and at the next meeting read it out, when it is discussed ... that will be certain agony!

The boy was intensely affected by Nature's beauty. On 20 February 1916, he wrote:

I woke up this morning to see the most lovely sunrise – I wonder whether you saw it? The whole of the Eastern sky was one great block of crimson – no fur clouds – but just this flawless sheen! And the dew was heavenly. Next holidays we must have some nocturnal expeditions – do you remember that blissful morning last Easter, when we all went – that is to say, all at home – to the badgers' holes? How we saw lots of cubs, badgers, foxes, but far best – a perfect forest sunrise

– as though veils of boiling gold were thrown over the trees – it was gorgeous! You must come down here (Harrow) as soon as you can – if possible on a fine day…

Your Devoted son Rupert.

His mother wasn't able to visit, owing to a bad cold. She sent Aunt Lulu instead.

On 12 March, Rupert wrote again:

My darling Mother, We had a most gorgeous concert last night – Plunket Green, Louise Dale, Ida Kiddus and the Russian singer Boris Lansky. It was absolutely glorious! Plunket Green of course was perfectly marvellous, but I think I liked the Russian the best. He sang in Russian, which is a lovely language to hear. And we had Maud Valerie White accompanying her own songs.

The boy was of course also interested in politics and like everything else he was interested in, he wanted to share it with his mother: 'I'm sending you Wells' book. I should advise you to read the chapter called "The Labour Market". I think it's awfully good. Yes, you must come down for the concert.'

But again – 19 March 1916 – Anne disappoints him; she is in bed with flu. Rupert, a Signaller in the school army corps, then turns to a subject that was particularly exercising his young mind:

I wonder what you think about conscientious objectors to the war? I think theirs is the most appalling position that any one could be put into … and as for the childish fury of those brave English people who brand them as cowards – well – it's merely mad!

… (At Harrow) there was a young temporary master who was both medically unfit for the war and a conscientious objector: he had the moral courage (which was, it is true, unnecessary) to say out, what he thought about it – and the school in body, with that particularly babyish inconsistency which forgets the facts and remembers only impressions, branded him a coward, refused to be taught by him, wrote a petition to the headmaster (which was received!) that he should be sacked, with the result that he was sacked! … This is Harrow's latest achievement and in spite of my being an Harrovian, I think it perfectly loathsome. Please don't tell anyone about it.

On 26 March 1916:

I am awfully glad you are better again. Today is an absolutely perfect day. I woke up this morning to a sudden freshness in the bluest of skies and softness of early morning [air]. At last Spring is here in earnest. I went round my form-master's garden this morning; he is a very enthusiastic gardener; and the daffodils were perfectly gorgeous! And the anemones, croci … were all looking their best in the glow of a real Spring morning; he had some lovely little irises out – tiny little purple flecks, with splendid gold centres. I do love a garden.

At Oxford, Rupert lodged in the Christ Church Deanery with a family friend later to become the Bishop of Ripon. In due course he would take rooms in college at Peck 6:8, across the quad from Michael. He passed his First Public Examination in Holy Scripture in Hilary term 1920. He then passed the preliminary examination of Second Public Examination in Modern History in Trinity term the same year.

At some point in the spring of 1920 Michael and Rupert, described as 6 ft 2 in. tall, athletic and 'of gigantic physical strength',[58] met. Before the beginning of Trinity term, they took themselves off for a reading holiday in preparation for their exams. On 4 April, Buxton wrote to his mother:

> I had a most successful time in Surrey with Michael Davis [sic]. I am sorry to say that I did not get through a great deal of work as the county was so lovely, and there was such a lot to do. Our last few days were the best – actually the last two. We took an expedition walking from the neighbourhood of Chichester to Beachy Head, the whole length of the South Downs … We did thirty-five miles a day, I have never known such a walk for views – south bound over the hills to the sea and naturally over the whole expanse of Sussex and Surrey on a narrow grassy plain with steep sides covered with primroses, violets, cowslips and anemones. A most inspiring place to walk and I can well understand the enthusiasm of Belloc and Kipling for the 'Great hills of the South County' and the patriotism that they breed.

Then, the following month – tragic news. Oxford undergraduate Alastair Grahame, the only child of Kenneth Grahame, author of *The Wind in the Willows*, committed suicide by lying across the railway line that runs down the east side of Port Meadow, an ancient grazing ground between the Thames (known as the Isis in Oxford) and the railway, to the north-west of the city.

There was already a literary association with the river here. In 1862 a lecturer in Mathematics at Christ Church, the Reverend Charles Dodgson (Lewis Carroll), and the Reverend Robinson Duckworth rowed up it with three young girls — Lorina, Alice, and Edith Liddell.

---

58   Nicholas McAulay.

Alastair Grahame's story is a wretched one. He, like Michael, had been born in 1900 and attended Eton before Christ Church, though this had not been his first public school.

The Wind in the Willows (1908) had not been made from the spark his father had got from Alastair in quite the same way as *Peter Pan* had been inspired by the Davies boys, but Grahame had given his son to believe that the character of Toad was based upon him. Like *Peter Pan*, it became a children's classic (both in book form and as a play written by A. A. Milne) at a time when the cult of the child was identified with all that was glorious about Edwardian England.

The attention it brought Alastair was especially unwanted, partly because he was born blind in one eye and with a squint in the other. To compensate, but in the process adding to his discomfort, his parents were determined to show that he was genius material. They exaggerated his gifts and pushed him hard in ways that didn't suit him, so that he developed a frustrated, angry temperament when he didn't measure up.

So unruly did Alastair become that when as a child he walked in Kensington Gardens – at the same time as Michael and Nico played there – complaints were received about his slapping and kicking other children. Only his father's bedtime stories about Mole, Ratty and Toad could calm him.

Antipathetic, squinting, half-blind and easy meat for bullies, he lasted at his first public school, Rugby, one term only. When Eton took him he had an emotional breakdown and in 1916 left. Afterwards, somehow, he was found a place at Oxford, where he was still referred to as Toad: 'Of course I was not surprised at the news,' wrote a friend after Alastair passed Mods, 'for we were both determined that nothing else should happen, were it only for the Toad's sake.'[59]

---

59   Jackie Wullschläger, *Inventing Wonderland* (1995).

Whereupon he had lain down on the tracks and a train had run over him.

The coroner's report stated that Alastair had lain down on the tracks and waited for the train; it had not knocked him down. But they recorded a verdict of accidental death anyway. Student suicide was not something any college wanted to acknowledge, and in those days, the establishment got what it wanted.

His death will have touched Michael more than some; because Alastair's close friend and confidant leading up to his suicide had been Rupert.

The man with the film star looks – Rupert did seriously consider becoming a film actor – had befriended the temperamental, seriously reserved, physically damaged boy. They were not mere acquaintances. Rupert had taken him on, taken him home to Woodredon, let him play the organ at Warlies (which Alastair greatly enjoyed). Then, one month after Rupert and Michael returned from their working holiday in Dorset, Alastair had committed suicide.

Bob Boothby told Michael that he had made a mistake about Rupert Buxton and thought he should ditch him. He said he recognised a 'dark force' in Rupert, and in an interview with Andrew Birkin sixty years later referred to him as saturnine, gloomy, sinister and very possessive. But, even in the light of Alastair's death, many assumed that Boothby was just jealous.

Chapter Thirty

1920: Michael Breaks Out

THE FIRST SUGGESTION of an unbalanced state of mind was evident very publicly on 4 December 1918, in Rupert's last year at Harrow, when he found his way into the pages of *The Times* in a most mysterious set of circumstances. A letter, unsigned and unstamped, had apparently been left for him at his house at the school. It read, 'You will be well advised to walk up Peterborough Hill alone at 10 minutes past 7 on Sunday night. Your help is needed.'

Peterborough Hill lay only a few yards from Rupert's house at the school. He sent a note to his housemaster, Archer Vassall, enclosing the letter and informing him that he was keeping the appointment. He had then mysteriously disappeared. Vassall and another master had watched the road for some time, but nothing was seen of the boy. The police were called in after he failed to appear on the last train from London.

The following day, a Monday, another letter, in the same hand as the first, was, according to *The Times*, received at Rupert's home, 'stating that he was safe, but that his brains were needed. The letter concluded – "Ill if he refuses, well if he agrees."'

The next anyone heard was apparently from Buxton himself. A telegram from Newcastle, signed 'Rupert' was received by his school and by his father stating that he would shortly be returning to London.

Extraordinary, one might think, that a national newspaper would be interested in carrying such a story. Being *The Times*, one might be tempted to conclude that Rupert's aristocratic and public school background was the reason for the interest of a newspaper which then appealed to the upper classes. But in fact *The Times* report followed an article the previous day (3 December) in the *Daily Mail*, which made the point that Rupert's disappearance was 'engaging the attention of New Scotland Yard officials and the police throughout the county'. The article also made some interesting points about the letter and about Rupert that *The Times* omitted.

In the *Mail*, the Headmaster admitted that he hadn't actually seen the letter. Only a few of Rupert's friends had seen it: '[Rupert] showed the letter to one or two other boys who ... advised him not to take any notice of it.' So, Rupert had taken the letter with him and it was never produced for Scotland Yard to investigate who might have sent it.

On 9 January 1919, a second, shorter article appeared in *The Times* newspaper, following a statement about his earlier disappearance made by Buxton's father, who had eventually found Rupert at King's Cross Station 'in a fainting condition'. According to *The*

Times, Rupert 'had, in the doctor's opinion, been suffering from overstrain resulting in some measure from preparing for a scholarship examination at Oxford ... He is already much better and it is confidently expected that a short period of rest will completely restore his health.'

In a case, without any solution or explanation in the offing, the *Mail* saw fit to mention a childhood accident that might explain it. Rupert 'was seriously injured cycling near Walton Abbey in August 1912, the shaft of a dogcart with which he collided penetrating his forehead...'

Buxton did not return to Harrow after the episode. 'Since then he has been having a "rest" with his elder brother,' wrote his house-master to the Provost, the senior academic administrator at his Cambridge college. 'He is quite recovered and there is no reason to anticipate a recurrence. The episode above appeared to have been entirely a medical question and does not in any way reflect on his character.'

The headmaster's letter to the Provost admitted that the episode was 'still unexplained ... I think myself that there was something histrionic and self-conscious about that strange episode at the end – but he was overwrought at the time, and not his normal self.'

The provost then wrote to Charles W. Cassington at Harrow, pre-sumably a master, but one who unfortunately had only just returned to the school and wrote back that 'I am afraid I can't tell you much,' except that 'all his story about the escapade was an illusion with no truth in it ... His family are rather cranks, as you know...'

This rather unkind, blanket dismissal of the Buxtons was probably levelled at their religious convictions. The family was not simply reli-gious, they were evangelical. Rupert's grandfather built St Thomas's Church, at Upshire, close to the family's two homes, as the focal point of their evangelical mission – prayer meetings, bible society, Band of Hope, etc – and he himself appointed a chaplain to run it.

'The keystone of Victor Buxton's life,' read Sir Victor's obituary in the *Essex County Chronicle*, 'was his entire dependence on God. He believed firmly and joyfully in the personal guidance of Christ.'

Rupert's mother Anne was the daughter of the Rector of Feltwell, near Thetford in Norfolk. Catherine Marsh, the evangelical writer and propagator of the Gospel among working people, was a close family friend. One of Rupert's early poems was entitled 'In Memoriam Catherine Marsh'.

Between 1915 and 1919, the family, like many others during the war, suffered a number of bereavements and it was in the context of death that Rupert's beliefs found form, just as it had been for Barrie.

In 1915, Rupert's grandfather Sir Thomas Fowell Buxton died and the following year his brother Jocelyn was wounded during the Battle of the Somme and went missing, strangely, only after he'd been rescued and delivered to the front-line hospital service station.

Rupert was just sixteen when he wrote:

My own darling Mother. This must be a very trying time for you and darling Father. You have always been so gentle and comforting to us all in our troubles; I wish I could return that sympathy.

I was sitting out in the garden when your letters came: all the wonderful peace of God's love was on the flowers. Do you know, I always like to think that He loves the flowers just as much as us – in fact we are all His garden flowers! Well, He seemed to whisper down through the evening scents of roses and carnations, that He would take care of our precious flower Jocelyn … Just as, when we pick a rose it soon fades; so when the life is picked from one of His Roses, it droops and dies – to revive in the great cool calm depths of Heaven's garden.

And the wonderful flower is revived by His gentle hands, and, the Night of Rest freshens its beauty for Tomorrow's Life.

I am glad you like the 'Dewdrop', though there is no depth to it: it was only a pretty sketch. Yes, I wrote a poem last night which I think is my best. But I will not send it to you as it is one that ought to be said – at least I think so; because it is the most serious I have written.

… May God's great gentle eyes look down and watch over our darling Jocelyn, as they watch over us; and may he give us all his Calm, and perhaps a little of His Wisdom for the trying days that are coming…

(Later)

My precious Mother,

I had not posted my Sunday letter to you when I got yours. My own dearest Mother, I know how awful it is to find another hope shattered: but, surely there is absolutely no reason to give up hoping as strongly as we did before.

Look at these statements:

From Captain Grey: 'Several men state that he [Jocelyn] was wounded in the shoulder, and that they saw Pte Ryecroft bring him into our trench'.

From a man in his section; 'This is to certify that I saw the above person (Rycroft) bringing in 2nd Lieut Buxton from the front of our barbed wire into the trench… (Pte. Gordon)'

Capt. Grey again: 'Several of his section informed me that he was brought into our trench from "No man's land" by his servant who was also wounded.'

Lieut. Norris: 'There is every reason to believe he was brought in safely as I was given to understand by one of our chaplains who knew him well, that he saw him arrive at the first dressing station…'

I do wish we were at home now, so as to be able to help somehow, but God will take care of him wherever he is, and if He has taken him, it is for his good…'

Later in July, Rupert learned of his grandmother Lady Victoria Buxton's death. On 27 July, he wrote that he was sorry to hear about 'darling Granny … but don't you think she would be better out of this emptiness of life, to go and join Grandfather Beyond. Perhaps this will be so.'

In November Rupert's brother Clarence was decorated with the Military Cross (for bravery) at Buckingham Palace. On 29 January 1917, Rupert wrote to his mother:

It is great news that I hear from your last two letters. How splendid that we shall all be together again – and how happy our dear Jocelyn [presumed dead] will be when he sees us all in church and sitting down to Sunday lunch; for he will be there too, and the circle will join hands with Heaven and those who will never die.

What a splendid fact it is – the Communion of Saints – the Communion of Souls. The continued taking part in all one's doings: the sharing of one's hopes, and the sharing of our disappointments. How glorious it is to think of him looking down to earth and joining in our prayers – which to us his soul 'beacons from the abode where the eternal are'.

This last is a quote from Shelley's 'Adonaïs: An Elegy on the Death of John Keats', in which the poet exhorts us not to mourn Keats, who is 'made one with Nature', where 'envy and calumny and hate and pain' cannot reach him. He is not dead; it is the living who are dead. His being has been withdrawn into the one Spirit, which is beauty.

Rupert echoed these ideas in a Sonnet, which begins:

> *Eternity! Man clutches at an hour,*
> *Feverish, to fill a quest of emptiness,*
> *While in him all thine ages, limitless*
> *Stretch through death's sunset in a mist of power.*
> *Why, in the tide-washed pool of mortal time*
> *Stays he to bathe, while God's infinity*
> *Lies all around him, and earth's vanity…*

Death, for Rupert, was the gateway to heaven, much to be desired: '…beyond Death's surf-washed crest Lies the blue ocean of a dreamless Rest!'

On 22 August, he wrote to his brother Clarence about their friends killed in the war: 'I think they are with us – actually taking part in our thoughts, moulding them, inspiring them, guiding them with the great love which they have found in Heaven.'

In a 24-stanza narrative poem, 'The Pilgrimage of Thala', Rupert told of a boy making his way gloriously into the presence of God by drowning:

> *XIX*
> *…he must either die upon the rock*
> *Or dive into this iridescent lake,*
> *And drown himself beneath its flowing rills.*
> *He chose the latter course, and throwing off*
> *His flask of wine and precious hunting knife,*
> *(He knew not why), he plunged into the pool*
> *To drown himself at once, and yet for aye.*

XX

But look what wondrous thing has come to pass!
Instead of suffocating beneath the wave,
He glided thro' the [slumbering] rills of green,
Down thro' the water, further, till he thought
He must be dashed against the bottom rocks.
But no! Thro' lovely flowers of blue and green
He glided, sinking more – and sinking yet!
Oblivion came, and after that he slept:
Yet onward thro' the limpid green he sank –
And died – yet lived in spirit one more day
Till two great scenes could shew him all this life,
And what it comes to in the sight of God.

Buxton found the image so deeply affecting that he illustrated these stanzas with a photograph of a real pool cut from a magazine.

It was but a short step from believing wholeheartedly in the glory beyond oblivion to welcoming it with open arms. By 30 September 1917, he was of the opinion that 'it was a terrible existence we are in'.

From the Monitors Room, Harrow he wrote to his mother:

> We have had very good views of the raids from here. Last night was a wondrous scene. There was a big silver moon and the sky was of that strange pale gold colour which seems to remind me of the Past. Great banks of saffron rested on the horizon.
>
> And there, amongst all this beauty; the scintillating, sinister beauty of soaring star-shells and crackling shrapnel; the blue green flashes of guns on the ground, and the darting, dashing lights of our air squadrons.
>
> It is a terrible existence we are in, Mother.

There is something so dreamlike about it, so like a nightmare from which we will awaken. But no, not now.

One staggers under the accumulated weight of sorrow which afflicts this sad sweet earth of ours.

Then, in May 1919, his father, who couldn't drive, bought a car and tried it out on the Warlies estate with one of his employees, who couldn't drive either. Somehow, Sir Victor fell out of the car onto the road and was run over by it. So serious were his injuries that he had to have a leg amputated. Gangrene set in and he died.

The family was then crippled by a tax bill and were forced to sell Warlies to Dr Barnardo's.

By the time Rupert arrived in Oxford he was understandably in quite a distressed state. His landlord at the Christ Church Deanery commented on this in a letter to Lady Buxton:

> I wish I had helped him more when he was with me. But I have always had a horror of forcing any man's confidence and though I think that this is an error on the right side, I have always felt that I have missed many opportunities. It haunts me rather, that he was often depressed and unhappy when he was with me, and I never succeeded in doing anything for him.

But then Rupert had met Michael and the depression had lifted. Rupert's thoughts about death were the thoughts of the Romantic poets he loved. Michael read Keats and Shelley as deeply as did his new friend. He empathised with glorious Shelley in particular, the poet touched by the maddening hand of the supernatural who searches restlessly for reconciliation with his lost vision of a world free of decay and change, through ultimate union with Nature.

None of this was strange to Michael. The only difference now was that together both young men's spirits soared to new heights by sharing the knowledge and looking at the vain world outside, and laughing.

There was very soon an intimacy between them that was near to love. Their talk brought them into a deadly nearness of contact. Reginald Colquhoun wrote that they were 'inseparable ... a peerless couple, and everyone who knew either of them loved them'. They burned with each other inwardly and in public now they could be 'arrogant and egotistical,' as another friend wrote after their death.[60] They

> did not go out of their way to please others, and they were by no means exceptionally useful members of Society in a material sense; but whoever came into contact with them recognised that they had in more than normal abundance the gift of personality. There glowed in them with unusual warmth a Promethean fire more valuable than words can describe. Either of them might have become an immortal genius or a martyr.

In April 1920, Michael had honoured an arrangement to visit the Welsh Lewises without Barrie, who was attending to the opening of *Mary Rose*. He and Nico went together and were back in time to see the play. As for Glan Hafren, well, suddenly it seemed an epoch distant from the world he shared with Rupert, as Michael indicated to Nanny Hodgson in a letter written from Wales on 18 April:

> Dear Mary,
>
> We return from this our native land tomorrow, so you may glimpse me before Oxford claims me on the Friday. The weather has not

---

60   Their obituary in *The Harrovian*.

been brilliant, but we've got along all right, Nico naturally I with an adjusted hypocrisy [OOOOH]. They must think yr humble servant a bit conceited, as many others do, but they're so outrageously Victorian at times, with all their charm, so utterly a family out of a book, that it's hard not to let an occasional gasp of remonstrance escape you.

On Wednesday I shall pursue my arrogant way to Ipswich, to see about buying a 60H[orse] P[owered] motor-car, of Italian origin, which should be very fine except that it is seven years old...

Au revoir,
Michael

Michael then wrote an apologetic thank-you letter to Eveline.

Dear Mrs Lewis,

Back again at Oxford, and it's looking lovely.

You know *Mary Rose* was a great success, and is likely to run well. I hope to see it again, and you must certainly go to it, and take Glan Hafren with you.

Nico and I have no complaints to make on our stay – we loved it thoroughly. I was angry to see I wasn't behaving very well occasionally. Nineteen is a tremendous age you know, and one at which self-satisfaction will out. I'll be more tolerable at thirty, p'raps a bit more at the 1923 Eisteddford. Very many thanks to you and Mr Lewis, & love to all –

Yrs Michael

Michael hadn't known how to love Eiluned. He had been looking not to love but for someone to love him. Rupert and he were like Narcissus, transfixed by the reflections of 'their own wan light' in each other's eyes. Each gave the other a reason to love himself. They could be arrogant and egotistical and cock a snook at earth's vanity, secure in the knowledge that 'God's infinity lay all around them'.

Inevitably the affair had a negative effect on their work: 'I am afraid I have not been at all comfortable in the [exam] papers,' wrote Rupert to his grandmother, 'and seriously consider it doubtful if I have passed. One must face the situation – still it is not very important, I find, to pass this time.'

However, the new self-confidence that their love gave Michael set his mind free to make his own choices. Busily he set about hatching a plan to leave Oxford and register with the Sorbonne in Paris to study art, and in July gave his notice to the University authorities.

Michael was drawing away from Barrie, but Barrie wasn't going to give up without a fight. To please him Barrie made great, even desperate and finally unsuccessful efforts to finish the murder mystery, *Shall We Join the Ladies?*, over which Michael had enthused. Also to please Michael he had discarded his idea for a novella entitled *Mrs Lapraik*, about an actress who is taken over by the character she has created on stage.

But Michael couldn't have been less interested. As Mackail observed: '[Michael] was conscious of an oppression in all his guardian's care and love.' Barrie became increasingly desperate and out of the blue bought Michael a cottage in Sussex, with the idea that he could be there with his friends. Again, Michael wasn't interested, and it cost Barrie a lot of money to get the cottage off his hands.

The solution, he felt, would be a holiday in Scotland, one to remember. He rented an entire island.

Chapter Thirty-One

1920: Between Earth and Paradise

EILEAN SHONA IN tidal Loch Moidart is situated on the west coast of Argyle, not far south of the Isle of Skye. 'A wild rocky romantic island it is too', Barrie wrote enthusiastically to Cynthia Asquith on 13 August 1920:

> It almost taketh the breath away to find so perfectly appointed a retreat on these wild shores ... Superb as is the scene from the door, Michael, who has already been to the top of things, says it's nought to what is revealed there – all the western isles of Scotland lying at our feet. A good spying-ground for discovering what really became of Mary Rose.

Shona is remote, exquisitely beautiful, located somewhere 'between Earth and Paradise' according to the writer and naturalist Mike Tomkies, who knew the island intimately half a century later and wrote a book about surviving on it living rough in the lap of Nature.

Being Scotland there is of course also history on its doorstep. A ruined castle – Tioram – guards the south-eastern approach. Built to control access to Loch Moidart and Loch Shiel in the thirteenth century, Tioram played a significant role in the many feuds between the kings of Scotland and the lords of the Western Isles. It fell to ruin when its chief left to become embroiled in the 1715 Jacobite Rising and ordered it burned. No more fanciful folly could possibly have been arranged.

Barrie was the guest of Thomas Evelyn Scott-Ellis, 8th Baron Howard de Walden, a prominent patron of the arts who, along with others, including G. K. Chesterton, Barrie had invited to join a film shoot six years earlier in Hertfordshire, the film something to do with a Revue he was preparing. 'Cowboy suits had been provided from a beer-barrel,' Mackail tells us, and we may imagine Barrie at his playful best.

Nothing came of the film, but de Walden responded some years later with an invitation to bring Michael on a fishing holiday at his thirteenth-century home Chirk Castle, near Wrexham, on their way to visit Glan Hafren.

Lord Howard de Walden was a rich man. He had inherited 100-odd acres of central London, the Marylebone Estate between Oxford Street and Marylebone Road, from his great-grandmother, Lady Lucy Cavendish-Bentinck (same family as Ottoline Morrell) – along with 8,000 acres in Ayrshire, various African and North American holdings, and the island of Shona.

On 15 August, Barrie had written to the Countess of Lytton:

We came up here three or four days ago and have got settled down for a month. It is the wildest sort of an island – 10 miles round with only this house on it, which Lord Howard de Walden has lent us in a grand spirit of generosity. Nothing could be more beautiful – in the heart of the Prince Charlie country. You blow horns from miles away when you want anything – an engaging way of telephoning that would please Davina [daughter]. We have mountains and lochs and boats and tennis and billiards, and most of the Western islands of Scotland lying at our feet.

Lovely weather till today when it is coming down in blankets.

Barrie had arrived with Michael and Nico and a number of their friends – Roger Senhouse and a puppy included (but not Rupert Buxton) – after an overnight train journey from London on 11 August. They had left the train at Glenfinnan and embarked on a steamer which took them on an unforgettable trip through Loch Shiel, which Barrie described to Lady Cynthia Asquith as

> an inland loch as calm as the Serpentine and not much wider though there were a score or so of miles, and we had to stop now and again to get a bottle of milk from a rowing boat or give a sack of flour to another. All through the Pretender's country – we lunched where he raised his standard and round about here he hid in caves when his sun went so quickly down ... This is a lovely spot, almost painfully so.

From Loch Shiel they took a single-track road to Doilinn, where they were met by a motor boat, which conveyed them across Loch Moidart, past Tioram – 'an aged keep where the last of the clan Ronald said farewell to his last acre' – to the island itself.

Eilean Shona House – 'The Ritz could not do us better. Such bathrooms!' – is spacious and interesting, beautifully appointed, set within gardens just a short walk from the jetty at this side of the island – banks of rhododendrons and trees facing south across a pond in those days, and a tennis court.

'That tennis court,' wrote Barrie to Lady Cynthia,

> as to which you seem to have doubts is I assure you a good deal played on and I myself have not only performed on it but have been read-ing the Badminton book on how to become a dab at it. I am now a dab, except for (a) my service, (b) my difficulty in taking other peo-ple's services, (c) the net bars my finest efforts. If Michael is not playing (he is extraordinarily energetic up here) he is drawing such oil-portraits of me that if I believed they did me justice I would throw myself from our highest peak. I have an uncomfortable feeling that his portraits of other persons are rather like them.

By this time, Rupert had met Barrie. He – 'sublime in mauve waistcoat', as Barrie observed, 'but otherwise commendable' – had accompanied Michael to the Adelphi Terrace apartment before the annual Eton–Harrow match in July. He may have blotted his copybook a little as he and Michael went to a dance and Rupert took the key of Barrie's desk instead of the key to the door, so that Michael had to sit in the lift at the foot of the stairs from midnight until 3 a.m. awaiting his return – 'with claret and a loaf'. Well, that was their story anyway.

It had been in Rupert's mind for some time to get Barrie on his own, and though the date is uncertain he did take him to dinner, just the two of them, in London, which would have required more courage than any other of Michael's friends had. The dialogue at that dinner – if it could be heard above the silences – would have been extremely interesting.

Rupert would surely not have invited him out alone unless he wanted to say things, or get Barrie to say things, that he didn't want Michael to hear. Whether this had anything to do with the young man's absence from Shona, or whether Rupert's simultaneous trip down the Nile with his mother had already been arranged before Barrie took Shona, there is no record. But in Barrie's increasingly desperate attempts to bring Michael back on side, Rupert's absence will have suited him.

Roger Senhouse, by comparison, was easy to handle. By 7 September, Barrie was writing:

> We are a very Etonian household and there is endless shop talked, during which I am expected to be merely the ladler out of food. If I speak to the owner of the puppy he shudders but answers politely and then edges away. Our longest conversation will be when he goes:
>
> He (with dry lips but facing the situation in the bull-dog way): *Thank you very much for having me. Awfully good of you.*
>
> Me: *Nice to have you here.* (Exeunt in opposite directions).
>
> Do my letters seem aged? I certainly feel so here. I have a conviction that they secretly think it indecent of me to play tennis, which however I am only suffered to do as a rare treat. They run about and gather the balls for me and in their politeness almost offer to hold me up when it is my turn to serve. By the way, what an extraordinarily polite game tennis is. The chief word in it seems to be 'sorry' and admiration of each other's play crosses the net as frequently as the ball. I fancy this is all part of the 'something' you get at public schools and can't get anywhere else. I feel sure that when any English public school boy shot a Boche he called out 'Sorry'. If he was hit himself he cried, 'Oh, well shot.'

Increasingly, Barrie found himself alone.

> This island has changed from sun to rain, and we have now had about
> 60 hours of it so wet that you get soaked if you dart across the lawn.
> It's dry for a moment and anon I will be observed – or rather I won't
> be, for there is no one to observe me playing clock golf by my lonely
> self. I am mostly by my lonely self; and a little island is not the best
> place for strenuous exercise in wet weather, the roads – or rather the
> road – ending as soon as it sets off and the heather so wet and slippery
> that as you ascend you suddenly disappear from view. The others are
> out sea-fishing with Jock Oliver and Audrey Lucas who have arrived,
> and the party is merrier without me.

The fishing was good. Thanks to the confluence of rivers and the
sea, salmon, sea trout, pollock, mackerel and even cod are available – but the party had become infected by the stand-off between
Michael and Barrie; Michael's desire to get away, and Barrie's
response, which was always to try to please him and return to the
old ways.

It was not going to happen, and the young men especially were
torn between their loyalty to Michael and their wish not to hurt
their host. It was better that they stayed apart. But an island is not
the best place to accommodate so difficult a situation, for there is
no escaping it.

With *Mary Rose* playing to packed houses in London and due to
open in New York early in 1921, Barrie turned to new work:

> The publishers clamour for more plays and I have brought *Kiss for
> Cinderella* with me in the pious hope of preparing it for them. It seems
> trumpery work … I am not naturally an idler, it was always a glory

to me to be at work, but I can get hooked on to nothing that seems worth playing.

To make matters worse, his decision to pursue his art had found a highly personal way to get further under Barrie's skin. Michael had begun to draw sketches of him and 'he has the diabolic aptitude for finding my worst attributes, so bad that I indignantly deny them, then I furtively examine myself in the privacy of my chamber, and lo, there they are'.

Some of the other guests had been trying to get Barrie to walk more – 'Of course I ought to bound up the hills like Robinson Crusoe after goats, but though I do climb a bit it isn't a daily joy.' And when, on 26 August, he took

> a prodigious walk over mountains whose very names call for stout climbers – was cheered all the way by thoughts of modest boasting about it over the tea-cups; but all is vain – it is flouted by Michael as a thing of nought and a mere beginning of his excursions. I am chastened and reminded of a Swiss mount I left with the same pleasant sensation, to be told at the hotel that it was the local cleric's favourite morning stroll and that he had done it 250 times.

Michael was preparing for his independence at Shona and in Rupert's absence loved nothing better than scrambling alone to the top of the mountain which, rising directly out of the sea, is the island. The highest point is marked by a permanent trig point and cairn. There is no path to it, but the climb is not arduous. Once up there, in good weather, there is an astonishing view across the Western Isles, the nearest of them Muck, Eigg and Rùm.

Here Michael wrote his two surviving poems, for which he had no great regard, but which are nonetheless a statement. At least one more was written on Shona, but was lost.

'Eilean Shona'

Throned on a cliff, secure, Man saw the sun
hold a red torch above the farthest seas,
and the fierce island pinnacles put on
in his defence their sombre panoplies;
Foremost the white mists eddied, trailed and spun
like seekers, emulous to clasp his knees,
till all the Duty of the scene seemed one,
led by the secret whispers of the breeze.

The sun's torch suddenly flashed upon his face
and died; and he sat content in subject night
and dreamed of an old dead foe that had sought and found him;
a beast stirred boldly in his resting place;
and the cold came; Man rose to his master-height,
shivered, and turned away; but the mists were round him.

Nico recalled Michael showing him the poem –

And my saying words to the effect that I liked it but I hadn't a clue what it was all about! Which I remember rather disappointed him as he thought it was 'so simple'. I've never tried to think who was his 'old dead foe', just taken it to be imaginary.

The old dead foe is the 'the same nameless enemy', a Mephisthophelean spirit, that pursued Michael in his nightmares as a boy. The 'seekers' are

Barrie's 'little gods', also already met. Barrie was convinced that Michael was attended by a malignant devil. Speaking to an uncomprehending gathering of students at St Andrew's University in 1922, he said:

> One can see him serene, astride a Scotch cliff, singing to the sun the farewell thanks of a boy … If there is any of you here so rare that the seekers have taken an ill-will to him, as to the boy who wrote those lines, I ask you to be careful.

In the second poem the process of rejection has begun.

'Island of Sleep'

Island of sleep where wreathéd Time delays,
Haven of things remote, indulgent, free,
Thou whose enriching mists in autumn days
Veiled the intruder on thy secrecy;
He there beheld bright flowers in a dream
Join with tall trees to cheat the Cyprian,
And heard in murmurs of a woodland stream
Arcadian incantations of resurgent Pan;

Yet will not touch again thy perfumed shore
And mount the coloured slopes beneath the trees
Or there release his senses ever more
To tread the foot-prints of old deities,
So thou do not send echoes to remind
Of those sweet pipes, and charm him from his kind.

He is telling us of the opportunity that so remote and time-lost a place as Shona affords the poet to hear 'in murmurs of a woodland stream Arcadian incantations of resurgent Pan'. The word 'incantations' is fairly illegible in the handwritten original and has been variously guessed at, but the rest is clear.

Michael is reminding us that Barrie chose to name Peter Pan after the goat-foot god of Greek myth, who ran with Dionysus, the god of ecstasy, on the mountains of Arcadia. We are back on the dark side. 'Yet [Pan] will not touch again thy perfumed shore … to tread the foot-prints of old deities, So thou do not send echoes to remind of those sweet pipes, and charm him from his kind.'

I have already mentioned his cousin Daphne's poem 'Another World', where the 'loathly keepers of the netherland' have 'cloven feet' and there is a 'horn that echoes from the further hill, Discordant, shrill'. Michael is commanding that it has to end. He is saying goodbye to Barrie's boy-cult.

It was far from certain that Barrie was going to let him have his way.

Chapter Thirty-Two

1920–21:
Barrie Gets His Way

ON 9 SEPTEMBER, while still in Scotland, Michael wrote to his tutor, Robert Dundas, presumably in case it hadn't filtered through to him, that he had given notice to the University:

Dear Mr Dundas.

Your emotions will not, I know, be violently stirred, when I say I am not going up to Oxford again; surprise, pity, or wrath, can scarcely have survived the thrashing of last term.

I feel very much the young fool; but wish to be obstinate into the bargain, even if the first step I take for myself be into the deepest of deep ditches; it will at least be an experiment; and I am a little strengthened by Stevenson's Apology for my kind.

I shall always be sorry for not having taken Greats for Mods; and shall look out for the O's on judgement day.

Yours sincerely

Michael Ll. Davies

I do incidentally hope to quit education for some trade, so as to give Mr Stevenson's immorality some sort of standing.[61]

The comment at the end is probably facetious. We must surely believe that Michael was still (in his mind) bound for the Sorbonne to study art.

At any rate no good honest work found him, and suddenly he did change his mind, writing to Dundas from rooms in the heart of old Oxford across the road from Christ Church at No. 84 St Aldates, a building full of character on the corner of Pembroke Street.

84 St Aldates.

Friday.

Dear Dundas (according to suggestion not since withdrawn) I'm sorry to be a bother; but should I possibly be allowed to creep into the House again in October, into some obscure corner? Of course it is

---

61　The comment about taking up a trade refers to Robert Louis Stevenson's 'An Apology for Idlers' (1877), which Stevenson said was written with himself in mind. Only a year later he was able to write to his mother: 'It was well I wrote my "Idlers" when I did; for I am now the busiest gent in Christendom.'

unprecedented. I am not in the least deserving; but reasons faintly sincere, these: if I stay in lodgings I should like to go with someone else after 2 terms of my own company; it would be rather foolish to go with natural non-Greats friends, and Marjoriebanks and I are not, in confidence, very good cohabitants. I know I could work if it were permitted. Now is the time arrangements are made, and the element of doubt which you must have about the use of me at Greats makes such rather more difficult. I'm sorry if this is at once trivial and impossible.

I dislike always bringing up the whole question of my existence before you.

Would you come to lunch here on, say, Friday, if I ask Charlie B-H? This is not a persuasive, nor a lenient, measure.

Yours,
Michael Davies

Edward Marjoribanks was an Old Etonian friend of Michael, later to become a Conservative politician. A telegram followed the letter some days later:

R H Dundas, Senior Common Room Christ Church Oxford
Have become moral and ask leave to return to work but is this possible as have opened no book this vacation. Query Collections and Verdict. Meanwhile starting to read.

By then Michael's address was Barrie's apartment off the Strand. These erratic missives will have done little to give Dundas confidence, but he was allowed to return to Oxford. A relation of his, Andrew Sellon, with an interest in the family tree, described Dundas as 'a somewhat notorious Fellow, I believe he had the same rooms that Lewis Carroll once had'. Carroll, or Charles Dodgson, became a lecturer in Mathematics there in 1855, publishing *Alice's Adventures in Wonderland* in 1865.

It seems that Elizabeth Lucas had taken Michael aside and persuaded him at least to finish his degree before going to Paris. On 19 December, Barrie wrote to her:

> It was nice of you to have that talk with Michael and I have no doubt that for the time at least it had a steadying effect. All sorts of things do set him 'furiously to think' and they seem to burn out like a piece of paper. He is at present I think really working well at Oxford and has at any rate spasms of happiness out of it, but one never knows of the morrow. I think few have suffered from the loss of a mother as he has done.

Elizabeth Lucas was a warm friend to Michael, relieving him of the necessity of spending Christmas 1920 with Barrie by taking him to Paris.

Macnagthen wrote of this difficult period being turned around after he was allowed to return to Oxford: 'Henceforward there was no wavering; he worked loyally and found increasing satisfaction in his work; he was at Eton for a day at the end of March (1921), full of quiet happiness.'

Barrie said much the same of Michael, writing to Elizabeth,

> He is working hard and really enjoying his life at Oxford for the present at least. He has the oddest way of alternating between extraordinary reserve and surprising intimacy. No medium. In his room at Oxford lately he suddenly unburdened himself marvellously. One has to wait for those times, but they are worth while when they come.

The description is not a happy one on the face of it, suggestive of stress at the very least.

Returning to Oxford had meant of course that his relationship with Rupert would continue as before. No doubt the business with Dundas about Michael's lodgings in college was connected to his being closer to Rupert, as the gates of Christ Church closed at night.

On 13 February, Rupert wrote to his mother of new rooms in college. 'My rooms are much better than they were: but as yet there are no pictures! ... you must give advice on the question. Blue furniture and curtains and a red carpet are the dominant colours.'

The week before, he had written to his mother that 'the Norway project is rather vague still, I'm sorry to say. Michael may not be able to go, in which case it will have to be given up.'

Whatever the Norway project was, it was evidently planned for the Easter holidays – Easter Day fell on 27 March – when Barrie had already planned to take Michael and Nico elsewhere. Reading between the lines, this looks like a further opportunity for disagreement between Barrie and Michael. In the event, Rupert and Michael spent Easter in Corfe Castle in Dorset, staying at a little inn by the sea. Barrie joined them for a few days at the end of it.

The next we hear is that Michael travelled to Oxford from London on 9 May, Barrie's sixty-first birthday. Nico to Eton, too, which suggests that Michael had been down for Nico's half term. Then, on 17 May, Barrie writes to Michael: 'The Mill House sounds like a good place, and you had lovely weather for it.' We know no more than this, but it seems likely that Michael and Rupert have again been away together.

Two days later, Thursday 19 May, was a warm summer's day in Oxford, a day in Eights Week, the main University rowing event, a big festive occasion which takes place over four days.

Edward Marjoribanks saw Rupert that morning and Michael around midday. Michael said he was going to swim in Sandford pool that afternoon, and would not be able to watch the Eights. Buxton had not mentioned he was going out. The two young men left the city together shortly after two o'clock.

There was nothing unusual or foolhardy about swimming in Sandford Pool. Arthur Bryant, a friend and contemporary of Rupert at both Harrow and Oxford, wrote that the couple had been to Sandford together to swim several times before. While on the following day Thomas Ripon said, 'There are bathers there almost every day in the summer, and I believe that Rupert was a good swimmer.'

The couple walked there through Christ Church Meadow, a spacious and beautiful pasture belonging to the college and a popular place for walking and picnicking during the day, when its wrought iron gates are open to all.

Moving southwards through the meadow, which is bounded on its west side by the Thames and on the east by the Cherwell, the couple approached the place where cattle graze and the two rivers converge. Here, on an island, the many college boathouses will have been busy, as this upstream stretch of the river is where the Eights Week rowing events occur.

The path, altogether the most lovely river walk in Oxford, leads past eights and fours and sculls, past river boats and flocks of grazing geese, and continues on its way south under a road bridge and a railway bridge, over Hinksey Stream by means of a footbridge and a further bridge over the weir stream, where a narrow path leaves the main one for Sandford lasher.

Here the river thunders through the weir into a large still pool, perhaps 100 metres across, by means of a series of sluice gates between concrete piers, which support a railed pathway, which Rupert and Michael took across the river to the west bank on the other side.

It led them past a nineteenth-century obelisk, which in their day would have carried the names of only three Christ Church students who died here – Richard Phillimore and William Gaisford who drowned in 1843, and George Dasent in 1872.

For, 'the pool under Sandford lasher, just behind the lock, is a very good place to drown yourself in', as du Maurier's great friend Jerome K. Jerome had written in *Three Men in a Boat* (1889).

Today, owing to these deaths and people's interest in an additional and more recent two, the railed pathway is barred and the single lifebelt by the obelisk is unobtainable. But it is still possible to find a way onto the side of the lasher where Rupert and Michael went that day by walking past Sandford Lock and through a field leading to the west bank.

It is an idyllic spot, the pools, high and low, separated by the weir, are quite beautiful and tranquil in summer. Hither the boys came, 'either wildly gay or very serious' (as Barrie wrote to Rupert's mother afterwards), gazing over their gloomy grave, sensing the gentle motion of the leaves on the trees, the grass springing under their feet and the soft thunder of the lasher in the distance.

Later it was reported that one of the men swam over to the weir and sat on it basking in the sun. It would have been the poor swimmer Michael left alone on the bank, gazing at the pool where two universes met.

Did he turn to Shelley, dreaming that he could somehow lose himself in the otherworld of the pool, wet and remote – 'What am I that I should linger here? – Vision and Love – Sleep and death Shall not divide us long'? Or, as he watched the muscular Rupert drop his clothes beside him and swim strongly out towards the weir, did Michael not know that death was on him?

> *When on the threshold of the green recess*
> *The wanderer's footsteps fell, he knew that death*
> *Was on him. Yet a little, ere it fled,*
> *Did he resign his high and holy soul*
> *To images of the majestic past,*
> *That paused within his passive being now,*
> *Like winds that bear sweet music, when they breathe*
> *Through some dim latticed chamber. He did place*
> *His pale lean hand upon the rugged trunk*
> *Of the old pine; upon an ivied stone*
> *Reclined his languid head; his limbs did rest,*
> *Diffused and motionless, on the smooth brink*
> *Of that obscurest chasm;— and thus he lay,*
> *Surrendering to their final impulses*
> *The hovering powers of life. Hope and Despair,*
> *The torturers, slept; no mortal pain or fear*
> *Marred his repose; the influxes of sense*
> *And his own being, unalloyed by pain,*
> *Yet feebler and more feeble, calmly fed*
> *The stream of thought, till he lay breathing there*
> *At peace, and faintly smiling...*[62]

---

62   From Shelley's poem, which foretold his own drowning, 'Alastor'.

Chapter Thirty-Three

1921: Disposal

THERE WERE TWO eye-witnesses to the drowning, Charles Henry Beecham, engineer's assistant at the nearby Sandford Paper Mills and his assistant Matthew Gaskell, both of whom testified that the pool was 'as still as a mill-pond'.

They gave their evidence on Saturday 21 May to a Coroner's Inquest, which was conducted by F. E. Marshall, described as 'one of the University's coroners', at the Settling Room, Gloucester Green, in the city.

Beecham said that when he went up to the weir with Gaskell to regulate the water which fed the paper mill, he was standing on the Oxford side [the east side].

Marshall: Did you hear a shout?

Beecham: Yes, I heard a shout. I looked in the direction and saw two men bathing in the pool in difficulties.

Marshall: Did they appear to be struggling – or what were they doing?

Beecham: I only just saw their heads above water.

Marshall: What did you do?

Beecham: I immediately ran across the bridge to get the lifebelt, and Gaskell followed. Gaskell held the line while I threw the belt, but the men had already disappeared.

Marshall: What did you do then?

Beecham: I left Gaskell at the weir and ran to Radley College boathouse for assistance. Some of the Radley students were bathing, but some of them came back with me and others brought a boat.

Marshall: How far is the boathouse from the pool?

Beecham: It would take about ten minutes to bring a boat from there to the pool. I ran to the weir but saw no sign of the deceased.

Marshall: Then what did you do?

Beecham: I pointed out to one of the Radley students where the men went down. We returned to the mill about a quarter of an hour afterwards. The accident had already been reported to the police in Oxford by telephone. I can swim very little. The pool I believe at the spot is between twenty and thirty feet deep. There are at present no weeds likely to cause danger and the water is unusually low at this time of year, and is still. I should say there is no backwash.

Marshall: Was there any sign of either of the men clinging to the other?

Beecham: I could not see that.

Gaskell was then called and corroborated the evidence of Beecham. Asked if he would like to add anything, he said: 'I think not.'

Answering a question from the Dean of Christ Church, the Very Reverend Dr H. J. Wright, he said that it had taken less than a minute from the time he heard the shout to get the lifebelt. Gaskell was then asked whether he could say whether the men were clinging to each other as though one was trying to help the other.

> Gaskell: Their heads were close together.
> Juror: You could not see anything else?
> Gaskell: They appeared as though they were just standing in the water with their heads above the surface.
> Another juror: Was there anything to suggest that one was supporting the other?
> Gaskell: I could not say. It was a very quick affair.

Thomas Frederick Carter, of 34 Nelson Street, Oxford, employed by the Thames Conservancy, then said he was in the depot at Osney, when, just before five o'clock, he received a call to go to Sandford Pool. The superintendent sent him to commence dragging in the pool for two undergraduates who had been reported drowned. When he got to the pool, dragging operations were commenced. With two other assistants, operations were continued, and up to dark neither of the bodies had been recovered. At seven o'clock the next morning dragging was recommenced. One body was recovered shortly after two o'clock about thirty yards from the weir, in about twenty feet of water.

> Carter: As I was hauling the body up I noticed something drop off when within about 8 ft. from the surface. At first I thought it was a limb of a tree, but have now come to the conclusion that it must have been one body dropping from the other.

One body was taken to the hotel while they dragged for the other, which was recovered an hour later.

> Marshall: Where?
>
> Carter: At the same spot I found the first.
>
> Marshall: Which body was first recovered?
>
> Carter: I do not know the gentleman's name, but he would be about 6 ft. 2 in. [Rupert Buxton].
>
> Juror: Did you form the impression that the bodies were clasped?
>
> Carter: Yes, that was my impression.
>
> Juror: And you thought they became separated when you were drawing them up?
>
> Carter: Yes.
>
> Dean: I suppose as you were pulling them up the weight suddenly became lighter?
>
> Carter: Yes.

Summing up for the jury, the Dean said,

> The deceased were seen bathing in Sandford Pool, and one of them swam to the weir and sat on one of the stones, and in a few minutes his friend proceeded to swim across to him. When he got half way across he appeared to be in difficulties and his friend at once dived off the stone on which he was sitting [and went] to his friend's assistance. He reached him but apparently he no sooner got to him than they both disappeared and were not seen alive again. In the ordinary way there was a great deal of water tumbling over the weir, which caused a suction towards the weir, and there were certain eddies which, unless a man was a strong swimmer were very dangerous, but the water just now was low.

The view of the jury was that Michael had accidentally drowned while bathing, and that Rupert lost his life trying to rescue him. As the Dean gave the jury's verdict, he was reported to have been overcome with emotion and burst into tears.

After the same verdict was reached in the case of Alastair Grahame a year earlier, this should come as no surprise. Oxford, and Christ Church in particular, did not want these deaths to look like suicide.

It was never likely that there would be a verdict of suicide for a number of reasons, not least that the court could not claim to be unprejudiced.

The coroner was connected to the University. The coroner for the Oxfordshire area at this time was one Harold Galpin. Mr Marshall was described as a 'University coroner'. It is not clear whether the University had sufficiently frequent cases of accident and suicide actually to run its own coroner's office, or whether Marshall had been drafted in from outside. Either way, Marshall was in the employ of the University.

The Foreman of the Jury was the Dean of Christ Church College, and according to a nephew of Barrington-Ward, who knew all of them, of the six other jurors four at least were dons at Christ Church – J. G. Barrington-Ward, the Reverend A. E. Rawlinson, J. C. Masterman and Theo Chaundy.

Further, there are clear discrepancies between the evidence of the witnesses and what the Dean, as Foreman of the Jury, said in his summing up about one of the deceased (Michael) getting into difficulties. On the day in question as both witnesses – Beecham and Gaskell – gave evidence, the water was calm and still, and Gaskell said that the water was low, free of reeds, and there was no backwash. Moreover, the Coroner pointed out that there could have been no suction towards the weir at the time, neither were there any eddies.

Beecham could not report any struggling to substantiate his statement that they two men were in difficulties. On the contrary, all that he had seen was 'their heads close together'. Gaskell had stated that the two men appeared as though they were just standing in the water with their heads above the surface.

Bedevilling any attempt to pick at the case in more detail is the disappearance of the transcript of the Inquest. Neither the Oxford University Archive, nor the Oxfordshire Record Office, the Christ Church College Archive, or the separately administered department of Bodleian Special Collections, has a copy of it.

Being a University court there should be a record in the University archive or in the Bodleian Library. The Oxfordshire Record Office is the most likely other source, but while they hold all the city Coroner's Inquest files for 1921, including some undertaken at the Settling Room, all of them in chronological and in numerical order (which would indicate if any was missing), there is no sign of the Llewelyn Davies–Buxton case. One is reliant on newspaper records.

Then, of course, there is the state of mind of the deceased, which was never a matter of analysis at the Inquest, even though when Rupert was lodging at the Deanery he was observed to have been depressed.

Much was made of Michael's ineptitude as a swimmer. But flatmate Edward Marjoribanks gave evidence that while 'Mr Davies could not swim very well ... It was his pride, however, to swim about twenty yards.' And again, as Peter Llewelyn Davies, a sober man who visited the site as I did, wrote to Dolly: 'The place is too calm, and the distance from bank to bank too small, for the question of swimming capacity to enter into it at all.'

Perhaps an open verdict would have been the better one.

On the evening of 19 May, Barrie was at home in the Adelphi

writing his daily letter to Michael. In it he wrote that he hoped he would be able to come down for the opening performance of their play, *Shall We Join the Ladies?*, now only a one-act play – he had been unable to take it further and decided to let the audience work it out – which starred Gerald du Maurier as Dolphin, a butler.

At eleven o'clock, with the intention of posting the letter, he walked out of the flat and took the lift to the ground floor. As he opened the gate of the lift and moved into the hallway, he was approached by a stranger who raised his hat, said he was from a newspaper and asked if Sir James could oblige him with a few words on the incident. Barrie asked what he was talking about. It was in this way that he learned of Michael's drowning.

He turned around and went back into the lift. In a daze, he telephoned Gerald and Peter first, and then his secretary Cynthia Asquith, who recalled that he spoke 'in a voice she hardly recognised': 'I have had the most terrible news. Michael has been drowned.'

When Cynthia arrived at the flat, Gerald and Peter were already there. They tried to persuade Barrie to go to bed, but he would not. Eventually they left for their own beds, and when Cynthia arrived the following morning, Barrie had still not slept. He had been pacing up and down the length of the study floor all night long.

Nico was playing cricket at Eton while Michael drowned, and in the evening sang at a Musical Society concert. He was told of his death after lights out, at around 10 p.m. by Macnaghten, but had gone to sleep not really believing it. The full import of the event only hit him when Peter arrived at his bedside the following morning, and Macnaghten, himself a suicide in later years, made it worse by coming in, kneeling by his bed and holding both their hands. The boys then drove to Slough for breakfast and on to Adelphi Terrace. Nico recalled, 'Uncle Jim's immediate reaction on seeing

me was "Oh – take him away!" Strangely I don't remember feeling
hurt at this.'

Nico was given the responsibility of telling Nanny, who was working as a midwife at Queen Charlotte's Hospital. He was excused from
the funeral and went to stay at Cannon Hall with the du Mauriers. In the 1970s, in interview with Andrew Birkin, he concluded
that suicide was likely: 'I've always had something of a hunch that
Michael's drowning was suicide – he was in a way the "type" i.e.
exceptionally clever, with varying moods.'

When D. H. Lawrence heard about it, he wrote from Hotel Krone,
Ebersteinberg, Baden Baden to Mary Ansell: 'My dear Mary, we had
your note after your second trip to England. No, I hadn't heard of
the boy's drowning. What was he doing to get drowned? J. M. Barrie
has a fatal touch for those he loves. They die.'

Two of Lawrence's master-ideas were that possessive love is a
deathly force, and that 'accidents' harbour a deep intentionality in
both perpetrators and victims.

For Boothby and Michael's close friends his death was devastating and a watershed. Boothby spoke to Andrew Birkin of the many
'desperate, hysterical letters … I can see Roger Senhouse being led
up the High in Oxford, sobbing.'

In the wake of the tragedy we can begin to see what Michael
meant to his friends, and how different their lives might have been
had he been released to carry the real Peter Pan into his own and
their lives. Nico said that Roger Senhouse used to tell him that
'for quite a long period after Michael was drowned, Boothby would
say, looking upwards! – "I think you'll be pleased with what I did
there, Michael!"' Boothby himself said that had Michael not died,
he would not have gone off the rails as he did, that Edward Marjoribanks, who 'was devoted to Michael', would not have committed

suicide after he got into Parliament. He said that Michael's death 'altered the whole course of Roger Senhouse's life', referring to his affair with Lytton Strachey, and Clive Burt, he believed, would have done far more with Michael still there as muse.

It was an extraordinary tribute, particularly that he might have made Boothby's life different to how it turned out. That would have been quite an achievement. After Michael died Boothby, who would enter Parliament in 1924, earned the nickname 'the Palladium' at Magdalen for his 'twice nightly' appetite for homosexual sex. In 1963, five years after he gave up his seat and was raised to the peerage, he began an affair with East End cat burglar Leslie Holt, who introduced him to the gangster Ronald Kray, one of the twins foremost in organised crime in London in the 1950s and '60s. Kray supplied Boothby with young men and arranged orgies in exchange for personal favours. When the *Sunday Mirror* broke the story in 1964 and the German magazine *Stern* named the parties, Boothby denied the story and threatened to sue the *Mirror*, and because senior Labour MP Tom Driberg was also involved the Labour-backed *Mirror* backed down, sacked its editor, apologised and paid Boothby £40,000 in an out-of-court settlement.

According to Peter Llewelyn Davies in a letter to Dolly Ponsonby, Barrie bore Michael's death 'somehow, with wonderful composure, and physically at least with better success than could have been expected'.

On 31 May, Barrie wrote to Rupert's mother:

Dear Lady Buxton,

I have just read your very kind letter, but I have been thinking a great deal about you since the 19th and feeling sorrowful for you. I am very glad that you have a daughter. Michael was son and daughter to me, and all I have been doing of any account in the last ten years was trying to be father and mother to him. I cared for him a great deal too much but the circumstances of our two lives perhaps excused it. I should like by and by to be allowed to see Rupert's sister, with the hope that she might come in time to look upon me as a friend.

I suppose I knew Rupert more intimately than you knew Michael. There is not any subject I can pretend to know much about, but I know more about boys than any other, and one of my grand ambitions for Michael was that he should form a deep friendship for someone who was worthy of him. This was slow in coming, for though there were a few at Eton for whom he had a warm attachment, continued at Oxford and elsewhere, Rupert was the one great friend of his life. [Michael] has often talked to me about this, sometimes for hours, far into the night, reappearing to do it after he had gone to bed, and the last letter I had from him, on the day they died, was largely about your boy. Rupert treated me quite differently from any other of my various boys' friends. They were always polite and edged away from me, as of a different generation, but he took for granted that Michael's friend should be mine also. Michael knew me and my ways as no other person did, and he was more amused than words can tell by the way Rupert took me in hand. I shall never forget the glee with which he told me one day that Rupert was going to ask me to dinner all alone, and how I hoped Rupert would, and how he did and also came to me. I was very proud of his treating me in that way, and Michael knew I liked it, and I daresay the two of them chuckled over it, for they could both be very gay tho' neither was facing life lightly.

They were either wildly gay or very serious as they walked together to Sandford…

Yours sincerely,
J. M. Barrie

There was never any likelihood that Rupert's sister would go any-where near him; nor did she. The letter seems to corroborate Peter's view that Barrie's state of mind was stable, but it was in contrast to Denis Mackail's view – 'He never got over it. It altered and darkened everything for the rest of his life' – and to Barrie's own statement in a letter to Dundas a year after the tragedy: 'What happened was in a way the end of me.' But then Peter was aware that it wasn't long before Barrie was making notes for a story based on the tragedy.

To be entitled *Water* or *The Silent Pool* or *The 19th*, it told of a dream he had of Michael returning from the dead. The boy was unaware that he had been drowned until 'the fatal nineteenth' approached again and he realised the inevitability of his death being repeated and went with Uncle Jim, holding his hand, into Sand-ford Pool – 'He said goodbye to me and went into it and sank just as before…'

Chillingly, he then added – 'Must be clear tht [*sic*] there is noth-ing suicidal about it.'

Afterword

T HE RECENT REVELATIONS and prosecutions of high-profile figures for sexual offences are bound to make one wonder whether Barrie's motivation in the matter of the Llewelyn Davies boys was sexual. Even in his day there were many who assumed that it was. According to Nico, the youngest of the boys, it was common talk on the literary cocktail party circuit.[63]

Homosexuality was illegal in England, even between consenting adults, until 1967, when the age of consent was set at twenty-one. Only occasionally would a court case break through the surface of Victorian respectability, most notably in 1895, just as Barrie began frequenting Kensington Gardens, when there were three.

The first of the trials of Oscar Wilde was brought by Wilde himself

---

63   Letter from Nicholas Llewelyn Davies to Andrew Birkin, 29 December 1975.

against the Marquess of Queensberry, who left a card at his club accusing him of 'posing as a sodomite' after the Marquess became aware that Wilde was having an affair with his son, the poet Lord Alfred Douglas. It opened at the Old Bailey on 26 April. The prosecution paraded a motley squadron of some dozen young male witnesses – many but not all of them rent boys – to testify that Wilde and Alfred Taylor (Wilde's procurer), were indeed guilty of twenty-five counts of gross indecency and conspiracy to commit gross indecencies, though sodomy wasn't specifically among them. Wilde therefore lost his case against Queensberry, and the Crown prosecution indicted Wilde with gross indecency and brought him to trial at the Old Bailey. This second trial produced a hung jury, but a third saw Wilde convicted and sent to prison for two years, an experience that assisted his passage to an early death at forty-six.

The aggressive nature of the Crown's prosecution of Wilde is said to have been linked to a homosexual affair between Liberal Prime Minister Archibald Philip Primrose, the 5th Earl of Rosebery, and the eldest of Queensberry's fetching sons, Francis Douglas. Queensberry is said to have threatened to expose this affair if the Crown didn't deal severely with Wilde. Rosebery, whose wife, the daughter of a Rothschild banker, had died and left him a bachelor some years before, suffered severe depression right up to Wilde's conviction, whereupon he made a remarkable recovery.

This is worth mentioning because Rosebery's private secretary was Barrie's closest friend, Thomas Gilmour, which suggests among other things that Barrie will have been privy to the whole case and well aware of the risks that a prominent citizen ran by importuning young boys.

Barrie himself became a correspondent of Rosebery, writing to him after the dust had settled, on 2 November 1897:

A play of mine – a version of my novel *The Little Minister* is to be produced at the Haymarket Theatre on Saturday next, and I have dared
to hope that if you were disengaged you might have sufficient interest in it to come. I think your children might enjoy it. A box would
be reserved if we thought it was a possibility that you would come.

In Wilde's case, it is likely that more than one of his sexual encounters
were with boys below the age of consent, which for heterosexuals
in Great Britain and Ireland was sixteen. The abuse of minors was
rampant. In a letter to Leonard Woolf in 1907, the Bloomsbury
sexual anarchist Lytton Strachey wrote:

> Have you ever been to the Trocadero? It's filled with little messen-
> ger boys, who do their best to play the catamite, but it hardly comes
> off. The nearest one of them got was to put his arm round [Maynard]
> Keynes' neck as he was helping him on with his coat! Remarkable?
> The truth is that sodomy is becoming generally recognised in Eng-
> land – but of such a degraded sort! Little boys of 13 are what the
> British Public love. There are choruses of them at most Comic Ope-
> ras, and they flood all but the most distinguished of the Restaurants.

When Michael's cousin Daphne du Maurier was fourteen she wrote
a story about Barrie,[64] whom she knew very well, she didn't think
twice about giving him a procurer – 'depressive Mr Tibbs', who picks
up a boy called Maurice, a thinly disguised Michael Llewelyn Davies,
in the West End of London close to the Trocadero, and takes him
to meet Tommy Strange, who, we learn, 'likes young gentlemen'.
    The Trocadero itself would hardly have suited Barrie as a point of

---

64   *The Seekers* (1921).

procurement. In those days cinemas were the more discreet pick-up joints, dark to the eyes of the law if not always to eagle-eyed managements. 'Barrie must have slipped into thousands of cinemas in his time,' his official biographer Denis Mackail recorded, but for some reason 'had to abandon one of the nearest to the Adelphi'.

In 1921, while the film of a night time shoot of London was being edited by a newsreel production company, a keen pair of eyes recognised Barrie lurking about in the area around the Adelphi. To everyone's surprise there he was, snuggled up in hat, scarf, and raincoat, refreshing himself at a coffee-stall at two in the morning.

The question posed was why would a 61-year-old man, who would never normally frequent a coffee stall, let alone at two in the morning, be propping one up around the corner of his apartment? Not only (to Barrie's embarrassment) did the news clip show at countless cinemas up and down the country, but a frame from it appeared in the press, with caption-writers wondering at Barrie's habit to prowl about the streets and patronise coffee-stalls in the small hours.

Perhaps we should be charitable: Michael had died but six months earlier.

When one looks at his autobiographical novel *The Little White Bird*, even hardened Barrie supporters throw up their hands when they read his description of the night he spent with young David, purportedly Michael's elder brother, George. The episode is pages long, but this is typical:

'Mother said I wasn't to want it unless you wanted it first,' he squeaked.

'It is what I have been wanting all the time,' said I, and then without more ado the little white figure rose and flung itself at me. For the rest of the night he lay on me and across me, and sometimes his feet were at the bottom of the bed and sometimes on the

pillow, but he always retained possession of my finger, and occasionally he woke me to say that he was sleeping with me. I had not
a good night. I lay thinking.

Of this little boy, who, in the midst of his play while I undressed
him, had suddenly buried his head on my knee.

Of David's dripping little form in the bath, and how when I essayed
to catch him he had slipped from my arms like a trout.

Of how I had stood by the open door listening to his sweet breathing, had stood so long that I forgot his name and called him Timothy.

In the book, Timothy is the name Barrie gives to the child he longs
to have fathered and many readers at the time felt not outraged but
sorry for him. Self-exposure beneath a veil of whimsy and sentimentality worked for Barrie and won him many a reader's sympathy. But
you never knew where the whimsy ended and the darker self took
over. Critics gave him the benefit of the doubt: 'Barrie, in the manner
of Lewis Carroll and his nude photographs of little girls, was consciously innocent,'[65] wrote James Harding in the 1980s.

There were indeed plenty of relationships with children other
than the Llewelyn Davies boys, clearly innocent. One very special
one was with Bevil – 'my favourite boy in the wide wide world' –
the son of the writer and academic Arthur Quiller-Couch. Barrie
engaged Bevil in adventures, taking photographs of them and making them into a book, exactly as he did with the Davies boys.

And long after Michael, his great love, passed from his life, Barrie
was to be seen with a boy close to hand, sometimes friends' children, but also sometimes a boy with just a name and very little pack
drill. One of these was Dick Rowe, 'a little boy' who appeared in

---

65   James Harding, *Gerald du Maurier* (1989).

his company on a holiday to Scotland as late as 1933 and was still
his consort two years later – brought along with him 'from the flat'.

In time, Barrie had a baronetcy and a great deal of power. He was
also of course a celebrity, and the Peter Pan association ensured constant homage from parents who desperately wanted their children
to meet him. So much so that when, in August 1933, he was staying at Balnaboth, just north of Kirriemuir in Scotland where he was
born, and was giving one of his regular young friends (his secretary's
son, Simon Asquith) a birthday tea party, who should come over
from nearby Glamis Castle but their Royal Highnesses the Duke and
Duchess of York with their children, Princess Margaret and Princess
Elizabeth, our future Queen who was seven. 'Crackers on the table,
and games in the garden afterwards,' were the order of the day, led
by the very artist of children's games, Sir James M. Barrie himself.

He liked to be with children. They made him the child he once
was.

So successful was the birthday party that he was invited to Glamis
the following day, for Princess Margaret's birthday, and was chosen
to sit next to the birthday girl at tea. He recalled later that observing some of her presents on the table, they

> seemed to be simple things that might have come from sixpenny
> shops, but she was in a frenzy of glee about them, especially about
> one to which she had given the place of honour by her plate. I said
> to her astounded: 'Is that really your very own?' And she saw how I
> envied her and immediately placed it between us with the words: 'It
> is yours *and* mine.'

Whatever little secrets passed between them thereafter, Margaret
clearly fell under his spell. Barrie was told that when later his name

had been mentioned, she had responded immediately: 'I know that man. He is my greatest friend, and I am *his* greatest friend.'

Barrie would see Margaret again, in London, when she was five. In a house in Regent's Park there were more games in which Barrie once again played a leading role, before confessing to her that he had taken the generous words she had uttered about her favourite present being 'yours *and* mine', and those about each being one another's 'greatest friend', and put them in his play, *The Boy David* – his final play as it turned out. By way of compensation, he told her, she would receive a penny for every utterance of her two phrases on stage. She didn't forgot this and in due course he received a letter from her father, by then King George VI, to the effect that if Barrie didn't pay up he'd be hearing from His Majesty's solicitors. Barrie responded to the effect that a proper Agreement would be drawn up by his solicitor, Sir Reginald Poole, and a ceremony was planned for the signing by himself and Princess Margaret at Buckingham Palace, when a bag of pennies would be handed over. But it never happened, because Barrie died before it could.

For the weaver's son from Kirriemuir this latter-day conjugation with royalty must have seemed a climax of sorts. But it is also instructive because, as in the case of the Llewelyn Davies boys and like most writers, life was for him the ground of his art and he lived life principally for his work, living it to invigorate and inspire his plays and novels. Theory was no good to him at all.

Also, to be fair, any judgement should be undertaken in the context of the time, not of our time. The Child was of special interest to late Victorian and Edwardian writers. Industrialisation had led to exploitation of children in the cotton mills of the north, and in 1839, almost half the funerals in London were for children under ten years of age. The Romantic ideal of the Child – the innocent soul untrammelled by 'the regular action of the world' – celebrated by Wordsworth and earlier by Rousseau, had given way to nineteenth-century exploitation, guilt and sentimentalism.

Dickens had mourned the loss of the idyll in *Oliver Twist*, in Little Nell's death in *The Old Curiosity Shop* and in Johnny's death in Great Ormond Street Hospital (to whom Barrie gave the *Peter Pan* copyright) in *Our Mutual Friend*. By the second half of the nineteenth century, the Child had come to represent something deep in us that had been sacrificed to materialism. As never before the symbol of the Child fascinated and gripped people dimly conscious that if what had been sacrificed were to be lost for good it would be Man's undoing.

In England, a number of adult males besides Barrie formed friendships with children outside the family that were inspirational and remained sexually pure. For example, John Millais, with what the newspapers called 'his schoolboy manner', had a relationship with Beatrix Potter when she was a little girl. Millais was one of a group of adult males, including Elizabeth Gaskell's husband and Quaker politician John Bright, who came alive in the company of young Beatrix, with her innocence, beauty and shy contemplative manner.

But there was also speculation about unscrupulous males turning the Cult of Child to lascivious advantage. The critic John Ruskin was divorced after he began a bizarre relationship with the artist Kate Greenaway, who liked 'to play child' with him and indulge in baby talk. The reason Ruskin (sixty-four) contacted Greenaway (twenty-nine) in the first place was that he found her drawings of pubescent girls irresistible. Likewise, the reason the Reverend Charles Dodgson/Lewis Carroll's friendship with the young Alice Liddell and her two sisters, famously the inspiration for *Alice's Adventures in Wonderland*, came to an abrupt end was that he began taking plainly provocative photographs of them.

To begin with, the fact that such relationships were creatively inspirational put parents at their ease, as no doubt Barrie's creative intentions put the Llewelyn Davies boys' mother, Sylvia, at her ease.

We watch as Sylvia falls over herself to facilitate his plan, while others (her husband Arthur, sister Trixy, mother Emma, the boys' Nanny Mary Hodgson, and Sylvia's close friend Dolly) become exasperated at how compliant she is.

We watch, too, as Barrie appears to derive a tremendous sense of power from the process of capturing Sylvia and the boys on the pages of his novels and plays.

And we listen to those who knew Barrie and Michael at the time, including in particular Denis Mackail, who was in a unique position to know and made the point, that while Michael and Barrie drew closer and closer, 'perhaps it isn't always Barrie who leads or steers'.

This book is not principally about Barrie, of whom I have written at length elsewhere. A struggle as it is to withdraw from this extraordinary figure as the chief focus, when we begin to look at his favourite boy we seem to move beyond the age-old question of whether they were having sex and see that Michael was the medium for something which Barrie desired even more, and watch as the boy brings it to such delicacy of interpretation that the coarser methods of love-making seem rarely, if ever, to be used.

For Michael not only led Barrie in his pursuit of what really interested him (as being a du Maurier he knew he would), he left him standing. It was Michael who clarified that being a little half-and-half meant more than remaining a little boy for life and having fun, that actually the Peter Pan in us has nothing to with escapism, playing at fairies or pirates and American Indians when you were an old man of sixty-three and hoping that no one will turn up and compel you to face reality. It has to do with lapsing out, as Michael did so successfully in the Scottish Highlands, and his grandfather did by dreaming true. It has to do with discovering the spiritual half of the betwixt-and-between in you in whatever way it takes you.

The reason our lives become trivial, and we find ourselves and our lives so boring, is simply that we do not pay enough attention to the half that makes Peter Pan special, the half that has nothing to do with Walt Disney or the Peter Pan bus company or that peanut butter company or Hummingbird candy.

To begin with, it involves the dying of the human half so that we may taste the half of Peter that transcends this, the spiritual dimension that returns us to the magical state of childhood, a time when we do not so much live life as are lived by forces outside us – the half which sometimes, as Barrie also indicated, can lead to ecstasy.

But then to carry that experience, that inspirational quality back into the hurly-burly of life, so that the human half benefits. This, Barrie did not allow Michael to do, because he didn't see it. On the contrary, as Boothby said, Michael felt pressured to do what would have been anathema for him to do. Barrie failed to realise that if you love someone the first thing you do is set them free. Eiluned was right; Michael should have been allowed to go to Paris. It was as simple as that.

So Rupert and Michael met. There was immediate empathy, but zeal got the better of them. 'There glowed in them with unusual warmth a Promethean fire,' wrote *The Harrovian*. They became high on the *effect* of their transcendence, so self-centred that attention to what they were really about declined and its essential value escaped them.

They went to their deaths either wildly gay or very serious, believing that only our mortality offers us the promise of our beliefs and intuitions. When in reality our beliefs can act upon the substance of the universe and shape it.

Acknowledgements

S INCE MY FIRST foray into the world of J. M. Barrie, *Captivated: J. M. Barrie, the du Mauriers & the Dark Side of Neverland* (Chatto & Windus, 2008), it is no longer possible to examine Barrie without reference to the du Mauriers, any more than it is possible to examine one of the du Mauriers without reference to Barrie. No surprise therefore that the tragic story of Michael Llewelyn Davies, whose mother was Sylvia du Maurier, puts *Peter Ibbetson* at its very core.

Since 2008, George du Maurier's *Peter Ibbetson* (the du Maurier family myth) has appeared in various paper and ebook editions. However, if you can get hold of a copy of the 1947 Pilot Press edition you will have the additional joy of John Masefield's reminiscence of what it meant to be a teenager when du Maurier's novel first appeared in 1894. Having said this, *The Real Peter Pan* depends ultimately, as did *Captivated*, on research undertaken by others into the lives of Barrie and the du Mauriers, albeit as virtually distinct biographical entities.

Notable in the Barrie camp are W. A. Darlington's biography, *J. M. Barrie* (1938), for its analysis of the plays, and the official biography by Denis Mackail, *The Story of J. M. B.* (1941), for its painstaking analysis of Barrie's notebooks. But the work of these is dwarfed by that of writer and film-maker Andrew Birkin, who, in the 1970s, drew together the thoughts of so many about Barrie for his film and book, *J. M. Barrie and the Lost Boys* (1979) – a vast archive which he now generously shares through the website jmbarrie.co.uk, and which includes letters of the Llewelyn Davies family by courtesy of Laura Duguid.

In the du Maurier camp, thanks go particularly to Kits Browning, Daphne du Maurier's son and literary executor, for his long-term support, and to Margaret Forster, whose official biography, *Daphne du Maurier*, was published in 1993.

The one source in which Barrie and the du Mauriers were never separate entities is the archive of Dorothea 'Dolly' Parry, later Lady Ponsonby of Shulbrede. Dolly was a close friend of Barrie, the Llewelyn Davies family and most especially Sylvia du Maurier. I am very grateful to the Hon. Laura Ponsonby of Shulbrede Priory for making her mother's many diaries and letters available.

Tracing the trajectory of Michael's short life also brings many other sources into focus, in particular the poetry of P. B. Shelley, notably 'Alastor', and the work of other poets, such as George Meredith, James Hogg and William Johnson Corey. I would like to thank Katrina Burnett for access to the work of her mother, Janet 'Eiluned' Lewis, including the poem 'Birthright' and novel *Dew on the Grass* (1934), which is finding a new audience today, and to Powys County Archives, where the family archive is lodged.

Thanks also to the Brotherton Collection, Leeds University Library for access to the Roger Senhouse archive and to Judith Curthoys at Christ Church College Library, and Oxford University and Bodleian libraries for consultation and access to material relating to Rupert Buxton and Michael Llewelyn Davies. I am also grateful to Timothy Young, Curator of Modern Books and Manuscripts at the Beinecke Rare Book and Manuscript Library, Yale University, and Dolores Colón, who processed the photographs of and by J. M. Barrie from the Llewelyn Davies and Barrie collections held there, as well as Eleanor Cracknell, the archivist at Eton College. Also, thanks are due to Mark Barrington-Ward, nephew of one of the jurors at the inquest into the drowning at Sandford Pool in 1921 (and acquaintance of three others).

Field research took me to Scotland and was greatly facilitated by many generous people met along the way, including Hans and Antonia de Gier and Colin Strang Steel at Edgerston; Neil and Rosie Hooper at Fortingall; Rhoda Robertson at Killiekrankie; Ken Brown and Roy and Cecilia Dyckhoff at Tomdoun; Wendy Harpe and John Szarkiewicz at Beauly; Gerald and Penny Klein, Patrick and Judy Price and Dorothy Dick at Scourie; Innes Morrison and Heather Mitchell at Amhuinnsuidhe; Vanessa Branson, Paul Waddington, Jon Easton and Jo O'Brien at Eilean Shona; Yvonne O'Shea at the Cuilfel, Kilmelford; and Graham and Moira Jackson on the Auch Estate. I am indebted also to Zilla Oddy at the Archive and Local History Service of the Scottish Borders Council for articles about, and photographs of, J. M. Barrie in Jedburgh.

Special thanks go to Neil Hooper, Ken Brown and Dr Henry Kaye for their careful editorial advice on various aspects of the landscape and fly-fishing in the book, and to the editor and author of two inspirational books: *Fish, Fishing and the Meaning of Life* (ed.) Jeremy Paxman (Penguin, 1995) and *The Fly Caster Who Tried to Make Peace with the World* by Randy Kadish (Saw Mill River Press, 2007).

I am grateful also to Faber & Faber for permission to quote from Neville Cardus's *Autobiography* (1984) and to all the publishers and authors of works quoted (see Sources). While every effort has been made to trace copyright holders, I would be grateful to hear from any unacknowledged sources.

Unless otherwise indicated, the illustrations in the plate sections are reproduced by kind permission of the Beinecke Rare Book and Manuscript Library, Yale University, USA. The landscape photographs were taken by the author, except for those connected to Amhuinnsuidhe, all of which are reproduced by kind permission of Amhuinnsuidhe and the North Harris Trust.

Finally I would like to thank my publisher Jeremy Robson of the Robson Press for giving me the opportunity to write this book, to my editors Olivia Beattie and Victoria Godden, and to the whole team at the Robson Press for engaging with it with enthusiasm.

Sources

Asquith, Cynthia (ed.), *The Flying Carpet* (Partridge, 1926).

_ _, *Lady Cynthia Asquith Diaries, 1915–1918* (Hutchinson, 1968).

Barrie, J. M., the Works. Those referred to are listed in Index under Barrie: Works by

Birkin, Andrew, *J. M. Barrie and the Lost Boys* (Constable, 1979; Yale UP, 2003).

Blake, George, *Barrie and the Kailyard School* (Barker, 1951).

Boothby, Robert, *My Yesterday. Your Tomorrow* (Hutchinson, 1962).

Braithwaite, Geoffrey G., *Fine Feathers and Fish* (T. & A. Constable, 1971).

Campbell, Duncan, *The Lairds of Glenlyon* (Cowan, 1886).

Cardus, Neville, *Autobiography* (Collins, 1947; Faber & Faber, 2008).

Carrington, Dora, *Letters and Diaries*, edited by David Garnett (Cape, 1975).

Connolly, Joseph, *Jerome K. Jerome* (Orbis, 1982).

Crane, David, *Scott of the Antarctic: A Life of Courage and Tragedy in the Extreme South* (HarperCollins, 2005).

Darlington, William Aubrey, *J. M. Barrie* (Blackie, 1938).

Day Lewis, Cecil, *The Buried Day* (Chatto & Windus, 1960).

Derwent, Lavinia, *A Breath of Border Air* (Hutchinson, 1975).

Douglas, George, *Scottish Fairy & Folk Tales* (London, 1893).

Dudgeon, Piers, *Captivated: J. M. Barrie, the du Mauriers & the Dark Side of Neverland* (Chatto & Windus, 2008).

du Maurier, Daphne, *The Breaking Point* (Gollancz, 1959; Virago, 2009).

_ _, *Rebecca* (Gollancz, 1938; Virago, 2003).

_ _, *The Rebecca Notebook and Other Memories* (Macmillan, 1982; Virago, 2012).

_ _, *The Young George du Maurier* (Peter Davies, 1951).

du Maurier, George, *Novels*, with an Introduction by John Masefield (Pilot Press, 1947).

Dunbar, Janet, *The Man and the Image* (Collins, 1970).

Farr, Diana, *Gilbert Cannan: A Georgian Prodigy* (Chatto &Windus, 1970).

Forster, Margaret, *Daphne du Maurier* (Chatto & Windus, 1993).

Harding, James, *Gerald du Maurier* (Hodder & Stoughton, 1989).

Holroyd, Michael, *Lytton Strachey: A Biography* (Chatto & Windus, 1994; Pimlico, 2004).

Jerome K. Jerome, *My Life and Times* (Hodder & Stoughton, 1925).

Jung, C. G., *Psychological Types* (Routledge, 1971).

Kadish, Randy, *The Fly Caster Who Tried to Make Peace with the World* (Saw Mill River Press, 2007).

Lawrence, D. H., *Women in Love* (Martin Secker, 1920).

Lewis, Eiluned, *Dew On the Grass* (Lovat Dickson & Thompson, 1934; Honno Classics, 2006).

Lucas, Audrey, *E. V. Lucas: A Portrait* (Methuen, 1939).

Mackail, Denis, *The Story of J. M. B.* (Peter Davies, 1941).

Magnaghten, Hugh Vibart, *Fifty Years of Eton* (Allen & Unwin, 1924).

Maude, Pamela, *Worlds Away* (Heinemann, 1964).

Moore, Harry T., *The Priest of Love: A Life of D. H. Lawrence* (Penguin, 1980)

Morrell, Ottoline, *Ottoline: The Early Memoirs* (Faber & Faber, 1963).

Moscheles, Felix, *In Bohemia with George du Maurier* (T. F. Unwin, 1896).

Ormond, Leonee, *George du Maurier* (Routledge, 1969).

Paxman, Jeremy, *Fish, Fishing and the Meaning of Life* (Penguin, 1995).

Read, Herbert, *The Innocent Eye* (Faber & Faber, 1933).

Rose, Jacqueline, *The Case of Peter Pan* (Macmillan, 1984).

Savage, Jon, *Teenage: The Creation of Youth, 1875–1945* (Chatto & Windus, 2007).

Scott, R. F., *The Personal Journals of Captain R. F. Scott, RN, CVO, on his Journey to the South Pole* (John Murray, 1923).

Telfer, Kevin, *Peter Pan's First XI* (Hodder & Stoughton, 2010).

Tomkies, Mike, *Between Earth and Paradise* (Whittles, 2006).

Wullschläger, Jackie, *Inventing Wonderland* (Methuen, 1995).

Index

Adams, Maude x, 81, 85, 171
'Adonaïs: An Elegy on the
    Death of John Keats' 338
Airlie Castle, Ogilvies of
    (Angus, Scotland) 110
'Alastor' vii, 287, 362
Albert, Prince Consort 112
Alexandre Dumas 36, 39
*Alice's Adventures in Wonder-
    land* 358, 382
Alpine Club 13, 162
America x, xiii, 39, 62, 81,
    82, 95, 140, 171, 199, 227,
    240, 350, 383
Amhuinnsuidhe, Outer Heb-
    rides 195–206, 284, 288,
    301, 303
Angus 109, 110
Ansell, Mary (see Barrie,
    Mary)
art 12, 26, 31, 37, 38, 44, 55,
    112, 114, 165, 265, 270,
    304, 308, 317, 318, 321,
    323, 344, 346, 356
Ashdon Farm, Exmoor 169,
Asquith, Herbert Henry (1st
    Earl Oxford) 198, 312
Asquith, Lady Cynthia 153,
    163, 181, 312, 316, 319,
    345, 347, 369
Asquith, Simon 380
Astor, Lord and Lady 276
Auch Lodge, Bridge of Orchy
    222–3
Auld Licht 116, 117, 156

Baldwin, Stanley 93
Balfour, Arthur 118
Ballantyne, R. M. 62
Balmoral Castle, Aberdeen-
    shire 112
Barrie, James Matthew
    absence of feeling 155
    adoption of Llewelyn
    Davies boys 177–8
    and Allahakbarries 92,
    94–6, 154, 183
    and Captain Scott
    88–90, 124, 131, 140–43
    'Castaway' games for
    Peter Pan 64–8, 70–73
    and children 20–24,
    34–5, 375–81
    development of Michael
    Pan 132, 134
    exploitation of Michael
    ix–x, 2, 62, 171, 176,
    181, 192, 204, 222, 271,
    275, 289, 302–3
    as fantasy weaver 6–7,
    23–4, 44–6, 54–5, 58–62,
    203–4, 291–5
    fishing 111, 121
    generosity to Michael
    189–90, 308
    George du Maurier man-
    tel, assumption of 11,
    35–40, 42–6, 54–5, 58,
    64–6, 154–6, 201–6, 285
    indifference to art 155–6
    'Kensington Gardens'

    games 17–29, 76, 87, 90
    loneliness, detachment
    32–4, 92, 164, 292, 300,
    301, 350
    love for Michael ix, 77,
    100, 140, 157, 172, 180,
    191, 213, 271, 272, 313,
    379
    menacing attitude to
    Michael 6, 67, 106, 134
    Michael's love for 159,
    180
    motivating interest in
    Michael's family 36–40,
    42–4, 58, 64–5, 154,
    206, 285
    notebooks 53, 66, 69, 91,
    97, 111, 126, 134, 155,
    177, 181, 223, 267, 373
    and parents of Michael
    31, 41, 70–71, 73–6
    predilection for games
    18–21, 92–5, 137–8, 176
    preoccupation with
    death 6–7, 10, 34, 99,
    102, 115, 119, 134, 190,
    191, 192, 198, 204, 205,
    216, 221, 268, 282, 283,
    285, 287, 288, 291, 303,
    370, 373
    reaction to Michael's
    drowning 369, 372
    sexuality 70, 141, 142,
    291, 318, 375–80
    snobbery 147, 176, 182–3

spiritualist beliefs 117–18, 221, 284, 285, 291, 301, 352
supernatural heritage 116, 118–19
winning of Michael's mother 44–6, 54–5, 74, 91, 117, 180
Works by:
Accursed Thing, The 100
Admirable Crichton, The 143
Auld Licht Idylls 116, 156
Boy David, The 381
Dear Brutus 266, 268, 270, 271, 272, 289
Kiss for Cinderella, A 350
Little White Bird, The x, 24, 27, 28, 36, 51, 74, 99, 180, 191, 231, 243, 267, 378
Little Minister, The 21, 32, 35, 116, 156, 377
Little Mary 179
Mary Rose 99, 119, 195, 196, 202–6, 288, 289, 292, 294, 301, 303, 342, 343, 345, 350
'Neil and Tintinnabulum' 106, 163, 193, 216, 272
Peter and Wendy x, 6–10, 49, 81, 134
Peter Pan ix, x, xi, xii, xiii, 4, 6–10, 66, 72, 73, 81, 85, 90, 99, 100, 104, 126, 131, 140, 143, 157, 159, 160, 231, 232, 233, 243, 278, 317, 318, 330

Peter Pan in Kensington Gardens 243
Sentimental Tommy 318
Shall We Join The Ladies? 150, 181, 344, 369
Tommy and Grizel 4, 44, 45, 117, 118, 182, 318
Well-Remembered Voice, A xiii, 119, 283, 286, 287, 288
What Every Woman Knows 143–4, 183
Window in Thrums, A 116, 156
Barrie, Maggie (sister) 293, 294
Barrie, Mary (wife, neé Ansell) 18, 22, 33, 34, 41, 44, 70, 73, 145, 148, 149, 151, 160, 182, 317, 318, 319, 370
Barrington-Ward, J. G. 367
Battle of the Somme 263, 336
Beauly, Inverness-shire 132
Bective, Lady Alice 317
Bedford Square, London 317
Belloc, Hilaire 329
Birkin, Andrew ix, xi, 107, 125, 145, 147, 159, 192, 203, 213, 232, 248, 272, 291, 309, 310, 331, 370, 375
Black Lake Cottage, Surrey 1, 4, 62, 63, 88, 90, 91, 92, 95, 96, 107, 140, 143, 148, 157, 160, 164
Blackmore, R. D. 169, 174
Bloomsbury Group 13, 14, 218, 315–21, 323, 377
Boer War 53, 198
Bonham Carter, Violet 312
Boothby, Robert ix, 213, 219,

309, 310, 311, 312, 315, 331, 370, 371, 384
Boucicault, Dion 160
Braithwaite, Geoffrey 236
Braques, Georges 323
Breath of Border Air, A 278
Bridge of Orchy, Argyle and Bute 223
Bright, John 382
Brighton, East Sussex 254, 265
Brittany 311
Brooke, Rupert 2, 14, 316
Browning, Robert 13
Bruce, Kathleen 140, 142, 143
Brunaval, Loch 201
Bryant, Arthur 360
Buckingham Palace 338, 381
Burke, Edmund 112
Burne-Jones, Edward 12
Burnett, Katrina 255, 258
Burns, Robert 277
Burt, Clive 211, 218, 310, 371
Butlers (Barrie's) 198, 202, 214, 222, 290, 292, 293, 294, 295, 369
Buxton, Clarence (brother) 338, 339
Buxton, Lady Anne (mother) 325, 326, 327, 341, 371
Buxton, Jocelyn (brother) 336–8
Buxton, Maurice (brother) 325
Buxton, Roden (brother) 325, 326
Buxton, Rupert Erroll Victor (Michael's friend) 324, 325, 329, 331, 333–5, 336–41, 344, 348–9, 359, 360–62, 384
preoccupation with beauty 326, 337, 339, 340

preoccupation with
death 331, 336–41
Buxton, Sir Thomas Fowell
(grandfather) 336
Buxton, Sir Thomas Fowell
Victor (4th Baronet Vic-
tor Buxton, father) 324,
336, 341
Byron, George Gordon (6th
Baron) 112

Café de Paris 222
Cambridge University 13,
14, 199, 206, 208, 242,
304, 308, 316, 320, 324,
335
Campbell, Mrs Patrick 197,
288
Campbell, Robert 115
Campbell chiefs of Glen-
lyon 114
cancer 102, 112, 126, 167
Cannan, Gilbert 12, 63, 140,
145, 148, 149, 150, 151,
160, 164, 317, 318
Captain Hook (character)
xii, 2, 5, 8–9, 67, 82, 84,
107, 131, 143, 231
Cardus, Neville 291–5
Carlyle, Thomas 13
Carrington, Dora 317, 320,
321
Carrington, Whateley 245
Carroll, Lewis ix, 329, 358,
379, 382
Cassington, Charles W. 335
Castle River, Amhu-
innsuidhe 201
Cavendish-Bentinck, Lady
Lucy 346
Censor 131, 140
Censor, Barrie's Abolition
Committee 148
Chaplin, Charlie 17, 18,
238, 290
Chase, Paulene 160

Chesterton, G. K. 346
Cholesbury, Buckingham-
shire 317, 318
Chopin 65, 324
Christ Church Meadow 360
Christ Church, Oxford 308,
324, 328, 329, 330, 341,
356, 357, 359, 361, 365,
367, 368
Coles, Edward (uncle) 291
Colquhoun, Reginald 342
Conan Doyle, Arthur 93,
118, 161
Corelli, Marie 118, 184, 221
Corfe Castle, Dorset 359
Coward, Noel 270
Crane, Walter 21
cricket 21, 22, 63, 92–5, 104,
106, 132, 138, 155, 162,
167, 168, 176, 186, 190,
197, 199, 209, 216, 222–4,
238, 259, 264, 265, 291,
294, 369
Crookes, William 118
Cubism 323
Cuilfel Hotel, Kimelford
240, 241
Currie, Sir Donald 115

Da Vinci, Leonardo 303
Daily Mail 334
Darlington, W. D. 179, 271,
288, 289
Day Lewis, Cecil 232,
De Girardin, Madame Del-
phine 284
Derwent, Lavinia 278
Dew on the Grass 248
Dhivach Lodge, Loch Ness
111, 130, 131, 133, 134, 237
Dickens, Charles 382
Disney (see Walt Disney)
Dodd, Elizabeth, see Der-
went, Lavinia
Dodgson, Charles (see Car-
roll, Lewis)

Douglas Henry, Norma 145
Douglas Pool, Amhu-
innsuidhe 201
Douglas, Lord Alfred 376
Douglas, Sir George 115, 117
Drumnadrochit, Scottish
Highlands 130
Du Maurier, Daphne
(cousin) 4, 5, 42, 66, 75,
76, 99, 125, 133, 146,
201, 269–71, 285, 302,
354, 377
Works by
'The Archduch-
ess' 285
Breaking Point, The
285,
Myself When Young
147
Rebecca 66
Rebecca Notebook
and Other Memories,
The 42, 133
Du Maurier, Emma (mater-
nal grandmother) 11, 31,
44, 71, 106, 125, 126,
128, 135, 154, 156, 157,
169, 170, 171, 173, 174,
177, 383
Du Maurier, George (maternal grandfather) 11,
35–40, 42–6, 54–5, 58,
64–6, 154–6, 201–6, 285
Works by
Peter Ibbetson 11,
36–40, 42, 44, 45,
58, 64–6, 154, 157,
201, 204, 206, 246,
285
Trilby 11, 26, 37, 44,
55, 79, 155, 176
Martian, The 11, 54
Du Maurier, Gerald (uncle)
125, 138, 141, 143, 144,
168, 269, 270, 271, 281,
369, 379

Du Maurier, Guy (uncle)
174, 177, 226, 229, 230
Du Maurier, May (aunt) 170,
173, 174, 177, 291
Du Maurier, Sylvia (see
Llewelyn Davies, Sylvia)
Du Maurier, Trixy (aunt) 42,
75, 383
Du Maurier 'other-world'
intimacy 42–3, 285
Duff, Lady Juliet 273
Duke of York Theatre 84,
207
Dulverton, Devon 175
Dundas, Robert (Oxford
tutor) 355–7, 359, 373
Dundee, Angus 109
Duneaves, highland Peth-
shire 113

Earl, Sebastian 218, 232,
310, 321
Eckhart, Meister (von Hoch-
heim) 246
Edgerston, Scottish Borders
276–7, 284, 305
Edinburgh 157, 273, 276, 309
education 110, 144, 208,
213, 216, 242, 356
Schools (boys)
Eton College 125,
126, 129, 130, 133,
138, 145, 163, 168,
176, 177, 187, 191,
199, 206, 207–24,
227, 229, 231, 243,
251, 253, 254, 258,
259, 262, 265, 282,
283, 284, 289, 300,
304, 305, 307, 309,
310, 311, 325, 330,
348, 349, 357, 358,
359, 369, 372
Norland Place pri-
mary and pre-prep
139, 159, 177

Osborne Naval
College 124, 125,
129, 133, 138, 139,
174, 222
Wilkinson's prepara-
tory school 57, 76,
139, 162, 163, 175,
176, 187, 198
Edward VII, King 1, 31, 103,
321
Edwardian Era 1, 2, 71, 91,
115, 321, 330, 381
Eights Week, Oxford 359,
360
Eilean Shona 345–54
Eilean Shona House 348
Elephant Man, The (see
Merrick, Joseph)
Eliot, T. S. 316, 317
Elizabeth II, Queen 380
Emery, Winifred 21
Eminent Victorians 321
Eton Chronicle 251, 252, 265,
283, 284, 300, 301
Eton College (see education)
Eton–Harrow cricket match
199, 209, 348

fairies 3, 21, 23, 24, 28, 35,
40, 51, 57, 58, 64, 67, 81,
82, 84, 85, 98, 99, 104, 114,
115, 116, 117, 197, 383
Farr, Diana 12, 45, 63, 148
Fenimore Cooper, James
39, 249
Fine Feathers and Fish 236
First World War xii, 2, 71,
89, 159, 222, 223, 224,
225–33, 239, 262–5, 283,
286–7, 304–5, 307, 315,
316, 318, 327, 328, 336,
339
conscientious objectors
318, 327, 328
as watershed xii, 315,
316, 318, 319

fishing 105, 108, 111, 112,
120, 121, 131–2, 135, 146,
170, 175, 183, 184, 185,
186–189, 190, 196, 198,
199–202, 221, 222, 223–4,
236–8, 240, 241, 275, 277,
285, 305, 325, 346, 350
fly-fishing 175, 184, 186–9,
190, 199–203, 221, 236,
237, 252, 285
flying 3, 5, 9, 27, 49, 51, 58,
70, 83, 85
Forfar, Angus 110, 115, 260
Forster, Margaret 5
Fort Augustus, Scottish
Highlands 130, 237, 276
Fort William, Scottish Highlands 235
Fortingall, highland Perthshire 108, 112, 113, 114,
115, 119, 120, 130
France 11, 26, 37, 39, 73, 74,
91, 100, 101, 110, 140,
160, 222, 223, 226, 238,
239, 254, 284, 304, 308,
311, 323, 344, 358, 384
Freyberg, Lieutenant General
Bernard 308
Frohman, Charles (impresario) 82, 95, 100, 101, 140,
160, 207

games 2, 5, 6, 18, 19, 41,
57–68, 70, 72, 76, 87, 89,
90, 93, 94, 95, 117–18,
132, 133, 134, 137–8,
176, 208, 217, 222, 247,
249, 251, 258, 311, 349,
380, 381
Garsington Manor 315–21
Gaskell, Elizabeth 382
George VI, King 381
Gertler, Mark 317, 318
ghillies 112, 186, 187, 196,
202, 223, 237, 240
Gibb, Geraldine ('Gerrie':

sister-in-law) 159, 271, 272, 273, 274, 281, 282, 290, 291, 297, 299
Gielgud, John 270
Gilbert Cannan and His Mill 318
Gilmour, Thomas 92, 100, 161, 162, 305, 376
Gladstone, William 13,
Glamis Castle, Angus 111, 380
Glan Hafren, Penstrowed, Wales 241–55, 257, 260, 262, 307, 342, 343, 346
Glen Garry, Invergarry 235
Glen Lyon 108, 112, 113, 114, 115
Glencoe 115, 223
Glenquoich Lodge 237
Gluck, Christoph Willibald 324
Goldsmith, Oliver 244
Grahame, Alastair ix, 329, 329, 367
Grahame, Kenneth ix, 329
Grampian mountains, Scottish Highlands 109, 223
Grand Hôtel, Caux (Switzerland) 145
Granville Barker, Harley 131
Great Ormond Street Hospital 382
Greenaway, Kate 382
Grundy, Sydney 281

Haddeo River, Devon 175
Haggard, Rider 207
Harding, James 379
Harrovian, The 342, 384
Harrow School 199, 209, 210, 324, 325, 326, 327, 328, 333, 335 340, 348, 360
Herbert, Auberon 'Bron' Herbert (9th Baron Lucas) 198, 199, 201, 223, 238

Herbert, Nan 198, 224, 247, 275
Hodgson, Mary (Nanny) 26, 29, 51, 61, 71, 74–5, 103, 107, 127, 133, 138, 139, 157, 159, 167, 169, 174, 175, 176, 177, 180, 192, 198, 202, 206, 224, 229, 231, 238, 271, 289, 290, 291, 298, 342, 383
    alerts Jack to odd goings-on 291, 297
    fears for Michael 133, 298
Hogg, James 97–9, 204, 205, 301, 302, 303
homosexuality 210, 211, 310, 371, 375, 376
Hope, Anthony 198
Hope, Betty 198, 199, 201
Hotel Meurice, Paris 222, 311
houses of main protagonists:
    Adelphi Terrace House, Robert Street, London (Barrie) 164, 198, 246, 258, 286, 289, 291–5, 298, 301, 304, 312, 348, 368, 378
    23 Campden Hill Square, London (Barrie and the boys) 130, 137, 139, 153, 174, 176, 177, 231, 232, 290, 297, 300, 308
    18 Craven Terrace (18), London (Llewelyn Davies) 25, 26
    Egerton House, Berkhamsted, Hertfordshire (Llewelyn Davies) 88, 101, 104, 126, 130
    133 Gloucester Road, London (Barrie) 17, 3
    31 Kensington Park Gardens, London (Llewelyn Davies) 11, 25,

    23 Kensington Park Gardens, London (Llewelyn Davies) 73
    Leinster Corner, Leinster Terrace, London (Barrie) 73, 138, 161
Housman, A. E. 248, 249
Hugo, Victor 284–5
Huxley, Aldous 317
hypnotism 5, 12, 23, 26, 37, 38, 40, 43, 44, 55, 79, 100, 155, 182

Impressionism 323, 324
Inverness, Scottish Highlands 130, 132
Isis, River (Oxford) 329

Jackson, Michael x
James, Henry 12, 118, 154, 155, 173, 174
James, William 118, 284
Jerome, Jerome K. 32, 33, 92, 94, 361
Joyce, James 315
Jung, Carl G. 246, 284

Kailyard school 156
Katrine, Loch 273, 275
Keats, John 218, 252, 264, 303, 338, 341
Kensington Gardens 2, 7, 11, 17–24, 26–8, 40, 49–51, 57–9, 62, 73, 74, 77, 87, 90, 106, 168, 330, 375
Keynes, John Maynard 14, 316, 377
Killiechassie Estate 114
'Kilmeny' 98, 99, 191, 203–5, 301, 302, 303
Kilvert, Francis 169
Kimelford, Argyll and Bute 239, 240
King's Cross Station, London 334

Kinglass River, Argyle and
    Bute 223
Kipling, Rudyard 329
Kirkby Lonsdale, Cumbria
    12, 13, 14, 26, 29, 90, 317
Kirriemuir, Angus 18, 82,
    110, 112, 115, 195, 380,
    381
Korsakov, Rimsky 310
Kyle of Lochalsh, Scottish
    Highlands 196, 236

Ladies Loch, Amhu-
    innsuidhe 201
Last of the Mohicans, The 249
Lavery, Sir John 286
Lawrence, D. H. 34, 141,
    201, 315, 317, 318, 319,
    370
Laxford River, Sutherland
    184, 188
Llewelyn Davies, Arthur
    (father) 2, 11, 12, 13, 15,
    25, 26, 31, 35, 41, 46, 51,
    70, 71, 72–4, 75, 78, 83,
    87–91, 101–8, 112, 121,
    123, 124, 125–30, 133,
    143, 145, 146, 168–9, 291
Llewelyn Davies, Crompton
    (uncle) 14, 44, 171, 174–
    5, 316, 317
Llewelyn Davies, George
    (brother) 3, 26–9, 40,
    49–53, 57–61, 64, 65, 76,
    88, 90, 123, 128, 129,
    130, 133, 138, 139, 145,
    146, 159, 172, 174, 175,
    176, 196, 199, 206, 211,
    219, 222, 224, 226, 229,
    230, 231, 232, 271, 283,
    287, 378
Llewelyn Davies, Jack
    (brother) 26, 29, 40, 49,
    53, 65, 76, 90, 91, 107,
    124, 125, 126, 128, 129,
    138, 139, 146, 147, 148,

159, 162, 172, 174, 179,
    183, 196, 199, 222, 224,
    231, 238, 254, 265, 271,
    273–5, 282, 290, 291,
    297, 298
Llewelyn Davies, John
    (paternal grandfather)
    12–14
Llewelyn Davies, Mary
    (paternal grandmother) 12
Llewelyn Davies, Margaret
    (aunt) 14, 101, 107, 123,
    138, 177, 189, 264, 317
Llewelyn Davies, Michael
    affair with Roger Sen-
    house 218–20, 257, 272,
    304, 309, 310, 311, 320,
    347, 349, 370–71
    affair with Rupert Bux-
    ton 328–9, 331, 341–2,
    344, 359–62
    Allahakbarries team
    mascot 96
    American Indian cos-
    tume 140
    to Amhuinnsuidhe Cas-
    tle, Outer Hebrides
    (1912) 195–206, 284,
    288, 301, 303
    on Armistice night 307
    artistic talent 265, 304,
    308, 312, 348
    aura of 4, 163, 171, 172,
    188, 201, 211, 218, 219
    Barrie's exploitation of
    ix, 2, 62, 171, 176, 181,
    192, 204, 222, 271, 275,
    289, 302–3
    Barrie's favourite ix, 69,
    77, 139, 139, 149, 180,
    222
    Barrie in love with ix,
    77, 100, 140, 157, 172,
    180, 191, 213, 271, 272,
    313, 379
    Barrie's menacing

attitude to 6, 67, 106,
    134
    to Beauly, Scottish High-
    lands 132–3
    bedroom at 23 Campden
    Hill Square 138
    billiards with Barrie 137
    birth 51–4
    at Black Lake Cottage 1
    and Bloomsbury Group
    315–21
    breaking through from
    Neverland 48, 51
    to Bridge of Orchy
    (2014), Scottish High-
    lands 223–4
    at Christ Church,
    Oxford 125, 308–13,
    324, 328, 343, 356–9
    death by drowning
    360–73
    discovers Tinkerbell 68
    to Dhivach Lodge, Scot-
    tish Highlands (1907)
    130–32, 238
    Dora Carrington on 321
    to Edgerston, Borders
    (1917, 1918) 276–9,
    284, 305
    to Eilean Shona (1920)
    345, 347–8, 349–54
    at Eton College 125,
    163, 187, 191, 207–21,
    227–9, 253–4, 259, 265,
    283–4, 300, 304, 305,
    307, 309, 349, 358, 372
    to Exmoor, Somerset-
    Devon 169–75
    father's death 101–5,
    121–4
    fear of water 106, 107,
    258, 311, 368
    first to fly 85
    first trip to Scotland
    (1906) 107, 112, 120
    as fisherman 120, 121,

131–2, 135, 175, 184, 186–189, 190, 199–202, 222, 223–4, 236–8, 275, 277, 285, 325, 346, 350
to Fort Augustus (1917) 275
to Fortingall, Scottish Highlands (1906) 108, 112–15, 119–21
to France 73, 90–91, 100, 101, 160, 222, 311
friendship with Eiluned Lewis 248–55, 257, 342–4
friendship with ghillie Johnny Mackay 186–8, 196–7, 201, 223
friendship with Robert Boothby 309–11, 331
at Glan Hafren, Wales (1915) 241, 245, 246–255, 257, 259–62, 342–3
horror looking for him 134
illness 71, 100, 126, 212, 227, 265
initiation into Pan cult 62, 68
as intellectual 216–17, 220, 257, 320–21
in Kensington Gardens 76, 87, 90
to Killiecrankie, Scottish Highlands (1913) 118, 221
to Kimelford, Scottish Highlands (1915) 239–41
letters from Barrie 140, 213
letter to Barrie 135
letters from parents 103, 104, 127
loneliness, detachment 171, 200, 202, 212, 221
love for Barrie 159, 180

Lytton Strachey on 320
at mermaids' lagoon 3–10, 96, 97, 106
as Michael Pan 132, 134
mother's death 151–3, 165–72
mother's doctors 128, 170
moves in with Barrie 290, 301
to New Forest, Dorset 144
nightmares 5, 106, 133, 146, 160, 192, 212, 303, 304, 352
no discernment of reality 104
at Norland Place School 139
and 'other-world' intimacy 99, 120, 156, 200–202, 203–4, 217, 218, 219, 283–6, 291, 341
Ottoline Morrell on 320–21
in Peter and Wendy 134
in Peter Pan 82
Peter Pan brought to his bed 100
Peter Pan costume gift 104, 106, 158
poetic nature 4, 200, 201, 219, 265, 283, 302, 310, 341, 351, 352, 353
reaction to father's cancer 105, 134
reaction to mother's death 171
reaction to mother's distress 133, 168
as real Peter Pan xiii, 200–202, 285, 286
resistance to Barrie's interest 144, 145, 157, 272, 304, 305, 307, 308,

344, 350, 351, 355, 356, 358
as Romeo to Sylvia's Juliet 91
to Postridge, Devon 161–2 to Sandford Pool, Oxford (1921) 360–61
to Scourie, Scottish Highlands (1911), 183–9
sense of beauty 120, 156, 187, 199, 200–202, 218, 220, 221, 251, 264, 284, 310, 323
sexuality 210, 219, 220, 221, 255, 248, 291, 309, 310, 321, 341–2, 344, 375, 377
at Shulbrede Priory, West Sussex 78
as sportsman 138, 187, 190, 217, 259, 262, 264
as statue in Kensington Gardens 158
to Switzerland 145–51, 222
Sylvia thoughts about death 123, 124, 131
to Tomdoun, Scottish Highlands (1915) 235–8, 305
to the Trossachs (1917) 273, 275
at Wilkinson's School 162, 190
Llewelyn Davies, Nico (brother) 65, 67, 76, 90, 91, 100, 105, 107, 108, 111, 130, 138, 139, 141, 143, 146, 147, 150, 167, 170, 174, 175, 176, 177, 188, 196, 198–9, 203–4, 206, 210–11, 217, 220, 223, 227, 231, 232, 235, 238, 242, 246, 247, 248, 251, 254, 255, 259–62, 271, 272, 273, 275, 277–8,

281, 282, 289, 290, 291,
   298, 299, 300, 301, 310,
   330, 342, 347, 352, 359,
   369, 370, 375
Llewelyn Davies, Sylvia
   (mother)
   birth 11, 12
   design sense 25, 26, 41, 88
   financial situation 25–6,
      91, 130, 139, 145, 149,
      160
   grieving for Arthur 128,
      133, 139, 162
   inner life 42–4
   love for Michael 53,
      146, 192
   marriage 15, 25, 70–71,
      73, 74, 75, 87, 90–91,
      102, 103, 105, 125
   as Grizel 44–6, 69, 117,
      178
   last will & testament
      138–9, 177–8
   as Mary Duchess of Tow-
      ers ('Mimsey') 42
   as Mary Rose 191, 203,
      204, 291
   as Mrs Darling 83
   as mother 26, 47–53, 69,
      76, 91
   paternal relationship 12,
      36, 42, 44, 54–5
   personality 12, 15, 36,
      40, 42, 43–4, 69, 70, 75,
      76, 139, 148, 173
   relationship with Barrie
      xi, 31, 36, 44–6, 54–5,
      69, 73, 77, 78, 83, 87,
      90–91, 100, 101, 103–4,
      117, 130, 139, 144–5,
      149–50, 154, 157, 159–
      60, 161, 162, 179–80,
      271, 319, 383
   terminal illness 151, 160,
      165, 167, 169–72
   as Trilby 44, 55

Llewelyn Davies, Theodore
   (uncle) 14, 316
Lewis, Eveline 241–51, 262,
   263, 307, 343
Lewis, Eiluned 242–58, 265,
   308, 343, 384
Lewis, Hugh 242, 244, 247,
   258, 259, 261
Lewis, May 242, 244, 248,
   254, 260
Lewis, Medina 241, 242–51,
   254, 259
Lewis, Peter 242–4, 246, 247,
   248, 254, 258
Lewis, Sir George and Lady
   31, 32, 35, 36, 160, 164,
   175–6, 188, 241
Liddell, Alice ix, 329, 382
Lloyd George, David 14
Loch Garry, Invergarry 235
Loch More, Sutherland 184
Loch Stack, Sutherland 184
Lodge, Oliver 118
Lorna Doone 169
Louvre, The 222
Loyne, River 236
Luath (Barrie's Newfound-
   land dog) 72, 83, 132,
   157, 318
Lucas, Audrey 198, 255,
   298, 350
Lucas, E. V. 96, 162, 165,
   198, 221, 238, 293, 298
Lucas, Elizabeth 238, 239,
   282, 298, 300, 308, 358
Lucas, Lord (see Herbert,
   Auberon)
Lutyens, Edwin 290
Lynton, Devon 169
Lyon, River 112, 113, 114,
   120, 121
Lytton, Countess of Glenfin-
   nan 346–7

McAulay, Nicholas 329
McCarthy, Desmond 176

McCarthy, Lilian 131
MacGregor's Leap, Glen
   Lyon 114
Mackail, Denis 63, 77, 79,
   88, 90, 93, 94, 95, 100,
   101, 130, 132, 141, 143,
   145, 148, 149, 151, 153,
   154, 155, 164, 177, 180,
   182, 206, 222, 224, 265,
   291, 316, 344, 346, 373,
   378, 383
Mackay, Johnny 186–8, 196–
   7, 201, 223
Macleod, Betty 139
Macnaghten, Hugh (Eton
   tutor) 129, 145, 146, 179,
   211, 213, 216, 217, 218,
   220, 221, 257, 304, 305,
   309, 369
Maeterlink, Maurice 245,
   252
Magdalen College, Oxford
   309, 371
Mansfield, Katherine 317,
   318
Margaret, Princess 110, 380,
   381
Marjoribanks, Edward 357,
   360, 368
Marlborough School 14
Marsh, Catherine 336
Mary Queen of Scots 277
Masefield, John 37, 66
Mason, A. E. W. 74, 88, 141,
   157, 161, 162, 164, 198
Maude, Cyril 21
Maude, Margery 21
Maude, Pamela 21, 34, 70,
   119
Maurice, F. D. 13
Maxwell, Gavin 236
Melfort, Loch 240
Mendelssohn 324
Meredith, George 154, 213–
   15, 216, 221, 242–4, 252,
Merrick, Joseph 103

Methuen, Field Marshal
  Paul 53
Methuen button 53
Michael Pan (character)
  132, 134
Millais, John 12, 382
Millar, Charles Hoyer
  (uncle) 42
Milne, A. A. 330
Mitchell-Innes, Norma 231,
  232, 286
Mocheles, Felix 37
Moidart, Loch 345, 346, 347
Mona Lisa, The 303
Montrose, Angus 109
Moore, G. E. 14, 316
Morrell, Julian 320
Morrell, Ottoline 13, 149,
  317, 318, 320, 346
Mull, Isle of 239
Murry, Middleton 317
Myer, Frederick W. H. 283–4

Nanny (see Hodgson, Mary)
National Council Against
  Conscription 318
Ness, Loch 111, 130, 237
New Forest, Dorset 144
New Scotland Yard 334
Nurse Loosemore 169, 171,
  173, 185, 198

Oare River and village, Som-
  erset 169, 174
Oban, Argyll and Bute 239,
  240
'Ode on a Grecian Urn' 252,
  303
Ogilvy clan 109–10
Oliver-Rutherford, William
  Edward 276
Oliver, Frederick S. 276
opium 11
Orchy River, Argyle and
  Bute 223, 224
Oxford University 125, 155,

213, 245, 307, 308–13,
  324, 328, 343, 356–9

paranormal 12, 43, 44, 65,
  118, 245, 284, 286, 291
Parry, Dorothea ('Dolly': see
  Ponsonby, Dorothea)
Parry, Sir Hubert 12, 13, 106
Peter Pan statue, Kensington
  Gardens 106, 158
Picasso, Pablo 156, 323, 324
Ponsonby, Arthur (1st
  Baron) 78, 144
Ponsonby, Dorothea ('Dolly')
  13, 14, 22, 25, 42, 43, 45,
  46, 76, 77, 78, 88, 102,
  103, 126, 128, 130, 139,
  144, 145, 147, 189, 291,
  368, 371, 383
Port Meadow, Oxford 328
Porthgwarra, Cornwall 25,
  102
Porthos (Barrie's St Bernard
  dog) 18–21, 23, 33, 36,
  37, 39, 67, 72, 73
Postbridge, Devon 161
Potter, Beatrix 382
Pound, Ezra 315
Price, Professor H. H. 245
Primrose, Archibald Philip
  (5th Earl of Rosebery) 376
Prisoner of Zenda, The 198
psychology xii, 42, 117, 138,
  147, 245, 285, 319
Punch magazine 11

'Queen's Wake' 97, 98
Queensberry, Marquess of
  376
Quiller-Couch, Bevil 379
Quiller-Couch, Sir Arthur
  99, 191, 379
Quoich forest, Scottish
  Highlands 236, 237

Raine, Kathleen 236

Ramsgate, Kent 71, 126, 127,
  135, 154, 158
Read, Herbert 120
Real Peter Pan, The xiii, 200–
  202, 285, 286
Rizzio, David 277
Robinson Crusoe 39, 351
Rossetti, Dante Gabriel 12
Rowe, Dick 379
Rowling, J. K. 114
Rowse, A. L. 225
Rumpelmayer's, Paris 222
Ruskin, John 382
Russell Wallace, Alfred 118
Rustington-by-the-sea, West
  Sussex 46, 106, 107, 108
Rutherford, Anne 276

St Malo, France 311
Sandaig, Scottish Highlands
  236
Sandford Pool 360, 363, 365,
  366, 373
Sassoon, Siegfried 243, 317
Schiehallion, Glen Lyon
  113, 114
schools (see education)
Scotland 34, 82, 97, 98, 99,
  100, 107, 109–22, 130,
  183, 184, 196, 198, 216,
  220, 231, 233, 236, 241,
  257, 273, 276, 277, 284,
  309, 311, 325, 326, 334,
  344, 345, 346, 347, 355,
  379, 380
Scots Guards Regiment 304,
  305
Scott-Ellis, Thomas Evelyn
  (Baron Howard de Wal-
  den) 346
Scott, Captain Robert
  Falcon 88–90, 124, 131,
  140, 141–4, 215–16
Scott, Sir Samuel 197
Scott, Sir Walter 112, 275,
  276, 277

Scourie, Sutherland 183–9

séance 12, 245, 284, 286, 291

Secker & Warburg (publisher) 219

Senhouse, Roger 218–20, 257, 272, 304, 309, 310, 311, 320, 347, 349, 370–71

Serpentine, The (Hyde Park) 24, 27, 49, 51

Shelley, P. B. vii, 51, 112, 252, 264, 287, 326, 338, 341, 361, 362

Shiel, Loch 346, 347

Shropshire Lad, A 248

Shulbrede Priory, West Sussex 78, 144

Skelton, George 131

Skye, Isle of 196, 236, 345

Smee (character) 8, 82, 131

Society for Psychical Research 118, 245, 284

Solomon Caw (character) 27, 49, 50, 51, 52, 53, 263

Sons and Lovers 141, 318

Sorbonne, Paris 344, 356

Sound of Sleat, Scottish Highlands 236

Spean Bridge, Scottish Highlands 235, 237

Spencer, Gilbert 317

Spiritualism 12, 117, 118, 221, 245, 284, 285, 286, 291

Stephen, Leslie 316

Stern magazine 371

Stevenson, Robert Louis 120, 356

Strachey, Lytton 14, 218, 317, 320, 321, 371, 377

Strathtay, highland Perthshire 107, 118, 119

Stuart, Prince Charles Edward, 133, 236, 277

Summer Fields, Oxford 324

Sunday Mirror 371

Sunday Times 248

Sutherland, Millicent Duchess of 147, 183

Swiss Family Robinson, The 39, 58, 61

Switzerland 19, 145, 161, 163, 222

Tay, Loch and River 107, 109, 112, 120

telepathy 43, 65, 245, 246

Telfer, Kevin 96

Terry, Ellen 26, 258

Thames, River 164, 290, 329, 360

The Unknown Guest 245

The Vicar of Wakefield 244

Three Musketeers, The 36, 39

Tilford, Surrey 62, 63, 71, 77

Tillington, West Sussex 298, 300

Times, The 118, 333, 334

Tinkerbell (character) 3, 68, 82, 84

Tomdoun, Invergarry 235–7, 305

Tomkies, Mike 346

Tootles (character) 82

Tour Solidor, France 311

Trevelyan, Hilda 131, 157

Treves, Sir Frederick 103

Trocadero, London 377

Trossachs National Park 111, 273

Turner, J. M. W. 112, 114, 115, 165

Twain, Mark x, 85

Vassall, Archer 325, 333

Victoria, Queen 112, 118

Voshimid, Loch 202, 206, 264, 301

Walpole, Sir Hugh 179

Walt Disney Company, The x, xi, xiii, 384

Waverley Abbey 67

Wendy Darling (character) 3, 6, 8, 9, 10, 53, 66, 82, 83, 84, 85, 134, 157, 231

Whiblet, Charles 288

Whistler, James McNeill 12, 38

Whiting, Paul 310

Wilde, Oscar 375–7

Wind in the Willows, The ix, 329, 330

Witchcraft 98, 113, 115, 116, 117, 119, 282

Women in Love 318, 319

Women's Co-operative Guild 14

Woolf, Leonard 14, 316, 377

Woolf, Virginia 315, 316, 321

Wordsworth, William 112, 218, 382

World War I (see First World War)

Young Pretender (see Stuart, Prince Charles Edward)